PRAISE FOR TAXES
FOR HUMANS

"An empathetic, spirited, straightforward, judgment-free tax guide for self-employed Americans. Not just a guide to doing your taxes, but a rallying cry for civic engagement. What a gift!"

—**William G. Gale**, co-director of the
Urban-Brookings Tax Policy Center

"This might just be the most approachable – and dare I say, funny – tax book you'll ever read."

—**Farnoosh Torabi**, bestselling author and
host of the Webby-winning podcast *So Money*

"If you've ever felt overwhelmed or discouraged by taxes, read this book. I've never felt so seen, supported, and encouraged when it comes to money. Hannah Cole is the go-to expert in the creative community for taxes and bookkeeping, and she has completely transformed how I think about money and taxes over the years. Compassionate, witty, and deeply knowledgeable, Hannah brings a much-needed human approach to a topic most of us avoid. This book is a game-changer."

—**Ekaterina Popova**, artist, founder of Create! Magazine,
and certified master coach

"Hannah truly understands the unique financial landscape artists, creatives, and freelancers are faced with. She is my go-to expert on all things taxes for the creative community and beyond!"

—**Scott Malloy**, senior career advisor
at Rhode Island School of Design

Hannah Cole

FOUNDER OF SUNLIGHT TAX

Taxes for Humans

Simplify Your Taxes and Change the World When You're Self-Employed

WILEY

Published by John Wiley & Sons, Inc., Hoboken, New Jersey.
Published simultaneously in Canada.

For general information on our other products and services or for technical support, please contact our Customer Care Department within the United States at (800) 762-2974, outside the United States at (317) 572-3993 or fax (317) 572-4002.

Wiley also publishes its books in a variety of electronic formats. Some content that appears in print may not be available in electronic formats. For more information about Wiley products, visit our web site at www.wiley.com.

Library of Congress Cataloging-in-Publication Data is Available:

ISBN 9781394298396 (Paperback)
ISBN 9781394298389 (ePub)
ISBN 9781394298402 (ePDF)

Cover Design: Wiley
Author Photo: © Nicole McConville

To the taxpayers of Massachusetts, for funding my public school education. Without it, this book would not exist. And to Farrah and Jade. Because you are the future.

CONTENTS

Contents

CONTENTS

PREFACE

Money obstacles may have brought you to this book—specifically a lack of tax knowledge and skills. It's my goal to bring you not just through your tax issues but all the way to financial savviness and confidence. You need to get your taxes done. And most of this book is for that. But you also need "f***-you money." That's money that allows you to walk away from toxic and disempowering situations without financial fear and say yes to your dream opportunities. When you get the hard stuff organized and your financial footing secure, you can get back to your important work.

If you're feeling especially confused about taxes, it's likely because you have self-employment income. Being self-employed means you have all the complexity of a larger business but often not the budget to pay an accountant. You have to do things that employees don't (like bookkeeping, keeping receipts, and paying quarterly taxes) because you get benefits they don't get (like deductible expenses, which require tracking).

WHAT THIS BOOK IS

This book is for you if you:

- Want to DIY your taxes
- Want to understand your freelance taxes, do things better, and get systems that keep you organized

- Had a tax whammy (like tax debt, an audit, or divorce fallout) and are looking to get out of it
- Want to get more out of an accountant relationship or communicate your needs to them better
- Want to feel seen and valued for the work you care about
- Care about making the world/your own life/democracy better—and holding your representatives accountable.

WHAT THIS BOOK ISN'T

A note on what this book does *not* cover.

This book is about your federal income taxes. I've distilled the *most important issues* that a self-employed person needs to know to make this book feel useful and readable. I'm skipping the laundry list of hyper-specific tax situations (for the record, that laundry list *does* exist, and it's called the Internal Revenue Code)—I can't cover every conceivable tax situation. Do you want to read 7,000 pages of technical detail? Me neither.

If you're looking for detailed tax info on real estate, investing, your spouse's income, agriculture rules, every state's income tax rules, sales tax, or local business franchise taxes, I'm sorry. I can't get to everything. But I *will* give you essential tools you need to understand how to do things yourself and when you should find an accountant to help you. I'll even help you get more out of your accountant by knowing what to look for and ask for. This book will also give you the foundation to do more than taxes; it will help you set up the systems to make your taxes smooth (and legally compliant) every year, find extra money each year through tax planning, and build savings with tax-smart accounts.

HOW TO USE THIS BOOK

How will we do all that? I'll use a simple framework: mindset, education, organization, and then the level-up. There's also a section that covers the "oh, shit!" scenarios (like audits, what to do if you can't pay or you make a mistake, and spouses who go rogue). Lastly, there's a section on making the world better through, yes, the tax code.

I recommend reading Chapters 1–11 first to understand how the pieces fit together and then come back to the "doing your taxes" chapters in Part 4 to actually do the work. If you're on the fast track, you can skip Parts 5 and 6, but these will help you get more money, and they are a trusty reference for getting out of a tax jam.

Throughout the book, I'll point to additional resources that you can find at www.sunlighttax.com/taxesforhumans.

While I'm here for the holistic tax education, I also know that you may be reading this in a hurry on a deadline (I've been there, too). For that, let me introduce my alter ego, the Tax Dominatrix.

Her role is to tell you exactly what to do, especially if you're in a tax deadline panic.

Skip straight to the Dom parts to get:

- Action items
- Warnings (she's a Dom, after all, but she's got your back and is here to keep you out of danger)
- Chapter summaries

I'll avoid jargon, define terms, and get you up to speed on financial basics you perhaps never learned. You'll get the hard stuff organized and your financial footing secure so you can get back to your important work. Because caring, creative people who are doing the kind of empathy-building work that you do are positioned to create massive change, especially when equipped with the right tools.

ACKNOWLEDGMENTS

Thanks first to my agent, Maeve MacLysaght, who cold emailed me after attending my tax workshop. We all have impulses that could help others, but your follow-through changed my life.

Thanks to my beta readers: the OG, Illysa Hamlin; the official, Annie "the scalpel" Norbeck; Nicole McConville; Beka Hedly; and Jackie Hanson. Thanks to my tax reader (and friend): Bryan Colvin of Colvin CPA and, unofficially, Natalie Bugalski and Aubrey Holland. Thank you to my fact checker, Nabilah Nathani, and to my amazing assistant, Mark de Leon. Thank you to the team at Wiley for making it all possible.

Thanks to Michael Klein, professor at the Fletcher School, Tufts University, and to William G. Gale, co-director of the Urban-Brookings Tax Policy Center, for your generosity and insights on fairer tax policy.

Thanks to Aubrey, whose love and belief I've got receipts for: household equality, snow day kidcare (chicken coop, zipline, cabinets. . .the list is long), and the time and space to do my work.

Thanks to John and Emily Cole, who modeled civics to me from day one, including protest and door knocking (Mom) and 25 years of Tuesday nights on Arlington's Permanent Town Building Committee, overseeing renovation or new construction of seven elementary schools, two middle schools, three fire stations, and the police station, and, separately, Arlington High School (Dad).

To the audience of Sunlight Tax, who lifted me in the darkest time, when Hurricane Helene's flooding destroyed my studio and the 20 years of artwork inside it. You prove to me that there is so much good in this country, and it's worth fighting for.

ABOUT THE AUTHOR

Hannah Cole is a tax expert who specializes in working with creative businesses and mission-driven solopreneurs. A long-time working artist herself (represented by the Tracey Morgan Gallery in Asheville, North Carolina), she's helped tens of thousands of self-employed people skill up with accessible tax and money education through her Money Bootcamp program, tax workshops, and speaking engagements from Florida to Alaska and on the Sunlight Tax podcast. She has some fancy degrees (BA in the history of art, Yale University, and MFA in painting, Boston University) and a tax license (she's an enrolled agent). But what she cares about most is building community and democracy through helping badass people like you do more of your amazing work. She founded her company, Sunlight Tax, with a mission to serve visionary people, just like you, who are self-employed, with relevant tax and financial education so you can bring your unique vision to the world.

You can find all the resources mentioned in this book at:

Website: www.sunlighttax.com
YouTube: @sunlighttax
Instagram: @sunlighttax

PART I

INTRODUCTION

This book is a judgment-free guide for freelancers, solopreneurs, creatives, students, weirdos, visionaries, their partners, and people who give a damn about democracy.

CHAPTER ONE

MY STORY, AND YOUR MINDSET TO MAKE IT WORK

"So, how long are you going to do this art thing before you get a real job?" my dad's accountant asked me.

When those words landed, I realized that I was in enemy territory. My pulse started racing.

I'd just started my life as a professional painter. I was paying a CPA to do my taxes for the first time in my adult life. I wanted to learn about self-employment's minefield of tax responsibilities and set up some tax-smart savings, but I needed help.

Honestly, I had entered that room feeling cocky. I had just graduated my MFA painting program with the Dean's Award, a prestigious grant, two upcoming artist residencies, and a gallery that was courting me for representation.

This accountant saw none of that. To him, I was just a naive girl dabbling in something unimportant, lacking the maturity to learn about taxes and business and join the world of "people to take seriously."

I was a weirdo from another world, and I was wasting his precious time.

My fellow misfit, I see you.

You picked up this book because you've got tax questions. And I'm going to answer them. But I'll do more than that. I want you to feel seen and respected for the unique work you do. The world becomes better when more people like us have thriving businesses.

As a creative person, a mission-driven person, a community-building person, you are the empathy muscle of our culture. You find new solutions to old problems and help people gain new perspectives. You bridge gaps between people, help foster understanding, and are visionary—showing others that a better world is possible. If you are from a historically marginalized group, you may experience problems and see solutions that others never noticed. Your voice has been missing, and it needs to be heard.

Many of us culture and care workers have felt alienated from the world of money, like I did with my dad's accountant. We don't see ourselves represented or respected. Our passion is seen as naive, and not as a gift. And we've been living on a shoestring for so long, we've started to think that having money might corrupt us. We've swallowed a message that tells us to play small.

Believing this hurts you. Your vision alone won't change the world. You need money.

WHY IS THIS BOOK DIFFERENT?

Well, because I'm an artist first. *Not* your dad's accountant.

And I've seen some shit as a woman, as a mother, as a creative, and, frankly, as a person without much money or power. Here are some examples: I was fired from a museum job for complaining that my pay was half that of my male colleagues, I've experienced pregnancy discrimination, and I had a gallerist cancel a once-in-a-lifetime studio visit when I asked for an extra 15 minutes because I was actively having a miscarriage.

I've been assumed to be financially incompetent because I'm an artist. The creative stereotype is harmful and untrue (you know it, right? The one that says you're a flaky creative and "bad with money?"). True, I care more about inspiring people than amassing money. But also, I'm not stupid. I know how fully capable *you* are, and if I can do it, you can too.

Your exact experiences are likely different, and yet you too may feel alienated in accounting spaces because your experience is so different from the accountant's. Maybe your perspective has been shaped by financial discrimination, being a different personality type, or having very different interests from people in accounting. Perhaps you have worked hard to become the expert you are, only to feel humiliated admitting you don't know much about taxes in front of a judgmental accountant. Many of us feel like a round peg in a square hole when we talk to financial professionals.

That's why I founded my company, Sunlight Tax. I went back to school for accounting and got my enrolled agent's license (aka a tax professional, licensed by the IRS). Sunlight, as you know, is warm and helps things grow. It's the antidote to shame and fear. And that's where you come in. To me, creative and care-based businesses, run by people who have been historically underrepresented, are the cure for what ails this world. Sunlight Tax is where weirdos like us get straightforward tax education that values who you are and what you do. All of the charts and resources in this book are available to you at www.sunlighttax.com/taxesforhumans.

To be clear, I come at this work from a place of imperfection, not superiority. I have had all the frustration, made all the mistakes, plus suffered the harsh judgment of money professionals (and sometimes my partner). And yet, I learned how to do it well, which is great—because if this misfit artist can do it, that means you can, too.

> More than a quarter of all couples split up over money.[1] My nastiest fights with my partner were prompted annually with the tax return that highlighted how low-paid my "high prestige" art career was. My disorganization did not help.

I never forgot that humiliating experience in my dad's accountant's office, and I'm here to make sure you feel seen and get the help you need.

Let's get to it.

WHY SHOULD YOU EVEN CARE ABOUT TAXES?

Taxes are our agreement as a society. They fuel our country—taxes build our social safety net, our roads, our schools, our military, our green energy initiatives, you name it. Taxes are the broccoli of democracy. You might prefer Jolly Ranchers, but if you base your whole diet on those, your democracy isn't going to function. Like it or hate it, we need taxes.

The tax code is built on incentives that encourage people to do things that are in the country's interest. We create incentives for things we value. This can change over time, and it varies quite a bit depending on who we elect. These incentives work well for people who know the law. But there is a disconnect when people don't know the law. Tax education would be very helpful for all US taxpayers.

I think taxes should be taught in high school, as part of civics.

In a capitalist society, taxes create a lot of incentives for businesses. What most freelancers don't realize are that your freelance work counts as a business and can access these incentives and that these incentives kick in quickly and are way more generous than you'd expect.

The tax code is built to give you a financial boost as you start a new business, even a tiny one. (Don't worry, I'll teach you about this in Chapter 3 and in Chapter 4.) Incentives like these are here, right now, for *you*.

I get it. We've been trained to have a knee-jerk feeling that taxes are burdensome. You've never really considered that the tax code does all kinds of cool things to put money in your pocket at key moments in your life, when you need it. But it does. Here are some examples: a bigger tax refund the year you start a business or have an unexpected loss in your business; tax savings when you set money aside for your retirement, your family's education, or healthcare; an ability to access cash in your retirement account without penalty when you buy your first home or when you're the victim of domestic violence; cash back when you've been hurt by a natural disaster; cash in your pocket when you are poor but working and supporting children. I can go on, but you get the idea.

This knee-jerk tax reaction is no accident. Most people want the rich to pay their fair tax share and pay back into the country that helped them build that wealth. If you're a billionaire, it's a bad look to want to cut taxes for billionaires, when it's self-interested and benefits only you and your friends with yachts. So you need a strategy to get middle-class people to not want you to pay taxes. How? The current strategy sows distrust in government so that people don't have faith in it and associate the word "burden" with "taxes." It positions politicians who cut taxes as "relieving" people's burden, rather than seeing what they are really doing, which is taking money from the poor and middle-class and giving it to billionaires.

Taxes don't just take from you. They give back, too. Know this, because it helps you get everything they're intended to give you.

Hell, you can even organize and advocate for more. God knows the billionaires are doing this.

Taxes give us societal benefits we can't get on our own—think military protection, roads and bridges, educated neighbors, food safety, scientific research, natural disaster recovery, and so on. If we chose to, taxes could also provide universal healthcare, free vocational and university education, affordable childcare for working families, and public transportation that reduces carbon emissions. Other democracies have chosen these benefits already.

Did you know that the US tax code subsidizes your business expenses to create an incentive for you to make investments in growing your business—even for a company of one or a weird niche micro-business? It's true. Giving you a deduction for what you buy for your business isn't a given. It's a societal choice, to incentivize you to grow, because businesses that invest in themselves are more likely to succeed. They spend a lot of money in the economy, and when they grow, they spend more, plus they start to hire. They grow the US GDP. And they pay taxes. It's a virtuous cycle. Helping US businesses grow is a top priority of the US government.

There's a reason that people come to the US to start businesses. The US tax code makes it So. Easy. Compare us to almost any other country, and suddenly, you start to understand why the United States has three times more startups than all of Europe[2] or that a whopping 44% of Fortune 500 companies were started in the United States by the children of immigrants.[3] It's good to be a business in the United States. People in the United States may feel down on this country—but these numbers prove that people in other countries want the opportunity that we in the United States often take for granted.

The face of US business is changing in exciting ways. More businesses today have missions to benefit society and the planet (see: the growing B Corp movement), and more and more women, BIPOC, queer folks, and other historically marginalized groups are forming businesses to reflect our values and serve the unique unmet needs of our communities. While the business world may still be more male and white than the overall population, more people of diverse backgrounds are stepping in and making change with new businesses of their own.

When you are self-employed, even when you are purpose-driven and anti-capitalist, you are still a business. Getting clear on this unlocks all your tax benefits. Also, it's not evil to be a business.

Purpose-driven businesses that solve real problems are doing incredible good for the world. Who better to have money and use tax rules to their full advantage? *You* are who this is for. Your work is important.

Also, you're a business before you think you are. That matters, because it means that you need to learn the system now, to utilize all the benefits available to you at the beginning, when you really need it. Don't wait and miss out.

The IRS recognizes your business's starting point way sooner than you thought. It's not at the moment you make your first sale or when you first break even or when you decide you're ready to incorporate.

Nope—the IRS sees you as a business the moment you first *advertise*. This means when your website goes live, you post about it on social media or when you send your first announcement email to friends and family. You might not even realize you're advertising. Are you chatting with someone in your DMs about how you can help them solve their problem? That's advertising.

For most freelancers, this entitles you to tax benefits *years* before you thought you would get any. Knowing this stuff is key to getting those benefits.

HOW TO DO IT ALL WITHOUT GETTING OVERWHELMED

How do you get your money organized, your tax-savvy kicking, and your systems set up to put taxes and savings on autopilot, especially when you don't feel anywhere close to that point? I have one mantra for you:

Aim for improvement, not perfection.

Seeking perfection will keep you stuck and give you excuses to delay. ("Wait, I'm not done yet. Just one more detail. . . .") It's an impossible standard that will ensure you never make it. Improvement, on the other hand, is 100% achievable.

You, me, and the IRS already know that you're not perfect. Tax law doesn't require you to be. Wanna know what the IRS really *does* care about, though? Being on time. That is not an impossible standard.

Also? The IRS is very consistent about penalties when you are late.

You might be skimming this book to get your taxes done. I get it— I promise to help you do that. But let's talk for a minute about why you might feel allergic to growing your own wealth and why that might be holding you back.

YOUR MINDSET MATTERS

The very thing that makes your work awesome can often be mistakenly tied to attitudes that keep you broke. What makes your work great? The fact that you really, truly give a shit. That you place your vision higher than your desire for money. This is a superpower. It will help you find true fulfillment, because once you meet your financial needs, more money doesn't make you happier. As someone who has done the taxes of several millionaires, they aren't happier than any of my other clients. When you are passionate about your work and money isn't your primary mission, it's possible to get your head on wrong about money in general.

Creative people, healers, and care-based people tend to be undervalued in society, and consequently, we're often underpaid. We interact daily with other like-minded people, so it's easy to absorb the prevailing do-gooder attitude about money—that money itself is bad, and people with money aren't good people.

When you believe that people with money are bad, you make decisions that undercut your ability to earn, save, and grow your money. It's not rocket science. If you believe you'd be kind of a jerk if you had more money and you value not being a jerk, are you going to really advocate for yourself and the (monetary) value of your work when you discuss your rates with your next client? No, you won't.[4]

Having done thousands of tax returns for creative people, I see that to successfully build wealth, you must address your feelings of anti-wealth. If you believe you'll lose your moral compass by having a fully funded solo 401k, then you'll never fully fund your solo 401k.

Here's a helpful mental shift: money is not evil. It's not good either. It's neutral. It's a tool. Think of a hammer: you can build a house with a hammer or destroy a house with it. A hammer is a tool that amplifies the power of the person holding it. An ethical person with money is a person with the power to do more good.

You started your business to change the world in some way (large or small), and taxes are part of doing that. They aren't just a thing you need to get done each year and pay each quarter (although they definitely are both of those things). Understanding the essentials of your taxes will help save you money every year, help you have a bigger impact with your work, squeeze more out of each dollar, and achieve financial security faster.

You might see the world of shareholders and tax-savvy businesspeople and think, "That's a straight, white, male world; that doesn't feel like me." But I think, "I wish more people like you—my misfit, visionary, queer, BIPOC, and/or historically marginalized friend—were building wealth, taking up (financial) space, and growing your visionary business not on a shoestring but with capital and power so you can make a huge impact in this world and even enjoy some leisure, comfort, and security along the way." That's the reason I do this work.

And that's why you need this book.

CHAPTER SUMMARY

- You're not alone. You may feel judged, alienated, and underestimated by financial professionals.
- But you do need to get good with your money. I'll help you do that while making sure you feel valued for your unique work.
- Money isn't evil. It's an amplifier. Let it boost your amazingness.
- Taxes can give you huge incentives for growing your business and enhancing your life (especially your savings). It's empowering to know these areas.
- Building wealth and leveraging your tax benefits is good for you and the people you support. Your work is important, and you deserve financial security.

ENDNOTES

1. Mark Gilman, "Young Couples Are Splitting Over Finances, But There's Help On The Way To Keep It All Separate But Equal," *Yahoo*, January 18, 2023, https://finance.yahoo.com/news/young-couples-splitting-over-finances-153242555.html?guccounter=1&guce_referrer=aHR0cHM6Ly93d3cuZ29vZ2 xlLmNvbS88&guce_referrer_sig=AQAAAGTP5GDhPrV7zlq8wzVKk3SEML2 mqktcuNtuAyazwrQ6NwK_xmCuoBpqqG83vkVnvk8rSnSHoDV9SG5l3gAf7 EDmkae32TNq_0c-bnk8vSpgTTNJUaDKAxVFjlFY1ONe6L1ljDsKf7rEYqG5 p7vHgxqb80o-jJjYl03-Oq5v5kxT.

2. Charlotte Reypens, Julie Delanote, and Désirée Rückert, *From starting to scaling: How to foster startup growth in Europe* (European Investment Bank, 2013), 3, https://www.eib.org/en/publications/from-starting-to-scaling.

3. Elyssa Pachico, "New American Fortune 500 Report Reveals Impact of Immigrant Entrepreneurship," *American Immigration Council*, June 9, 2022, https://www.americanimmigrationcouncil.org/news/new-american-fortune-500-report-reveals-impact-immigrant-entrepreneurship#:~:text=The%20report%2C%20%E2%80%9CNew%20American%20Fortune,by%20immigrants%20or%20their%20children.

4. If this resonates, I've got a bonus chapter for you, about the "wealth gap," available at www.sunlighttax.com/taxesforhumans.

PART II

THE TAX EDUCATION YOU NEVER GOT

You already know this dirty little secret: there's no tax education in this country. Don't feel bad that you don't know this stuff. *Most* people don't, because it's not taught in school. And that's bananas. Taxes are more mandatory than military service. They're less optional than voting. Taxes are the bricks that build our society. They are part of civics.

CHAPTER TWO

TAX BASICS

L et's start with *you*, the self-employed person (and maybe your spouse).

WHO COUNTS AS SELF-EMPLOYED?

Self-employment income can mean a lot of different things: side hustle, freelancing, gig work, consulting, sole proprietorship, or an LLC (with one owner). And if you are married to (and file jointly with) someone with any of those things, then your tax return includes this stuff too (see Figure 2.1).

See Chapter 12 for info on LLCs. They can be confusing. For now, please know that they don't affect how you are taxed when you're the sole owner.

Figure 2.1   Your taxes are based on all your taxable income.

Source: © Hannah Cole/Sunlight Tax.

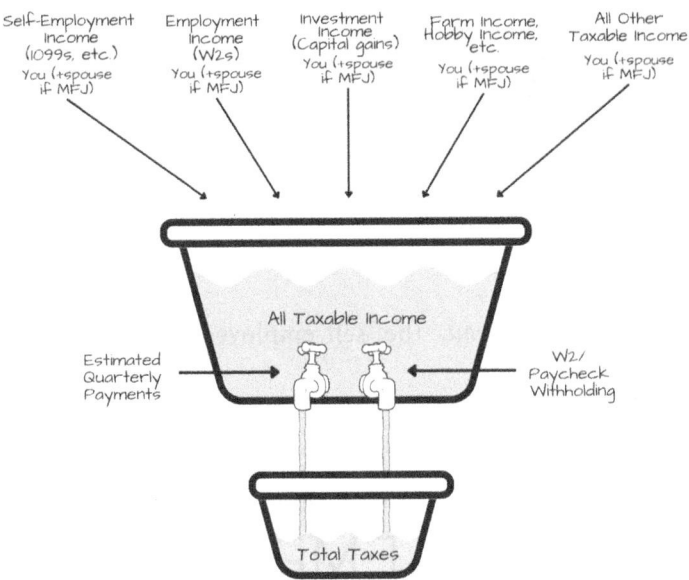

What the groups I just mentioned have in common is that they all report self-employment income on a form called (tax term alert!) a **Schedule C**. That's part of your personal income tax return. It's also where you get to deduct the costs of your work (aka your business deductions). I'll get into all the benefits and rules of the Schedule C in the next chapter, but for now, understand whether you have to file one.

WHO HAS A SCHEDULE C?

Figure 2.2 shows who files a Schedule C. These terms may feel very different to you, but for income tax purposes, these are all treated *the same*.

Figure 2.2 Who files a Schedule C?

Source: © Hannah Cole/Sunlight Tax.

Who files a Schedule C?

✓ Schedule C

- ✓ Self-employment
- ✓ Freelancing
- ✓ 1099 income for contracting
- ✓ Single-member LLC ●
- ✓ Sole proprietorship
- ✓ Consulting
- ✓ Gig work
- ✓ Side hustle
- ✓ Grant income related to your self-employment
- ✓ Royalty income from self-employment or if you've got an operating oil, gas or mineral interest
- ✓ Gambling winnings if you're a pro-gambler
- ✓ 2 spouses who equally share a business ★

● Unless you file paperwork with the IRS to be taxed as an S Corp, C Corp or nonprofit

★ In which case, mark "qualified joint venture" on the Schedule C. Unless you formed a legal business partnership or elected to be taxed as a partnership, S Corp or C Corp

Note: if you're married to someone on this list and you file jointly, that Schedule C is part of your tax return, too

Ø Schedule C

	Instead, you report the income HERE →
Ø Hobby income	Line 8j, Schedule 1
Ø Farming	SCHEDULE F
Ø Fishing	SCHEDULE F
Ø Rental income ●	SCHEDULE E
Ø Royalty income that's not from self-employment or an operating oil, gas, or mineral interest	SCHEDULE E
Ø Gambling winnings if you're not a pro-gambler	Line 8b, Schedule 1
Ø Scholarship and fellowship grants	Line r, Schedule 1
Ø S Corporation	1120 S
Ø C Corporation	1120
Ø Partnership	1065
Ø Multi-member LLC	1065 ★
Ø Nonprofit	990

★ But you can elect to be taxed as an S Corp or C Corp instead

● unless you provide "substantial services" like coaching, or guests's breakfast everyday, in which case, report on a Schedule C

19

There's also a Schedule C in your tax return if you are married to *and file jointly with* anyone in this graphic. That's because filing jointly means you're responsible for everything on the tax return, including your spouse's stuff.

Is It Possible to Have a Business and Not Have a Schedule C?

Short answer: yes.

However, the Schedule C is the default; it takes effort to form a different kind of tax entity, so if you aren't sure how you file, you almost certainly file a Schedule C. Unless you took a whole lot of Ambien and zombie-filed IRS paperwork in the dark of night. . .but that's unlikely, right?

This book will guide you through filing the Schedule C. Later, in Part 5, "The Level-Up: Smarter Taxes to Get You More Money," I will teach you about when and why you might choose to elect a different tax entity, like an "S Corporation."

Before we leave the subject of different tax entities, the Tax Dom has one quick piece of advice.

Please don't take legal or tax advice from some rando lady on TikTok. It could get you an unnecessary LLC or an S Corp that costs you $2,000 in new accounting fees and the State of Arizona chasing you down for unpaid unemployment and worker's comp. Instead, slow down and consider your unique business needs, which may be very different from that TikTok lady's audience. She might not be qualified to give legal or tax advice in the first place. See Chapter 12 for help deciding what's right for *your* business structure.

WHAT'S AN INCOME TAX RETURN ACTUALLY FOR?

Here's the simplest high-level version of what your income tax return is. It's a reconciliation document that compares the tax you paid throughout the year (which is estimated) with the actual tax you owe, when the year is over, and with tax credits and deductions factored in. The result is a refund if you've overpaid, or a tax bill, if you underpaid.

The US taxes the income a household makes each year. It also provides numerous benefits to taxpayers via the tax code, through reductions to taxable income (like deductions and tax-advantaged accounts) and direct reductions of tax (tax credits).

> We do not tax wealth. Wealth is the amount of money sitting in your accounts. Income is what comes in during a given period.

You communicate this information to the IRS by filing a personal income tax return (aka your "1040" or "ten-forty"). For starters, you will have a 1040 for each tax year, which is generally the same as a calendar year.

This makes taxes *retroactive*. You can't file your 2026 tax return until 2026 is over—in other words, until 2027. That is so you know what happened for the year. It's done, and you have a limited ability to change it after the fact—mostly through taking deductions and tax credits.

The purpose of your income tax return is to:

- Total how much income you, your spouse, and possibly your kids/dependents made throughout the year from all sources.
- Reduce it by the amount of any tax deductions you're eligible for.
- Then calculate the tax due on it (your total tax for the year).
- You subtract out the taxes you've already paid from your total tax (payroll withholding plus estimated payments for self-employment income).
- Lastly, subtract any tax credits you're eligible for, to get your *tax due or refund amount.*
- If you owe any penalties, those get added to the final amount.

Having tax due means you didn't prepay all of your tax, and you owe some more. A tax refund means you paid more than you owed[1] and therefore will receive the overpayment back.

Figure 2.3 shows a visual of tax return math.

Your tax return goal each year is to owe close to zero, because you've paid your taxes throughout the year. This can go sideways when you have a big income change. That's okay—your tax return's job is to reconcile and get you settled up. But use the new information to get the current year's payments back on track, or else you risk a fall-behind, get-caught-up-again cycle. It doesn't need to be that stressful.

Figure 2.3   What does a tax return track?

Source: © Hannah Cole/Sunlight Tax.

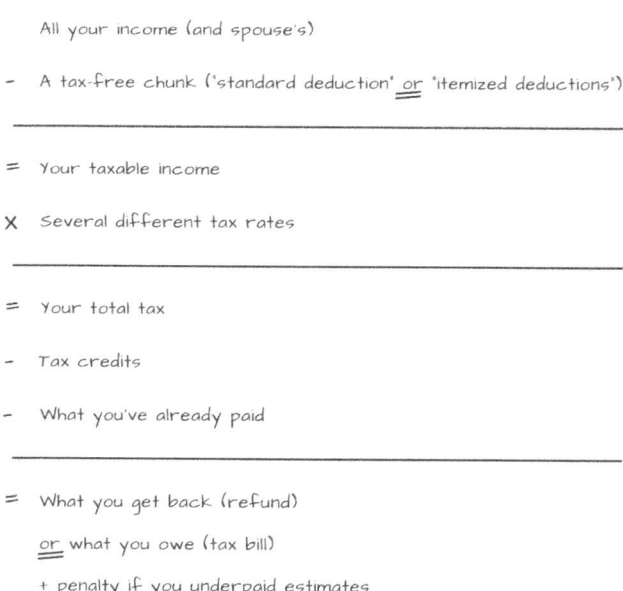

What does a tax return track?

All your income (and spouse's)

− A tax-free chunk ('standard deduction' or 'itemized deductions')

= Your taxable income

X Several different tax rates

= Your total tax

− Tax credits

− What you've already paid

= What you get back (refund)

or what you owe (tax bill)

+ penalty if you underpaid estimates

Your Business Deductions Are *Not* Itemized Deductions

The word *itemizing* often gets confused with business deductions. It's critical that you know the difference. They are not related. And whether you itemize deductions says nothing about whether you get to take business deductions. Business deductions are about having a "profit motive." (I cover that in Chapter 3.)

All US taxpayers get a tax-free chunk of income, and it's a binary choice between **Itemized Deductions** or taking the **Standard Deduction**. You get to take the one that's bigger.[2] Figure 2.4 explains itemizing.

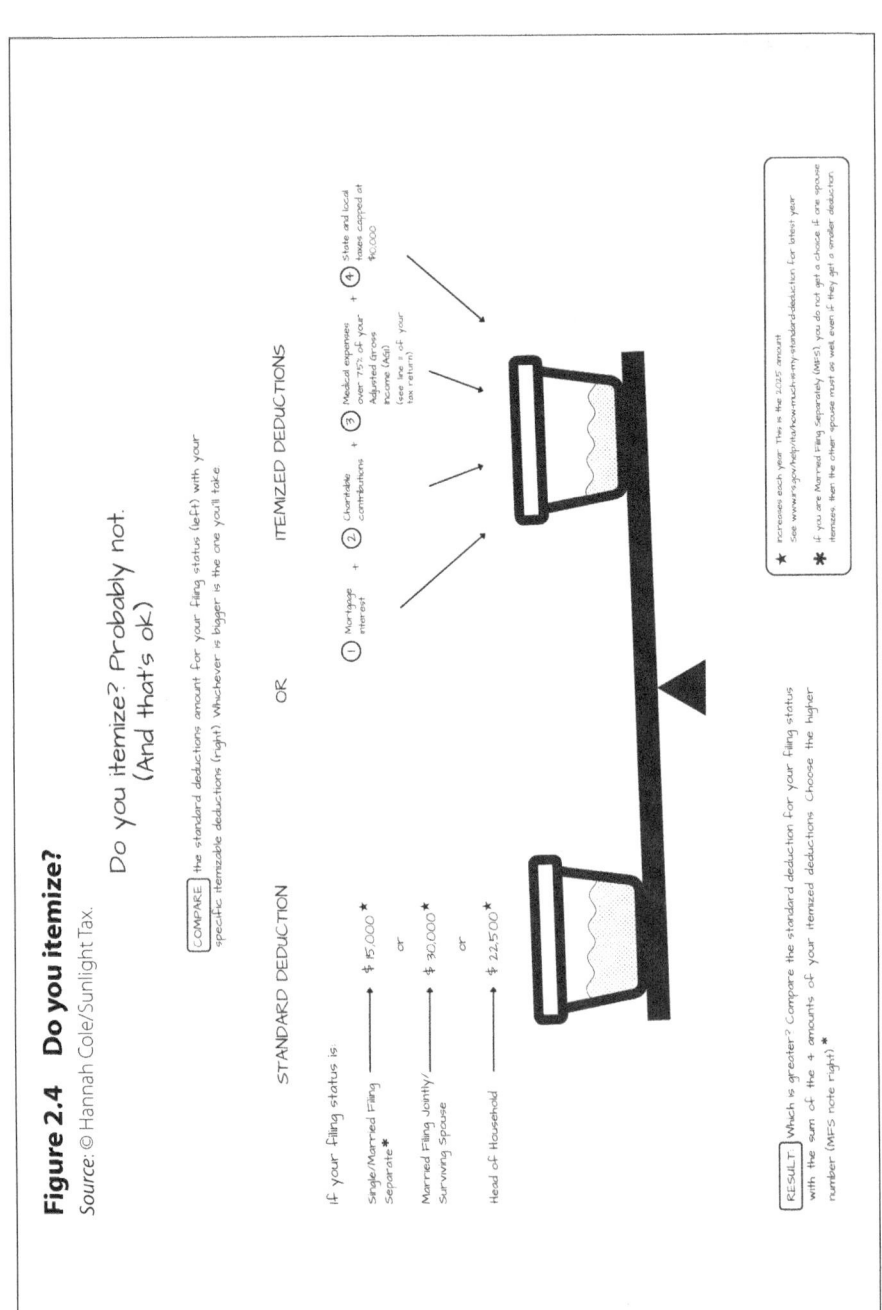

Figure 2.4 Do you itemize?
Source: © Hannah Cole/Sunlight Tax.

WHAT TAXES DO WE OWE ON OUR INCOME?

What taxes do you owe in the first place and on what part of your business income? An important goal of tax law is to treat all working taxpayers equitably. So taxes for an employee are related to taxes for self-employed people. But the taxes are smoother and paid automatically through payroll, when you're an employee, so that system is easier to learn. Let's start there. Then we'll translate to how they apply to self-employment income. It's easier to understand self-employment taxes when you know how it works for employees.

How Employees Get Taxed

Employees are paid by payroll.[3] If you're an employee, you get a regular paycheck. And in January, after a calendar year has ended, you get a tax-reporting summary of all your paychecks from each employer, called a W2.

> Employees are protected by (lovely) employment laws. It's one reason there's been a multidecade trend to classify workers as contractors, *not* employees. Businesses do not need to treat their contractors with the same rights under the law. But I digress.

If you've ever earned money as an employee, you've likely noticed that your full earnings don't enter your bank account. Why?

Medicare and Social Security: How Employees Pay

That's because 7.65% of your pay is taken from your paycheck and sent to the US Treasury to pay for your Medicare and Social Security.[4] This requires no input from you; it's mandatory. But interestingly, this 7.65% isn't the end of your Medicare and Social Security. Your boss matches your contribution with her own dollars, out of her business's pocket. She pays an equal 7.65% of your pay into your Medicare and Social Security taxes. That piece has its own name: **payroll tax**.[5]

Many people never notice that this is happening, and that's because the boss's contribution to your Medicare and Social Security never appears on your paystub or W2. Why? Because your paystubs and W2s only reflect *your* money. Understand that your "credit" for Medicare and Social Security is 15.3% (7.65 × 2 = 15.3) of your earnings, not 7.65%.[6] That's because both you and your employer are paying into it in equal parts.

Here's the civics behind that. Taxes are our societal agreement about how we want to run this joint. When we set up Medicare and Social Security withholding requirements, we decided as a society that the employee and the employer equally share the responsibility of paying into that individual employee's future health benefit (Medicare) and future retirement benefit (Social Security). In a system with work-based healthcare, this allows the worker to continue to get healthcare after they no longer work. Likewise, prepaying into a future retirement benefit during their most able-bodied working years helps the worker have some guaranteed income when they no longer earn any.

Note that Medicare and Social Security contributions come out of your very first dollar of earnings. When we translate these rules into the self-employment zone, this will become relevant.

Federal Income Tax for Employees

That's not the only money deducted from your paycheck as an employee. By law, your boss must withhold both federal and state income taxes. Federal income tax rates vary between 0% and 37%.[7] This number is confusing—your income tax rate is based on *all your income*, not just this job. This includes any additional jobs you have, such as rental income, royalties, farm or fishery income, stock and bond trades (aka capital gains), and real estate sales, plus all the income that your spouse earns, if you file jointly. So remember, a married couple who files jointly shares one tax rate. The more income you earn, the higher your tax rate, as shown in Figure 2.1.

So two employees earning the same pay could actually be taxed at radically different rates. One employee might have no other income and be in a low tax bracket. The second employee, earning exactly the same amount, could have a bunch of other income and be in a high tax bracket. For example, they could be Megan Thee Stallion and have a multimillion-dollar, multi-Grammy award-winning music career that is all self-employed income. Or they could be married to a super-high income earner, like the top neurosurgeon at Mass General Hospital in Boston, so their joint income with their spouse is more than $700,000. That would put their marginal tax rate at the top, which is 37%.[8]

HOW TAX RATES ACTUALLY WORK

Your income tax rates are a rainbow, not a single color. It's a myth that your "tax bracket" determines the rate of tax on all of your earnings. Believe this myth, and you fear that earning one extra dollar pushes you into the next tax bracket and suddenly spikes your taxes.

Nope. False. We have what's called a "graduated income tax" system for earned income (aka labor).[9] Each slice of income that every US taxpayer earns is taxed at exactly the same rate. We all get one slice of income taxed at 0% (roughly your first $12,000).[10] And if you earn more income, above the range of the previous bracket, your next chunk of income is taxed at the next rate. Not all your income—only the income above the last threshold.

Understand that "earned income tax" is tax on labor. People see that 37% marginal rate and think, oh, the rich really do pay more. That's a misdirect. The 1% live off of capital, not labor. Capital is taxed at highly favorable "capital gains tax rates": between 0% and 20%. When Warren Buffett says he pays a lower tax rate than his secretary, it's the truth. He does.

This continues through each tax bracket until your last earned dollar. Each slice of your income is taxed at the rate of that slice. The name for these tax rates is **marginal tax rates.**[11] They show you only what your very highest dollar earned is taxed at. Identifying the whole shebang by the outermost dollar feels misleading to me. It makes people feel more upset about their taxes than what reality warrants. It's like if you saw me at my brother's wedding, dressed in my black Jackie-O dress, with my hair done, and decided that I'm an elegant dresser. This would ignore that I'm in "soft pants" with the sweater I call "big nasty" on top six days a week. Jackie-O I am not. And while I aspire to the 37% tax bracket, my average tax rate is nowhere near that. And neither is yours.

Since Medicare and Social Security is the same percentage for everyone, employee payroll pulls out exactly the right amount of Medicare and Social Security all year long, so you never have any reconciling to do there.

But your boss has no clue what your federal income tax rate is. She doesn't know all your other financial details, like your spouse's income or your other jobs, so you have to indicate to her what level of federal income tax withholding you want taken out of your paychecks. You do this on a form called a W4.

There's State Income Tax, Too

Don't forget state-level income tax. Your state may also require you to fill out a form for your employee withholding. Some states use the federal form W4, and some states have their own form. Nine states don't have any income tax and don't require any form.

Those states are Alaska, Florida, Nevada, New Hampshire, South Dakota, Tennessee, Texas, Washington, and Wyoming.

State withholding tends to be easier and smaller. There are some states that require you to pay a few dollars into paid family and medical leave insurance, or other programs, through payroll. And keep in mind that Medicare and Social Security are federal programs, which you don't pay at the state level.

PUTTING THE TAX LAYERS TOGETHER

Withholding is required by law when you are an employee, so you pay taxes "as you go" throughout the year. If your only income is through a W2 and you didn't have a big tax change during the year, like a marriage or an untaxed bonus, you usually get a refund. Remember, the act of preparing a tax return is to reconcile your amount of tax already paid with the amount you actually owe, once you tally all your income and calculate whatever credits you're eligible for. It's rare that someone with only W2 income has a tax bill, and doing those taxes is simple and relatively painless.

To recap, an employee has three layers of tax taken out of each paycheck and prepaid to the federal or state government: Medicare and Social Security, federal income tax, and state income tax. Remember that Medicare and Social Security payments begin at the first dollar earned and are withheld at a flat rate of 7.65% of your pay as an employee.[12] Federal income taxes are based on your withholding decision on the W4 you submitted to your employer, and the marginal tax rates on earned income (labor) range from 0% to 37%, while your average tax rate is a blend of all the rates until your last (marginal) dollar. State withholding happens only if your state has income tax but is typically a smaller amount than your federal withholding.

HOW THESE TAXES WORK WHEN YOU'RE SELF-EMPLOYED

What happens when we earn our money on our own? In that scenario, things get harder—not because we're being punished. It's because the mechanism of payroll that forces all-year prepayment of tax isn't there. Furthermore, we get a sweet benefit that employees do not: tax-free business deductions. The only way to get those deductions is to track our spending on them and do basic math (bookkeeping!) to figure out what income remains after those expenses are subtracted. We're taxed only on the profit after these deductions. But for that sweet perk, we're responsible for doing the calculations (and saving our receipts to prove these expenses really happened).

Let's return to the tax withholding rules for employees, by applying it to us self-employed weirdos (without a payroll system automatically paying our taxes). We've got math to do before we know what our taxable income is.

What Part of My Self-Employed Income Is Taxed?

When you're self-employed, are you taxed on all the money you make through your work?

Hell no! Which is awesome. When you're self-employed, you're treated with all the benefits of a genuine business, so you get to spend all kinds of money on your business and not pay tax on those expenses (more on business deduction specifics in Chapter 4).

Employees don't get tax deductions. So they have no math to do—their employer says, "This is what I'm paying you." And the IRS says, "We'll tax all of that."

As a self-employed person, it's different—you earn money in a variety of ways (client billings, sales of products and services, Eventbrite ticket sales, Etsy sales, cash payments, grant income, contract jobs, 1099 income, etc.). It is your legal obligation to tally all of your self-employment income up and report that gross income to the government. Small amounts, cash, grants—all of it. If you understate this number by more than 25%, you are committing a felony. Some people use the phrase "under the table" like it's cute. The IRS doesn't do "cute" — they say, "felony." So, you know, toMAYto, toMAHto.

Check out Chapter 8 for an explainer on some types of income that aren't taxable or are partly taxable.

On the other hand, you don't pay any tax on the money you've earned but then spent to run your business. Hell yes. That's a huge benefit. But this does obligate you to do some math. You must track and report all your expenses.

Here's a visual:

	GROSS INCOME
—	BUSINESS EXPENSES
=	PROFIT (or LOSS if it's a negative number)

Only your profit is taxable. A negative profit, aka a loss, is not taxable at all. This is a generous benefit you get under the US tax code to help protect US businesses during the delicate "startup phase" and in years of hardship. Ultimately, a strong, well-resourced business can better weather the slings and arrows of the economy, life circumstances, disruptions, competition, etc. And when businesses grow, both the US GDP and the US tax base grow, which is a beneficial cycle.

But the flipside is that when you take deductions, you have to document them properly. Mostly this means keeping receipts. For a few categories, more is required (see Chapter 4). A good rule of thumb is that if you're not keeping the receipt or doing the IRS-required documentation for that deduction, don't put it on your tax return. So keeping receipts and documentation is mandatory, as is bookkeeping. This can be simple, like a spreadsheet.

Bummed about this? Tell you what. If you don't like the idea of bothering with receipts or bookkeeping, don't!

Wait, what?

Sure. If you don't want to track your deductions or keep your receipts, it's okay. *You just don't get to take them.* In other words, if you want to pay taxes on all your gross income—a dramatically larger amount of income than what your legal right is, that's fine. The IRS is fine with you overpaying taxes.

For the rest of us, I hope that offers some perspective on taking your deductions. You don't have to. But if you *want* to, you have to do the IRS-required stuff to prove that you are not making shit up. Think about it. Most years (in any year you're not audited), the IRS is taking your word for it when you list your business deductions. Wow. The employees of the world don't get this benefit. You self-report your income and your deductions. Most years, the IRS is trusting you to be honest.

How Far Back an Audit Can Go

I hope this makes clear the IRS's right to check (aka audit). In any given tax year, the IRS can ask to see your records (usually receipts, but other stuff, too). This happens retroactively, so your last three years of tax returns can get scooped at any time, for anything you put on them.[13] They can review six years of tax returns if you have misstated things, if you made substantial mistakes, and/or especially if you've understated your income (remember that word, *felony*?). There's no statute of limitations if you never filed a tax return that year or if you've committed fraud.

The reality is, those of us with self-employed income are in a group that the IRS audits frequently. They take our word for it most years on our income and expenses. Do you think there might be a few taxpayers out there not reporting all their income, because it's cash, or they didn't get a 1099 for it, and think no one will notice? Are folks maybe putting the odd vacation on the business card or using that card for meals out with friends that have no business purpose? You can thank those folks for your next audit. They are the reason we get looked at from time to time. If you report all your income and never put a deduction on your tax return without having the documentation, you will be fine—even if the IRS asks to see it and you have to show your work.

We've reviewed the fact that you only pay taxes on your profit, and not on your gross income. To do that, you have to follow the IRS rules for documenting those deductions, and that requires enough of a bookkeeping setup to track what's left over after you subtract expenses out of your gross income.

WHAT TAX DO YOU PAY ON YOUR PROFIT?

Good news. You already know what tax to pay on your profit, because it's exactly the same as the employee–employer scenario I laid out a minute ago. You'll find that some of it gets a little funky when we translate it from two parties (employee/employer) to one (you!).

Self-Employment Tax: Paying Medicare and Social Security

Like the employee, you also pay 7.65% of your profit toward Medicare and Social Security. Now think about the matching half of Medicare and Social Security that the employer pays. Who pays your boss half? Yep. You. Because you're the boss.

When you add the boss 7.65% and the employee 7.65%, that equals 15.3%. Take a mental snapshot of that number—it's important. You, as a self-employed person, pay 15.3% of your profit, every year, into Medicare and Social Security. This boss/employee combo has a name: it's called **self-employment tax.**

You are just as entitled to Medicare and Social Security in your later years as any employee, because you've been paying 15.3% of your profits into that system for your entire career.

See how scrupulously equally the law is applied to you here? You might be bummed about paying double the payment into Medicare and Social Security, but think about the full picture here. Who else would pay the other half? It's just you, no one else. You truly are the boss. What's more, you get the full boss ability to deduct all your business expenses out of your taxable income. No employee gets to do that. So you have the boss responsibility, but also the boss benefit.

Furthermore, if you've ever noticed in the fine print of your tax return that half of your self-employment tax is deductible[14] (it is!), you might wonder why tax law is so weird and complicated. Here's the reason: in the employee/employer situation, the employee doesn't get any deductions, including their contribution to Medicare and Social Security. The boss gets to deduct their contributions to their employees' Medicare and Social Security (aka payroll taxes) from their taxable income, because that is an expense of running the business. So the law is applied equally to you. You get to deduct your boss half but not your employee half. It just feels funny because in the first scenario, the law is applied to two different people, and in your scenario, you are both people in one.

You Also Owe Federal Income Tax

We're not quite done outlining all the taxes that you owe on your profit. Like the employee, in addition to your self-employment tax, you still owe federal income tax. Remember that your marginal income tax rate is the same as anyone else's—somewhere within the range of 0–37%.

Plus You Owe State Income Tax

Last but not least, you owe state income tax too, if you work in one of the 41 states with income tax.

Here is a quick visual summary of that:

GROSS INCOME

—EXPENSES

_____

PROFIT———————> this is your taxable income

PROFIT × 15.3% SELF-EMPLOYMENT TAX

+ PROFIT × (YOUR INCOME TAX RATE, a blend of rates between 0% and 37%)

= TOTAL TAX YOU OWE TO THE US TREASURY

And

PROFIT × (YOUR STATE INCOME TAX RATE, a range between 0% and 13.3%)

= TOTAL TAX YOU OWE TO YOUR STATE

SELF-EMPLOYMENT TAX: WHY YOU MIGHT UNDERESTIMATE YOUR TAX BILL

Self-employed people tend to underestimate the amount of tax they owe, because they don't realize how big self-employment tax is.

Self-employment tax kicks in immediately. You owe it on all the profit you make. This is quite different from federal income tax, where you are taxed in the zero income tax bracket for your first roughly $12,000 of profit. If you were to assume you owed nothing on a profit in your newish business of $10,000, because you mistakenly thought your self-employment kicks after a certain threshold the way your income tax does, you'd be wrong.

How wrong? While you wouldn't owe any federal income tax on $10,000 of profit (assuming no other income, of course), you'd still owe $1,530 in self-employment tax.[15] That's because 15.3% × $10,000 = $1,530. $1,530 is not nothing. And if it's a surprise, it will feel high. Make sure you understand that self-employment tax kicks in immediately.

The IRS gives you wiggle room to make a tiny profit before you have to file a tax return to settle up your Medicare and Social Security. Technically, your obligation to file a tax return to pay into your self-employment tax, when you have no other income to reconcile, begins at $400 in profit.

If you're wondering what happens with your taxes when your business has a loss, I'll ask you a rhetorical question. When you multiply a negative number times a tax rate (any tax rate), do you get a positive number? No? Well then, it looks like you don't owe anything. You don't owe taxes on zero or on a loss in your business.

How Do You Pay the Taxes During the Year?

We know what we owe on our self-employment profit, so how do we pay it?

Think about the employee, where payroll pays an approximation of what they owe in taxes every two weeks to the IRS and to their state. That's what we're trying to emulate.

We live in what is called a "pay-as-you-go" tax system, meaning you are required by law to pay your taxes as you go. What you're not allowed to do is to earn money all year and accumulate a giant outstanding tax bill. The potential in that scenario is for you to spend all your cash, forget to save some, and face a giant tax bill that you can't pay. That's not a smart way fund a country through taxes. Which is why we don't allow it.

> You: "Wait, what?" I'm kinda freaking out as I read that. "That scenario describes exactly what I have been doing, and now I'm worried I might be in trouble."
>
> Me: "I know. In our bananas system, where we don't teach people about taxes, as we should, most of us learn this rule by breaking it. Don't worry. It's fixable. By waiting until April 15, you pay penalties and interest every year; but once you start paying estimated quarterly taxes on time each quarter, your penalties and interest will stop. Let's learn how to quit those penalties and shrink your tax payments into smaller pieces that you pay quarterly. Ultimately, this will save you money and stress."

Many US taxpayers make money in ways where taxes aren't withheld. You, my self-employed friend, are in this boat. Also in this boat are people selling real estate, living off of stock and bond trades, taking in rents or royalties, or operating an orchard or cattle ranch.

The system built for all of us nonemployees requires us to pay taxes "as we go." That system is called **estimated quarterly taxes**.[16] The point of this system is to keep you out of tax debt. It keeps your tax payments smaller and more manageable and paid more frequently so you don't fall behind or have a stressfully large bill that is tough to pay.

ESTIMATED QUARTERLY TAXES: WHO, WHEN, AND HOW

First, who. Who has to pay their taxes quarterly? If you had a tax bill last year that was greater than $1,000, then you're now required to pay your taxes *quarterly*.[17] If you don't, you'll be assessed a penalty for each quarter that goes by where no payment came in from you, plus daily interest on your unpaid balance.

Why does this threshold exist? For good reason. Have you ever thought about what a tax bill is? It's an unpaid balance. It's tax you still owe after your tax return reconciles your estimated tax payments with the actual amount due. In the employee world, where payroll rules mandate this prepayment, most employees have a refund at tax time, because they've done what the system intends. Barring big income changes, the employee's prepayment through payroll withholding means they are mostly settled up each April 15.

You might recognize that this isn't what's going on with your taxes in your self-employment.

A tax bill means you didn't prepay the full amount of taxes you owed during the year. It's an underpayment. In other words, if your underpayment was greater than $1,000 last year, you need to bump up your payments this year, starting now, so you don't face a bill bigger than $1,000 next year.

This is based on data that says the average US taxpayer, if faced with a bill greater than $1,000, would struggle to pay it.[18] So that's where the IRS set the threshold. They don't want you struggling to pay. They want the amounts to feel relatively small and manageable. For that reason, when your bill gets past the "manageable" zone, they ask you to make those payments smaller but more frequently throughout the year. And, because our society built tax laws on incentives (both positive and negative), we put penalties and interest in there to encourage your compliance with this law rather than ignore it. If you're curious if you've been paying penalties and interest, look at line 38 of last year's 1040. That's your penalty for not making estimated payments. It's my goal to get you to a blank line 38 from here on out.

Honestly, this data is a little old. Current data puts this number closer to $400. Thankfully the IRS held the rule where it was.

Take out last year's tax return and look at line 37 to see if your bill was over $1,000. Of course, if this is your first time filing a tax return, you won't have anything to reference yet.

Your last tax return is a tool with useful information that helps you improve your systems. The big tax companies' whole marketing schtick is to encourage you to find your taxes scary and inaccessible so you bury your tax return in a drawer without looking. They profit from your fear. Why would you pay them if you realized you had all the resources necessary to do it yourself? The civic side of me hates this. I'd like you to feel that your tax return is a tool that you can use. It's expensive when you are reliant on a $300/hour accountant to answer tax questions that you could look up easily if you knew how to review your own tax return. I will be happy if you occasionally pull out your last tax return to check different numbers for yourself. Then use that money you didn't pay a tax company or an accountant and treat yourself to drinks with a friend. In Chapter 11 I'll teach you how to review your tax return.

Contrast this with estimated quarterly taxes. Notice the first word? They are estimates. You won't know your tax rate for the current year until the year is over—because it's only then that you'll know how much money you earned and determine your tax rate.

Perfectionists (and I'm a still-reforming perfectionist myself), be kinder to yourself, please. You cannot know the future. The law doesn't require you to. When we call these estimates, we mean it. Lean into that word. You will have to do a little math and take a stab at what you owe in the absence of "the right answer." And for us perfectionists, that's scary as hell.

I've seen people get freaked out by the uncertainty around making a calculation for estimated quarterly taxes and assumed they were doing it wrong, because they didn't know the "right" number, froze, and did nothing. The only wrong thing you can do regarding estimated tax payments is to freeze and do nothing. If you make an estimate that is off, even radically off but you do make a payment, then you avoid the "failure to pay" penalty.[19] You may still owe a little interest on your unpaid balance, but even in that scenario, you've reduced your unpaid balance with that payment, so your interest is smaller than it would be if you froze and paid nothing. See how taking a stab at it, and being a little off, is still better than doing nothing? It's hard to get your head around this, I know. I see you. It's okay. This will make things better, I promise. Even if the first time you do it feels weird and uncertain.

How Do I Calculate My Estimated Tax Payment?

How do you make this calculation? The goal is to *approximate* the amount of tax that you will actually owe, in real time, as you're earning it, so that next April 15, your tax bill is pretty close to zero. We won't know what your tax rate for this year is until you do that tax return next year, so we're going to need to guesstimate.

How to Estimate: The Safe Harbor Rules

The IRS created two so-called "safe harbor" rules to help you estimate. While they can't guarantee that you've paid exactly the right amount of tax, the goal is to prepay approximately what tax you owe throughout the year and then settle up the difference (by paying a small bill or getting a refund) with your annual tax return, on April 15. The safe harbor rules have a technical aim and a practical one. The technical side of meeting either one of the safe harbor rules is that it guarantees you will not owe penalties or interest. The practical aim is probably more important, and that is to give you a target when estimating what tax you owe, before you know your actual income for the year.

Safe Harbor Rule #1

Safe harbor rule #1 is the easiest, and it's the one that your software or accountant will give you. It says that you can pay 100% of last year's tax, broken up into four chunks. (If you make over $150,000 in profit, the percentage bumps up to 110% of last year's tax.)[20]

To do this, take your full tax from last year (see line 24 of your 1040), divide it into four parts (one for each quarter), and pay it at IRS.gov before each of the quarterly deadlines.

> For example, let's say that last year, I made about $100,000 in profit from my painting sales, and my total (federal) tax on that was $20,000. My quarterly taxes this year are paid like this; before April 15, I will log into IRS.gov and click the "Make a Payment" button. I'll select the reason "estimated payment," and I will make a payment of $5,000.

Then, before the next deadline, on June 15, I will log in again and make my second payment of $5,000, and then rinse and repeat in September and in January. If you add up all four of my payments, they equal $20,000. Did I pay 100% of last year's tax? Yes. In other words, I met the first safe harbor threshold.

Does doing this mean that I paid the right amount of tax?

No.

There's nothing about this rule that guarantees what income I will make *this* year. If I make more money this year than expected and my total tax turns out to be $23,000, then when I do my tax return, then I still have to pay that additional $3,000 in tax by the April 15 deadline. But, because I met one of the safe harbor rules, I will owe only the tax itself, *not* penalties or interest.

If I make less money than expected and have a smaller tax bill than last year, then I receive the excess back as a refund.

What Happens When Your Income Varies Year to Year?

What happens if my income this year is very different from last year's?

Let's say I have a huge drop in income from last year. Instead of $100,000, I made only $25,000 of profit.

In this case, my tax bill will be nowhere close to $20,000. In fact, paying $20,000 of tax will be difficult because I'll barely have enough cash to cover it. And also, there's no way I'm going to owe $20,000 tax on $25,000 worth of profit. When your income goes down, your tax rate goes down.

The reality in many fields, especially creative ones, is that our income can vary wildly from one year to the next, whether from your career itself or from life circumstances. If you get sick, if there's an economic down-turn, if a competitor starts taking business away from yours, or if you get hit by a natural disaster—there are a million scenarios that could drastically change your income this year compared to your earnings last year. In any of those scenarios, you won't owe as much tax as you did last year.

I live in Asheville, North Carolina. Midway through writing this book, Hurricane Helene hit my region with flooding and land-slides, destroying my studio and 20 years of my artwork. My art income from 2024 was down dramatically from 2023. This issue is alive in my world.

Of course, paying 100% of last year's tax is both difficult (in terms of you having the cash to pay it) and inaccurate, because your taxes will almost certainly be lower. What's a girl to do?

Safe Harbor Rule #2

Safe harbor rule #2 comes in here. This rule stays closer to your actual cash in hand. To me, honestly, it's a much more practical rule, but you won't see your tax software spit it out to you. That's because rule #1 references an actual, knowable number on your tax return, whereas rule #2 requires ongoing knowledge of your numbers.

But safe harbor rule #2 is the one that I think will help you the most. Here's how: you can pay 90% of *this* year's tax[21] (or, 100% of this year's tax if your profit is over $150,000). Think for a second about why that rule is weird. . .this year isn't over yet. How am I supposed to know what 90% of an unknown number is?

How Do I Know This Year's Tax? Bookkeeping

You don't completely. Remember to lean into that word *estimate* here. Here's how you do this: bookkeeping.

You need to do bookkeeping at least once per quarter to determine your profit for that quarter. When you know your profit for the quarter, you can calculate an approximate amount of tax you owe on it.

How Official Does My Bookkeeping Need to Be?

When I say bookkeeping, I don't mean you have to set yourself up on fancy expensive software. It can be as minimal as a spreadsheet. Each quarter, track and total your gross income and then track and total up your expenses. With those two numbers, subtract the expenses out of the gross income, and you're left with your approximate profit for that time period. Not so hard.

For example, if I want to meet the second safe harbor rule, then I will do my bookkeeping one quarter at a time. For Quarter 1, I'll add up my total income between January 1 and March 31 and add up my expenses for the same time period and then subtract the expenses from the income to determine my profit for that quarter.

Let's say that my gross income was $30,000, my expenses were $20,000, and my profit is therefore $10,000. I know for sure that I owe self-employment tax on that money, and I know that self-employment tax is going to be 15.3%. So my first calculation will be 15.3% * $10,000. That gives me $1,530 that I owe in self-employment tax.

I'm trying to keep the math simple for you. Technically, half your self-employment tax is deductible, so this calculation will overshoot what you actually owe. But I think this is good. Overestimating your self-employment tax is going to give you more wiggle room when estimating your federal income tax, which is a harder number to pin down. Lean into the idea of estimating, even if you're a little bit off, which is a lot better than not paying your estimates at all. You're doing great.

Next, let's calculate what I think I owe for federal income tax. This is the hard part. The fact is, I won't know my actual income tax rate on my profit until I do next year's tax return. This is where most people panic. These are *estimates* for exactly that reason. Take a stab at a number—really. I'll guesstimate here that my average tax rate for income tax will be about 12%. So I'll multiply my $10,000 profit for the quarter by 12% to get $1,200.

Add my self-employment tax amount to that federal income tax amount ($1,530 + $1,200) to get my guesstimate for what I owe the IRS in total tax for this quarter: $2,730.

See? We did an estimated tax calculation.

Where Do You Pay?

This one's easy. Pay your estimates on the IRS.gov website, before each quarterly deadline.[22] Once you're there, click the "Make a Payment" button. Where it asks you to select your reason for payment, select the dropdown menu item that says "estimated tax." Make sure you attribute your payment to the right place. If you accidentally pick a different option, like "balance due," the IRS computer thinks you're settling up last year's tax bill and that you missed your estimated tax payment. This can be sorted out (through a couple of letters back and forth with the IRS), but it's annoying to correct, so pay attention to it in the first place.

When Do You Pay?

When do you pay? Also easy. Estimated quarterly tax payment deadlines are the same every year (plus an extra day or two if one falls on a weekend)[23]:

April 15

June 15

September 15

January 15

Note that the first one also falls on tax day. Yes, you have two things due that day. Your balance due (if any) from last year's taxes, plus your first estimated tax payment for this year.

This is important. Estimated taxes are your tax payments, broken up into quarterly chunks, for *this* year. Not for last year, the way your tax bill is. This can cause confusion, so let's clarify.

First, many people freeze and get scared when it comes to calculating their estimated payments. Here's why I think that happens. If you're new to the system, then the only taxes you've seen are *last year's* taxes. We file our tax return in this country retroactively. You don't file your 2029 tax return until 2030. In other words, the whole year has happened by the time you file your tax return, so you know an exact tax number. That's the whole point of a tax filing—it's to reconcile any prepayments, which were guesses, with your actual tax owed. So the annual filing is the one time you do see an exact number.

Remember, filing is just the once per year paperwork.

46

What If I Make Really Different Amounts Each Quarter?

You might wonder what to do if your earnings are really different from one quarter to the next. That's the beauty of safe harbor rule #2. This method accounts for that.

Let's continue the previous scenario. Say my income drops in the second quarter of this year and I make only half what I made in quarter one. When I estimate my tax, the number will be about half what it was in the first quarter. On June 15 I log into IRS.gov, and pay $1,400 (instead of the $2,730 from Q1).

Then I spend the summer jumping in swimming holes and hiking mountains with my girls, so my income is waaaaaaay down over the summer. For the September 15 deadline, I log in and make a pretty small payment of around $500.

In the last quarter of the year, my income kicks back into gear. Like almost anyone in retail, I make a lot of sales during the holiday season, accounting for a large part of my annual income. For the fourth quarter, my profit is radically different from the first three quarters. Let's say it's $80,000. I log into IRS.gov on January 15 and make a much bigger payment of $20,000.

Review what I just did here.

I paid:

Deadline:	For dates:	My estimated tax payment:
4/15	1/1–3/31	$2,730
6/15	4/1–5/31	$1,400
9/15	6/1–8/31	$500
1/15	9/1–12/31	$20,000

Those numbers are not even. See how they correspond with my actual quarterly earnings and not a guess based on one quarter of the tax I paid last year?

This is so much better. Paying this way means that I pay taxes when I have the money. I pay less when I have less, and more when I have more. Even though I'm guessing at my tax rate and it might not be completely accurate, that somewhat inaccurate guess is still dramatically more accurate than basing my numbers on last year, if I tend not to make the same amount from one year to the next.

> Want a shortcut? The cheat-sheet version of how to estimate taxes on your income for each quarter is to do your bookkeeping to determine your profit for the quarter. Plug your profit into an *online income tax calculator* to calculate your tax. (Don't forget to categorize it correctly as self-employment income in the calculator, or it will underestimate your taxes.) Done.
>
> This is a really good one: https://www.aarp.org/money/taxes/1040-tax-calculator.
>
> If you read the whole explanation, you get a prize for understanding how it works. If you didn't, you can still get your taxes paid.

Doing my estimated tax payments this way is pretty damn accurate, even when it's a guess. It follows the spirit of the law—to pay what I owe as I owe it—whereas the first safe harbor rule works best for businesses with super-consistent income (unlike me).

I still need to settle up the final amount when I file my annual tax return. That's what my tax return is for! This is just a payment. I don't have to factor in any other things like tax credits, my home office, and the deductibility of one-half of my self-employment tax. Those are details that wait for my once-per-year tax return.[24] These are estimates.

My goal is to get close to the number that I actually owe and meet or exceed one of the two safe harbor thresholds. The beauty of the safe harbors is that I don't owe penalties and interest if I pay estimated quarterly taxes by each deadline. Most gorgeously, when tax day comes, my tax bill should be close to zero, because I've prepaid approximately the whole amount I owed for the year already. Can you feel the relief of knowing that you owe nothing on tax day? Good. That is the point of estimated quarterly taxes.

A Note for Higher-Income Taxpayers: Higher Rates

One last very important note for when you earn higher amounts. Once you earn over $150,000 in profit for the year, both safe harbor rules require you to increase the amount that you prepay.

For safe harbor rule #1, you need to pay 110% of last year's tax (rather than 100%). For rule #2, you need to pay 100% of this year's tax (rather than 90%). This follows the general rule for taxes that as you earn more income, your tax rate increases.

CHAPTER SUMMARY

- Self-employment income includes a bunch of stuff: free-lancing, contracting, consulting, small business income, single-member LLC income, and gig work. If you're married and file jointly, your spouse's self-employment income counts, too.

- Self-employment income is reported on a Schedule C. This is also where you deduct your business expenses and calculate what profit is subject to self-employment tax.

- Your income tax return reconciles the tax you paid throughout the year (an estimate) with what you actually owe, factoring in all your deductions and credits.
- Employees have taxes withheld from their paychecks for Medicare, Social Security, federal, and state income taxes. This system is simpler because it's automatic.
- As a self-employed person, you get to deduct business expenses from your gross income, which employees can't do. This means you're taxed only on your profit.
- To take deductions, you must keep receipts, follow some special IRS rules, and do bookkeeping. If you don't want to track expenses, you won't get to deduct them. But you're missing a huge benefit.
- The IRS can audit your last six years of tax returns. Keep your documentation for seven years in case of an audit.
- Self-employment tax is 15.3% of your profit, and it's how you pay into Medicare and Social Security when you work for yourself.
- On top of self-employment tax, you owe federal and state income taxes based on your profit.
- If your tax bill last year was over $1,000, you need to pay estimated quarterly taxes to avoid penalties and interest and to stay on top of your tax. This system spreads your payments throughout the year and helps you owe little to nothing at tax time.

ENDNOTES

1. It can also mean you're getting a big refundable tax credit, like the earned income credit (EIC). The EIC is a massive anti-poverty program that is administered through our tax system. It gives money to people who work but make very low wages, especially those with kids.
2. Unless you're Married Filing Separately. In that case, both spouses must itemize if one spouse itemizes, even if it's not advantageous.

3. David Weil, "Lots of Employees Get Misclassified as Contractors. Here's Why It Matters," *Harvard Business Review*, July 5, 2017, https://hbr.org/2017/07/lots-of-employees-get-misclassified-as-contractors-heres-why-it-matters.

4. "Topic no. 756, Employment taxes for household employees," *U.S. Department of the Treasury, Internal Revenue Service*, accessed December 2, 2024, https://www.irs.gov/taxtopics/tc756#:~:text=Social%20Security%20tax%20and%20Medicare,of%20FICA%20tax%20from%20wages.

5. "Payroll Tax," TaxEdu, *Tax Foundation*, accessed February 7, 2025, https://taxfoundation.org/taxedu/glossary/payroll-tax/#:~:text=A%20payroll%20tax%20is%20a,%2C%20Medicare%2C%20and%20unemployment%20insurance.

6. "Small business payroll taxes for employers & employees," *ADP*, accessed December 2, 2024, https://www.adp.com/resources/articles-and-insights/articles/s/small-business-payroll-taxes.aspx.

7. "How do federal income tax rates work?," *Tax Policy Center*, last modified January 2024, https://taxpolicycenter.org/briefing-book/how-do-federal-income-tax-rates-work#:~:text=The%20federal%20individual%20income%20tax%20has%20seven%20tax%20rates%20ranging,taxed%20at%20a%20zero%20rate.

8. Accurate at the time of writing, February 2025, but it could change.

9. "Graduated Rate Income Tax," TaxEdu, *Tax Foundation*, accessed February 7, 2025, https://taxfoundation.org/taxedu/glossary/graduated-rate-income-tax/#:~:text=A%20graduated%20rate%20income%20tax,rates%20increase%20as%20income%20increases.

10. This increases slightly each year. Check the current brackets here: "Federal income tax rates and brackets," *U.S. Department of the Treasury, Internal Revenue Service*, last modified February 13, 2025, https://www.irs.gov/filing/federal-income-tax-rates-and-brackets.

11. "Marginal Tax Rate," TaxEdu, *Tax Foundation*, accessed February 7, 2025, https://taxfoundation.org/taxedu/glossary/marginal-tax-rate/#:~:text=The%20marginal%20tax%20rate%20is,would%20be%20taken%20as%20tax.

12. "Topic no. 751, Social Security and Medicare withholding rates," *U.S. Department of the Treasury, Internal Revenue Service*, accessed December 2, 2024, https://www.irs.gov/taxtopics/tc751.

13. "How long should I keep records?," *U.S. Department of the Treasury, Internal Revenue Service*, last modified August 20, 2024, https://www.irs.gov/businesses/small-businesses-self-employed/how-long-should-i-keep-records.

14. Don't stress about this. It's something that gets calculated at tax time by your tax software or tax preparer, not something you need to track.

15. Technically I'm overestimating. At tax time, your tax software or accountant will calculate a deduction for half your self-employment tax, so it'll be closer to 14ish percent. But this overestimate makes the math easier to follow.

16. "Pay as you go, so you won't owe: A guide to withholding, estimated taxes and ways to avoid the estimated tax penalty," U.S. Department of the Treasury, Internal Revenue Service, last modified December 17, 2024, https://www.irs.gov/payments/pay-as-you-go-so-you-wont-owe-a-guide-to-withholding-estimated-taxes-and-ways-to-avoid-the-estimated-tax-penalty.

17. "Form 1040-ES: Estimated Tax for Individuals," U.S. Department of the Treasury, Internal Revenue Service, last modified December 7, 2023, /www.irs.gov/pub/irs-pdf/f1040es.pdf.

18. Lorie Konish, "44% of Americans can't pay an unexpected $1,000 expense from savings. 'We're just not wired to save', expert says," CNBC, January 24, 2024, https://www.cnbc.com/2024/01/24/many-americans-cannot-pay-for-an-unexpected-1000-expense-heres-why.html; "Report on the Economic Well-Being of U.S. Households in 2022—May 2023," Board of Governors of the Federal Reserve System, accessed December 3, 2024, https://www.federalreserve.gov/publications/2023-economic-well-being-of-us-households-in-2022-expenses.htm.

19. "Estimated taxes," U.S. Department of the Treasury, Internal Revenue Service, last modified December 10, 2024, https://www.irs.gov/businesses/small-businesses-self-employed/estimated-taxes.

20. "How the safe harbor for estimated tax can help you avoid underpayment penalties," H&R Block, accessed December 3, 2024, https://www.hrblock.com/tax-center/irs/tax-responsibilities/avoiding-underpayment-tax-penalty/?srsltid=AfmBOoo-2Mkm1CMqAAgItRBkG9pf4XgW4ic-uAfVO4UCR4P884ZgTzCH.

21. "How the safe harbor for estimated tax can help you avoid underpayment penalties."

22. "Online account for individuals," U.S. Department of the Treasury, Internal Revenue Service, last modified January 30, 2025, https://www.irs.gov/payments/online-account-for-individuals.

23. "Estimated taxes," U.S. Department of the Treasury, Internal Revenue Service, last modified February 6, 2024, https://www.irs.gov/businesses/small-businesses-self-employed/estimated-taxes.

24. "When a taxpayer should make estimated payments during the tax year," Nixon Peabody, March 18, 2021, accessed December 3, 2024, https://www.nixonpeabody.com/insights/articles/2021/03/18/when-a-taxpayer-should-make-estimated-payments-during-the-tax-year.

CHAPTER THREE

THE SCHEDULE C: CONGRATULATIONS, YOU'RE A BUSINESS

Now that you know how your self-employment tax works and how you pay taxes "as you go" when your income comes from self-employment, let's answer the question of where on your tax return you report this self-employment income.

Let's zoom out and talk about the basic structure of your personal income tax return, which is also called a **1040 ("ten-forty")**. Under US tax law, not all income is treated the same, and for that reason, there are plug-in parts of a tax return called **schedules**, whose job it is to separate different types of income for different tax treatments. You use a schedule if that only specific type of income applies to you.[1]

If you were an employee with W2 income and no other sources of income like stocks, rental income, self-employment, etc., your tax return would be simple, and you would have only a 1040. For the rest of us, we'll have one or more schedules that attach to the 1040. See my website, www.sunlighttax.com/taxesforhumans, for an illustration of each of the schedules.

You report your self-employment income on the **Schedule C** (Figure 3.1).

The Schedule C's main function is to separate income from self-employment, because the profit reported there is subject to self-employment tax. There are lots of benefits to the Schedule C and a few warnings. Let's get into it.

Figure 3.1   Schedule C's basic job.
Source: © Hannah Cole/Sunlight Tax.

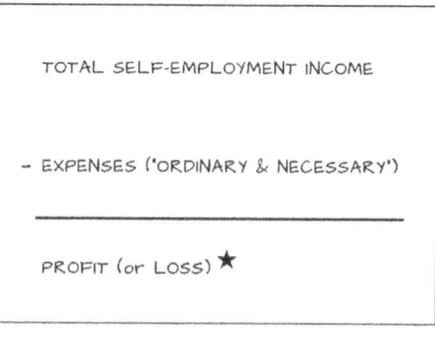

The Schedule C:
Profit or Loss from Business
(Sole Proprietorship)

Its job is to calculate your profit from self-employment that's subject to self-employment tax.

TOTAL SELF-EMPLOYMENT INCOME

– EXPENSES ("ORDINARY & NECESSARY")

PROFIT (or LOSS) ★

★ This amount is subject to self-employment tax, 15.3%

The Schedule C has a title. I want you to notice not one but *two key pieces of info* right in the title (see Figure 3.2). The title is "Profit or Loss from Business (Sole Proprietorship)."

Figure 3.2 Top of a Schedule C.

Source: Internal Revenue Service(IRS)/https://www.irs.gov/pub/irs-pdf/f1040sc.pdf./Public domain/last accessed on March 21,2025.

SCHEDULE C (Form 1040)	**Profit or Loss From Business** (Sole Proprietorship)	OMB No. 1545-0074
Department of the Treasury Internal Revenue Service	Attach to Form 1040, 1040-SR, 1040-SS, 1040-NR, or 1041; partnerships must generally file Form 1065. Go to *www.irs.gov/ScheduleC* for instructions and the latest information.	20**24** Attachment Sequence No. **09**

Name of proprietor	Social security number (SSN)

A	Principal business or profession, including product or service (see instructions)	**B** Enter code from instructions
C	Business name. If no separate business name, leave blank.	**D** Employer ID number (EIN) (see instr.)

E	Business address (including suite or room no.)
	City, town or post office, state, and ZIP code
F	Accounting method: **(1)** ☐ Cash **(2)** ☐ Accrual **(3)** ☐ Other (specify)
G	Did you "materially participate" in the operation of this business during 2024? If "No," see instructions for limit on losses . ☐ Yes ☐ No
H	If you started or acquired this business during 2024, check here . . . . ☐
I	Did you make any payments in 2024 that would require you to file Form(s) 1099? See instructions . . . . ☐ Yes ☐ No
J	If "Yes," did you or will you file required Form(s) 1099? . . . . ☐ Yes ☐ No

Part I Income

1	Gross receipts or sales. See instructions for line 1 and check the box if this income was reported to you on Form W-2 and the "Statutory employee" box on that form was checked . . . . ☐	1	
2	Returns and allowances	2	
3	Subtract line 2 from line 1	3	
4	Cost of goods sold (from line 42)	4	
5	**Gross profit.** Subtract line 4 from line 3	5	
6	Other income, including federal and state gasoline or fuel tax credit or refund (see instructions)	6	
7	**Gross income.** Add lines 5 and 6	7	

WHAT MAKES YOU A BUSINESS? YOUR PROFIT MOTIVE

What actually makes you a business, to the IRS? It's your **profit motive**.[2] Do you intend to make money from it? Yes? Okay, then you're a business. You're entitled to (and required) to file a Schedule C.

What's the alternative? What are you if you don't have a profit motive? You're a hobbyist.

No judgment. Hobbies are great. But hobbies aren't subsidized under US tax law. So you can have yourself a lovely hobby and even make occasional money from it. And if you do, you'll need to report that hobby income (on line J in Part 1 of your Schedule 1).[3] But you do not get to deduct any expenses.

As a business, you can deduct the "ordinary and necessary[4]" expenses of running your business. As a business in the United States, you receive the amazing tax benefit of not paying any income tax or self-employment tax on money you earn in your business that you funnel back into building or running that business.

You Can Have a Profit Motive Without Having a Profit

Your profit motive is the key; it makes you a business and entitles you to all those tax benefits. And you can have a profit motive before you have a profit.[5] Think about this: you and I have both eaten in a restaurant that isn't profitable yet. Does that make the restaurant a hobby? Hell, no. That's a business that has not hit the "break-even point" yet. Yet. They are definitely trying to.

It Takes Money to Make Money

Spending money before you make money is not just normal; it's *productive* (within reason). The US tax code encourages you to do this, by making those expenses tax-free and allowing you to treat your early-stage losses as a tax benefit.[8] You heard me right. When you have a loss, that loss is subtracted off your other taxable income. In other words, it creates a **tax shelter**. A tax shelter is a method of reducing taxable income. In this case, it's a legal one.

I wish someone had taught me about the "break-even point" in art school. All businesses start out in the negative. As an artist, I wasted energy thinking I was bad at business. It wasn't until I studied business law and economics when I went back to school for accounting that I learned that this is completely normal. The "break-even point," I learned, is a magical moment in business when you go from having more expenses than income to having exactly the same expenses as income.[6] If you subtract expenses from your income at this point, the number

---

will be zero—instead of negative—for the first time. The significance of breaking even is that from this point on, any additional income will be profit. In other words, this is the moment when your business becomes profitable.

Business school teaches people that this is normal and sets the realistic expectation that business is hard and turning a profit takes some time.[7] In fact, aggressively pursuing profit often means *investing more* in the business—not less—before you have income. You buy better materials, help, and space to increase your market share and make your product or service better, cheaper, and more competitive.

GOING NEGATIVE: A LOSS IS POSSIBLE

Remember the word *loss* in the Schedule C title, a few pages ago? I talk to many people who have small DIY businesses who have either a lack of knowledge or a mindset block that stops them from filing a Schedule C when they should. They say things like, "Hannah, I haven't filed a Schedule C because I'm not profitable yet." Or, "but I haven't made *enough* profit yet." (Please, someone tell me what "enough" is? I suspect that if you asked most billionaires, they'll all tell you they don't have "enough.")

Look again at the title. It tells you that profit is not a requirement for filing a Schedule C.[9] In fact, you miss one of its biggest benefits by not filing your Schedule C as soon as you're entitled to: the tax benefit of writing off startup expenses and the tax-savings of a business loss, which offsets your other taxable income.

I also see people skip filing a Schedule C because they don't feel that they are "official" yet. This is another false belief. Other entities may have other rules about what might make your business official (for example, your municipality might want you to get a business license, your state might want you to register to collect sales tax, or your spouse might prefer you form an LLC to protect your joint/personal assets from a lawsuit targeting your business). These are not things the IRS concerns itself with. From the standpoint of your income tax, consider Big Mama IRS to be the warmest, most inclusive entity out there. Your business, however informal, however not-yet-profitable, or however "unofficial," still counts as a business to the IRS. Why? Because the IRS is the tax collector. The IRS doesn't wait until the magic moment that you decide it's time to talk to a lawyer and file paperwork to form an LLC or until you do the self-work to get to feeling "ready." The IRS is there the moment you earn your very first dollar of profit. Its job is to collect the tax on it, thank you very much.

The IRS has a different standard of what makes you a business. You are a business when you have a "profit motive." This makes sense, because everyone earning a little money, from driving for Uber, or selling empanadas at a Little League game, or being paid as a contractor instead of as an employee, falls under the same rules when it comes to taxes. Not all of these folks are going to form an LLC or get a "Doing Business As (DBA)" or a business license—some might not even have a Social Security number. And yet the IRS still needs them to file their Schedule C. And you, too.

How Does a Loss Work?

Let me illustrate how a loss creates a tax benefit.

Let's say I support myself working a "day job" where I make $60,000 on salary, and meanwhile I start my business as a professional painter, and, say, spend $10,000 securing a studio space, and buy lumber, paint, and lighting to build it out so I have a productive place to make my work. I don't yet have any income from my business, even though I've gotten started and am spreading the word about my work. So far I have only expenses. My taxable income for the year will actually be $50,000, not $60,000. Why? My Schedule C will have $0 listed as income and $10,000 listed as an expense, and that equals a −$10,000 loss. Normally, I would pay taxes on my full $60,000 of salary. But here's where the loss comes in: it gets subtracted off my other income. So I only pay taxes on $50,000.

Here's the more amazing part. If I happen to have had taxes withheld from my salary (if it was W2, that would be required), then I have been prepaying taxes all year based on $60,000 of income. So when I actually do my taxes, I will have overpaid tax on that $10,000. In other words, I get a refund. A big one. Right in the most critical moment of my business, when cash is low and I'm most vulnerable. This is my favorite part of the tax code. It's poetic. The US government is nurturing your baby business through its infancy, with a big fat direct deposit into your bank account when you need it the most.

Art school never taught me any of this. And I'm a little salty about it.

You can have a rough year in business, lose money, and still very much have a profit motive. Think about it—shit happens. Say you have a studio in a warehouse building on the Swannanoa River, in Asheville, North Carolina, like I did. Hurricane Helene hits your mountain region, dumping trillions of gallons of water[10] down the mountains into the rivers. The Swannanoa River rises an unimaginable 30 feet, and every warehouse along that river is destroyed.

Yes, friend. On September 27, 2024, this happened to me. My studio was destroyed by flooding from Hurricane Helene, along with an enormous number of my neighbors. I lost 20 years of work. This is not a hypothetical example.

60

Are those businesses going to take a financial hit this year? Definitely. Some might even close forever—but many will try to rebuild.

Did they suddenly become hobbies overnight, because they were thrust into a very difficult financial situation? Of course not. They remain businesses. Their motives didn't change because of a random act of nature. A business can go through rough times, and at some point, most do.

It's a lot less disruptive to those businesses (and frankly, to the US economy) to rebuild, preferably with support from the government, than to close shop, lay off all their employees, end operations, and attempt employment in another field. From a purely economic standpoint, it's more efficient for them to learn from this event and rebuild their business better. That is the reason that the IRS allows businesses to take a loss on their Schedule C.[11] It helps businesses through rough times.

Understanding how to prove you have a profit motive to the IRS is critical if you have a business struggling to make income. That struggle can be because you're in the startup phase, or because your business suffered a disaster along the way.

Here's a practical example of what a "profit motive" looks like, since it's the key to proving that your operation is a business—not a hobby—when you have a loss. Remember, the practical difference is that as a business, you're entitled to the tax benefit of losses, plus tax-free business deductions. In other words, as a business, you pay much lower taxes, because you're taxed only on your profit, and not on your entire gross income, the way hobbies are.[12]

PROVING YOUR PROFIT MOTIVE: THE IRS NINE-POINT TEST

The IRS uses a nine-point test to determine whether a taxpayer has a profit motive or not.[13] In reality, you will see this test actually used only if you are being audited to determine whether your operation is a business or a hobby. This type of audit is often triggered by your Schedule C having multiple years of losses. This makes sense, because from the IRS perspective, a loss is a tax shelter; it's their right to check on taxpayers to be sure that these are being used legitimately. It also makes sense because if you abuse the tax code by taking tax-sheltering losses year after year on your Schedule C for what is truly just a hobby, you should be caught and stopped. Realize that there are legitimate losses and illegitimate ones. If you have a genuine profit motive, document it and follow the tax rules, despite the chance of audit (because audits are the check in our system), your losses remain legal, and you'll emerge from that audit with your legitimate losses intact.[14] No one loves an audit, but this system is fair, and if you're following the law, you'll be okay. The intention of the IRS nine-point test is to sniff out scammy tax-grab losses from a hobby vs. those losses that are the legitimate product of a real business. The IRS nine-point test also shows you that tax law is *law*, and it may ultimately come down to a judgment (in court), rather than something black and white. My clients ask me all the time to tell them The Answer—and I'm sorry that all I can give you to prepare yourself is the same metric the IRS uses to judge you. Ultimately, your unique facts and circumstances and the life experience and determination of an individual judge may be the ultimate decider. It's not a case of yes/no certainty.

Let's look at the IRS nine-point test for determining profit motive:

Factor 1 —Manner in Which the Taxpayer Carries on the Activity

Factor 2 — Expertise of the Taxpayer or His Advisors

Factor 3 — Time and Effort Expended by the Taxpayer in Carrying on the Activity

Factor 4 — Expectation That Assets Used in the Activity May Appreciate in Value

Factor 5 — Success of the Taxpayer in Carrying on Other Similar or Dissimilar Activities

Factor 6 — Taxpayer's History of Income or Losses with Respect to the Activity

Factor 7 — Amount of any Occasional Profits That Are Earned

Factor 8 — Financial Status of the Taxpayer

Factor 9 — Elements of Personal Pleasure or Recreation

No one factor is the decider here. The IRS must weigh all nine factors to determine whether you have a profit motive or not.[15] What's important for you to understand is that treating your activity like a genuine business is very important. It protects you. It could be the difference between you winning or losing a "Hobby/Loss Audit."

I've seen people in creative fields get in trouble by being so driven by artistic integrity and plagued by money mindset issues that they don't speak honestly about their *genuine actual profit motive*. Or the field they are in disguises its money motives altogether, even though they exist. For example, I'm a painter operating in the gallery/museum world. As such, I've been trained in my art career to signal nothing but pure artistic integrity. Despite the fact that there's absolutely nothing wrong with me earning money from art, the culture in my corner of the art world is to never openly speak about our desire to make money. We don't call art openings "networking and sales events" —that feels too baldly "businessy." We disguise them as parties—we serve wine, play music, wear cool clothes, and have them after business hours. But an art opening is a networking and sales event. If I were to talk to my gallerist about maximizing my return on every painting sold, she would look at me with horror and question my artistic integrity. I would be laughed out of the art world. But does my gallerist want to make sales, and do I? Absolutely!

Imagine the pickle I'll be in, if an artist like me faces a Hobby/Loss Audit, and I repeat the language of the fine art world to the IRS—because that language *hides* my profit motive, when my job during this type of audit is exactly the opposite—to *prove* my profit motive. You're allowed to operate within the norms of your field, and not speak like a Wall Street tycoon or used car salesman. That's fine. But be aware of those norms, and understand the goal when it comes to *your taxes*. Profit motive is your protection; it allows you all those juicy deductions, and if you genuinely have one, you may need to *code switch* to be more straightforward while speaking to the IRS.

Examples of How to Use the Nine-Point Test

If you work in a straightforward business, you can skip this next section. But if you're in a field where people consistently—despite genuine effort to make a living or to make money—struggle to make a profit, then let me elaborate on some of the points for you to help you understand the nuances of demonstrating your genuine intent to make a profit.

Factor 1 — The Manner in Which the Taxpayer Carries on the Activity

What's the manner you want to operate in? A *businesslike* manner.[16] What are key indicators of that? Having a separate business bank account and a business plan. The plan can be written on a napkin or even be in your head (the IRS Audit Technique Guide actually says this), but it should exist. It's important to understand that all businesses have a "startup phase," and if you are in the startup phase for your type of business, it will be normal for you to not yet have a profit. But you'll need to be very clear about what the startup phase norms are in your field and that you fall within them.

Factor 2 — Expertise of the Taxpayer or His Advisors

This factor asks if you have the requisite knowledge or have consulted with experts who have the requisite knowledge to carry out the business.[17] Did you get some training? Take courses? Engage with mentors? How did you study the field of business you are operating in, and is it enough?

Factor 3 — Time and Effort Expended by the Taxpayer in Carrying on the Activity

This is simple. If you engage in the activity in question for one hour per month, it's a hobby. Businesses take dedicated time and effort.[18] The more time you spend on the activity, the better the odds are that it's a business. Your calendar is a useful tool for proving this. Don't forget that time spent on your business is more than just studio time for a sculptor or recording time for a musician. It includes time spent communicating with collaborators, clients, and your audience; time spent professionally documenting your work; time spent bookkeeping, marketing, and networking. I like to say that if you hate doing it, it's great proof of being in business—because hobbyists only do the fun parts. A hobbyist painter only paints. A professional artist applies for grants, cultivates an audience of interested viewers on Instagram, communicates with collectors, curators, and gallerists by email or meets with them in person, does bookkeeping, website building, networking, takes professional photos of their work and more. All of that time is time spent on the business—not just the studio time.

Factor 4 — Expectation That Assets Used in the Activity May Appreciate in Value

This factor is usually related to the appreciation of land, but I think there's a case to be made that artists do much of their work at a discount (or for free) in exchange for publicity or prestige, whose ultimate aim is to appreciate the value of their artwork.[19] Many artists donate work to large charity auctions to increase their visibility or give discounts in exchange for press coverage or visibility among a collector friend group. Press and prestige are regular forms of currency in the art world, and they are often exchanged for discounts. (Also, yuck.)

I remember my scrappy, struggling artist self in my early days. I did all of those things and all for genuine business reasons. But it makes me angry, thinking back on it. I would say to that younger version of myself, "Honey, that collector is an opportunistic jerk. He is dangling promises of 'visibility' or introducing you to his art critic friend, but if he genuinely wanted to support your work, he would pay full price." That is not a tax recommendation! But it is life advice.

Factor 5 — Success of the Taxpayer in Carrying on Other Similar or Dissimilar Activities

This one is only relevant to folks with more experience. If you've been successful in turning around other unprofitable businesses into profitable ones, demonstrating that will help you.[20]

Factor 6 — Taxpayer's History of Income or Losses with Respect to the Activity

Losses beyond your control, like those due to disease, flooding, theft, or within the normal startup period for your field, aren't proof of a hobby. But a sustained period of profit can be helpful to show, even if the years you point to are outside the scope of your audit.[21]

Factor 7 — Amount of any Occasional Profits That Are Earned

If you have large occasional profits despite multiple losses, that will gener-ally help your case.[22] For example, if you struggle to achieve profitability in your dance company for years but are then awarded the MacArthur Fellowship (the so-called "genius grant," which is currently $800,000, paid out over five years), your large grant will be an important factor helping you to prove profit motive in the prior years. However, small, occasional profits do not outweigh large frequent losses.

Factor 8 — Financial Status of the Taxpayer

If you depend on income from the activity, that weighs in your favor. But if you do not, that can be counted against you; as you have the financial abil-ity to weather the losses, the chances are greater that those losses are being used fraudulently to offset your other income.[23] Before 2014, the IRS would sometimes argue that having a "day job" precluded your Schedule C from being a business. However, in *Susan Crile vs. Commissioner of Internal Revenue (2014)*, the US Tax Court judge found this argument to be invalid, citing the example of law professors (day job) with law practices (business) as a commonplace counterpoint.[24]

Factor 9 — Elements of Personal Pleasure or Recreation

This is a tough one if you're in a field that is "fun," like acting, music, horse breeding, or chartering fishing boats. Having work you love does not pre-clude it from being a business (just ask Taylor Swift).[25] But if you're an accountant, great news! No one ever accuses accountants of having an accounting hobby. Why? No one assumes our work is fun or that we would do it without being paid.

WAYS TO DOCUMENT YOUR PROFIT MOTIVE

The best way to prove your profit motive is to make a profit. If you are profitable, congratulations! If you're not yet profitable, that's when you need to worry about being able to prove that you have a profit motive. Makes sense, right?

Absent the best proof—actual profit—how can you show that you have a profit motive, and are therefore a business, and not a hobby? [26] Here's a list:

- Advertising.
- Grant applications.
- Your website.
- Your books and records.
- A written business plan.
- Your separate business bank account (not mixing your business money with your personal account).
- Your Instagram/TikTok/social media where you are building an audience for your work, or communicating en masse or one on one in DMs with collectors, clients, potential customers, etc.
- Your emails to collectors, clients, potential customers, etc. These can be direct, one-on-one emails, or blasts to a list.
- Your email newsletter/customer relations manager (CRM) service, like MailChimp, ConstantContact, Convertkit, etc.
- Brushing up on professional skills in your field through courses, coaching, professional development programs, etc.
- Anything you do for "visibility."
- Your calendar—remember that time spent on the business is an important factor in the nine-point test, and the "not fun" parts are good proof that you're not a hobby. Your schedule shows time spent,

not just in studio/on stage/doing the "fun" part, but on admin, books, marketing, networking, research, meeting with accountants and lawyers, etc. The more you dislike doing it, the better the proof that it's for business. (I'm serious: hobbyists only do the fun stuff.)

- Networking events. (What do these look like in your field? In the visual arts, art openings are networking/sales events, even though we pretend they are parties.)
- Anything else that proves you are trying to make money.

CHAPTER SUMMARY

- Your Schedule C means you're a business to the IRS. Nothing more "official" is required. This entitles you to business deductions and the ability to report a loss.
- What makes you a business? Your profit motive. If you lack a profit motive, you have a hobby, not a business. Hobbies don't get the tax benefits of a business.
- You can have a profit motive without making a profit yet. Genuine businesses can have unprofitable years, like during the "startup phase" or because of an unforeseen hardship.
- Spending money before your business makes money is normal and productive. The tax code encourages these investments by making them tax-free, and allowing losses as a tax benefit.
- A loss on your Schedule C can offset other taxable income, reducing your overall tax bill. This is a huge benefit, especially in the early, delicate stage of your business.
- To judge your profit motive, the IRS uses a nine-point test. This includes factors like how you carry on the activity, your expertise, and time spent.

- Keep good records to prove your profit motive. This includes advertising, grant applications, a business plan, and a separate business bank account.
- If you're audited over the issue of losses, the IRS will look at your profit motive. Treating your activity like a genuine business protects you and helps you get through the audit unscathed.

ENDNOTES

1. Nancy Ashburn, "Tax schedules and forms related to Form 1040, U.S. Individual Tax Income Tax Return," *Britannica Money*, accessed December 3, 2024, https://www.britannica.com/money/income-tax-schedule-meaning.
2. Sandra Feldman, "Profit motive required to claim business deductions," *Wolters Kluwer*, last modified January 22, 2022, https://www.wolterskluwer.com/en/expert-insights/profit-motive-required-to-claim-business-deductions#:~:text=The%20nine%2Dfactor%20test%20to%20determine%20profit%20motive&text=Among%20the%20factors%20the%20IRS,the%20income%20for%20your%20livelihood.
3. "Here's what taxpayers need to know about paying taxes on their hobby activities," *U.S. Department of the Treasury, Internal Revenue Service*, last modified December 10, 2024, https://www.irs.gov/instructions/i1040sc.
4. Those are the IRS's words. Officially. See U.S. Department of the Treasury, Internal Revenue Service. *Business Expenses*. 2022, Pub. 535, Washington, DC.
5. Feldman, "Profit motive required to claim business deductions."
6. "Break-even point," *U.S. Small Business Administration*, accessed May 22, 2024, https://www.sba.gov/breakevenpointcalculator.
7. Amy Gallo, "A Quick Guide to Breakeven Analysis," *Harvard Business Review*, last modified July 2, 2014, https://hbr.org/2014/07/a-quick-guide-to-breakeven-analysis.
8. See U.S. Department of the Treasury, Internal Revenue Service. Tax Guide for Small Businesses (For Individuals Who Use Schedule C). 2023, Pub. 334, Washington, DC.
9. "Schedule C & Schedule SE 2," *U.S. Department of the Treasury, Internal Revenue Service*, accessed December 3, 2024, https://www.irs.gov/faqs/small-business-self-employed-other-business/schedule-c-schedule-se/schedule-c-schedule-se-2.

10. Seth Borenstein, "Helene and other storms dumped 40 trillion gallons of rain on the South," *PBS*, last modified October 1, 2024, https://www.pbs.org/news hour/nation/helene-and-other-storms-dumped-40-trillion-gallons-of-rain-on-the-south.

11. U.S. Department of the Treasury, Internal Revenue Service. *Tax Guide for Small Businesses (For Individuals Who Use Schedule C)*. 2023, Pub. 334, Washington, DC.

12. "Here's how to tell the difference between a hobby and a business for tax purposes," *U.S. Department of the Treasury, Internal Revenue Service*, last modified January 30, 2024, https://www.irs.gov/newsroom/heres-how-to-tell-the-difference-between-a-hobby-and-a-business-for-tax-purposes.

13. Feldman, "Profit motive required to claim business deductions."

14. Feldman, "Profit motive required to claim business deductions."

15. Feldman, "Profit motive required to claim business deductions."

16. Robert Gard, "Business or hobby? The nine factors," *Journal of Accountancy*, last modified October 1, 2013, https://www.journalofaccountancy.com/ issues/2013/oct/20138370.html. See "Activity not engaged in for profit defined," *Code of Federal Regulations*, title 26 (1972): § 1.183-2, https://www .law.cornell.edu/cfr/text/26/1.183-2.

17. Gard, "Business or hobby? The nine factors."

18. Gard, "Business or hobby? The nine factors."

19. Gard, "Business or hobby? The nine factors."

20. Gard, "Business or hobby? The nine factors."

21. Gard, "Business or hobby? The nine factors."

22. Gard, "Business or hobby? The nine factors."

23. Gard, "Business or hobby? The nine factors."

24. *Susan Crile v. Commissioner of Internal Revenue, T.C. Memo 2014-202*, 23-27 (U.S.T.C. 2014).

25. See "Activity not engaged in for profit defined," *Code of Federal Regulations*, title 26 (1972): § 1.183-2, https://www.law.cornell.edu/cfr/text/26/1.183-2.

26. Craig W. Smalley, "How to determine profit motive," *The Tax Adviser*, last modified March 23, 2017, https://www.thetaxadviser.com/newsletters/2017/ mar/determine-profit-motive.html.

CHAPTER FOUR
BUSINESS EXPENSES

N ow that you understand the power of the Schedule C loss, that you need to be a business (not a hobby) to take one, and how to document your profit motive, let's talk about the benefit you've been waiting for: deducting business expenses.

WHAT COUNTS AS A BUSINESS DEDUCTION

This chapter is the reason you bought this book, right? We all want to know what's deductible for us—and business deductions are the most straightforward benefit of running a business.

US tax law is generous when it comes to allowing you business deductions. According to the IRS, you may deduct any business expense so long as it is both "ordinary and necessary."[1] Ordinary means accepted and normal within your field. Necessary means helpful and appropriate, but it doesn't have to be indispensable. For example, I don't *need* to attend a business conference that will be useful for making new business contacts (I can decide that the timing or cost isn't right for me), but it will be helpful to go, so it counts as a deductible business expense.

BASELINE DOCUMENTATION RULE

The baseline business deduction documentation rule is that you need a receipt. This serves as your proof that the expense on your tax return actually happened.[2] The IRS has the right to review your receipts, so you need to keep them for seven years, to cover you for the full IRS's six-year statute of limitations (see Chapter 19 for audit timing rules).

SPECIAL RULES FOR SPECIAL DEDUCTION CATEGORIES

There are special rules for deductions where you either don't normally get a receipt (like renting office space or driving to a business meeting) or where a deduction tends toward abuse (think "fun" categories: business meals and business travel).[3]

Business Meals

There are two types of deductible business meals. Meals with a business contact and meals while traveling for business. All business meals are only *half* deductible. Here's the logic: whether you're doing business or not, you have to eat. So the IRS splits the difference and allows you half of the expense.[4]

Meals with a Business Contact

Meals are a way to win new business, exchange contacts and ideas, and develop business relationships. That's why they are (partly) deductible.

While business meals are a great deduction, they tend to get abused. For that reason, the IRS has an extra-stringent rule. You must keep the receipt *and* list who the business contact is and what the business purpose was.[5] This means that if you can only produce the receipts for your business meals but are missing the contact name and business purpose, *your meal deduction will be disallowed.*

My method for tracking this is simple: I keep a calendar. When I plan to meet with someone for a business meeting over coffee, drinks, or a meal, I put it in my calendar, and I jot down the purpose of the meeting. As long as I get the receipt during the meal itself, I've now satisfied the documentation requirement. Note that this means that if your business meals category is audited, you'll need to show the IRS your calendar on top of the receipts themselves.

If you prefer, you can also jot down the contact name and purpose of the meeting directly on the receipt, and then stash it in your wallet or snap a quick photo for your digitized files.

You may not throw out your business credit card at any meal where you briefly mentioned business. You must have a business purpose in mind *going in*. Tread carefully. This category is a frequent IRS target, because they know people get loosey-goosey with it.

Business meals are for cultivating business relationships. This means that if you are dining solo and not traveling away from home, it's not a deductible meal.

Travel Meals

When you travel for business, your meals are deductible (50% of them).[6] These you *can* do alone. To be a valid travel meal, you must be away from home on business for long enough to require rest (usually this means overnight). The IRS believes in brown-bagging, so if you just have a long day but you come home to sleep, you don't get to take a meals deduction.

There are two different methods for taking a deduction for travel meals.

- **Method 1:** The actual expense method. This is what it sounds like. You track the actual expense of the meal, and you keep the receipt.[7]
- **Method 2:** Alternatively, you can take what's called a standard meals allowance expense when you travel. The standard meal allowance is an average rate set for meals based on the costs in that geographic area.[8] The GSA provides a rate table for domestic business travel, and the State Department keeps the rate table for foreign travel.[9] To use this method, you simply track the area you traveled to and the number of days you were there. At tax time, you look up the rate table for the place you traveled to, on either the GSA or State Department per diem website, and calculate the deductible amount at the standard meal allowance rate.[10]
- There's a little extra math for first and last days: you can only take 75% of the full standard meal allowance rate for those days, but you get 100% for the days in the middle. Add all of this up, and that's your reportable amount for these travel meals. Note that you still will be getting a deduction for only 50% of this total.[11]

- Although you don't need a receipt to take the standard meal allowance, you do need valid proof of the time, place, and business purpose of your travel.[12]
- The cool thing about the standard meal allowance for travel meals is that you don't need to keep receipts.[13] I love this, because I'm a light eater, so my meals are often cheaper than the average. This is one of the few dreamy places in the tax code where I can deduct a higher amount than what I actually spent. That said, if you order the filet mignon and three top-shelf martinis while traveling for business, you might prefer the actual expense method.

Mileage for Business

Mileage is one of the key areas I see people miss out on a deduction. When you travel for business in a car that you own or lease, your mileage is deductible as a business expense.[14] But as you know, you don't get a receipt for it. So here's how to track what's deductible.

For most small businesses, you're doing this business driving in a car that you also use for personal trips. You know it, I know it, and the IRS knows it. For this reason, the spirit of the mileage rules is to allow you to take the business trips as a deduction while separating out the personal use, which is never deductible. There are two options.

For either method, you will need to track your business mileage. You need to know the total number of miles you drive for the year.[15] Here's a simple tip: put a reminder in your calendar recurring on January 1 to note your odometer. This gives you both an ending mileage for last year, plus a starting mileage for this year. Don't forget to note your odometer before you sell a car and when you buy a new one. And also note it right now—so that if you are reading this on any day besides 1/1, you can have an accurate number at least starting from this point.

> As with all things in taxes, people are not perfect, nor are their files, and it's always better to take an attitude of "Let me start now" rather than "I didn't get it 100% right, so I won't do anything at all."

In addition to your total mileage for the year, you must track your business mileage. This is important, because it shows the IRS that you're not trying to deduct 100% of the miles you drove. Business mileage is anything that is for a business purpose *other than a commute*.[16] Your commute is a personal expense, and not deductible. So traveling to and from your main place of business is not deductible. If you have a home office—booya! You have no commute, so pretty much all your business drives are deductible.

The IRS requires you to have a mileage log.[17] It might sound intimidating, but mileage apps make it easy and give you an airtight mileage log that you can keep for your records—voilà! I personally like and use MileIQ. But there are others, so find the one you like best.

Actual Expense Method

Mileage method 1 is the **actual expense method**. To use this, you track your full auto costs (gas, insurance, repairs, tires, oil changes, etc.) and take a percentage of those based on business miles vs. personal miles.[18] In other words, you add up all your car expenses and then you divide that number by your business mileage for the year to give you the deductible amount of your total auto costs. Note that if you don't mark your odometer each year, this math is impossible.

A quick warning on this method. First, it's rarely as good a deal over the life of your business as the standard mileage method, which I'm about to talk about. But the one year it is really good is the year you buy the car. For this reason, look out. If you start with the actual expense method, you are stuck with it.[19] And after a few years, you'll get a lot less of a deduction for it, but you can't switch.

Standard Mileage Method

Method two is called the **standard mileage method**.[20] This one is often the better deduction. But you can't start out with the actual expense method and then switch to standard mileage.[21] Take the standard mileage method in year 1, or don't take it at all.

Using this method, you'll track all your business mileage and then multiply those miles by the IRS-determined standard mileage rate for that year to get your deductible amount.[22] This deduction is generous. Most people don't realize how expensive driving really is. This method gives all US taxpayers a standard rate, based on the average US fleet vehicle, and includes the real cost of driving—meaning not just gas but repairs, maintenance, insurance, and even depreciation.[23] This is one of those rare places in the tax code where you can reap a bigger deduction than what you spent. If you drive a small or electric vehicle, you're getting an extra juicy deduction.

You don't need to keep your car receipts when you use the standard mileage method. Your mileage log is the documentation you need.[24]

The standard mileage rate changes every year, so you'll want to look up the rate for the current tax year.[25] I have a free visual guide to tax deductions on my website, with the latest rates. If you'd like that, you can get it at www.sunlighttax.com/deductionsguide.

Although I'm writing this book primarily for self-employed people, if you're a farmer, these mileage rules apply to your farm activities, on your Schedule F.

Parking and Tolls for Business

Bonus tip: Keep business parking and tolls expenses separated from other car expenses in your bookkeeping, and keep *those* receipts. These are deductible as a separate expense, on top of either of the two IRS mileage methods.[26] In other words, parking and tolls count separately and get you an additional deduction.

Business Travel

Business travel can be both fun and necessary to your business. But because it is ripe for abuse, the rules are both detailed and strict.

When you travel for a 100% business purpose, the rules are straightforward. It's deductible. But what counts as business travel?

Business travel is defined by the IRS as when your duties require you to be away from your *tax home*, for substantially longer than a normal day's work.[27] And that the time away is long enough for you to require rest (think a night's sleep and not a nap in the car).

What Is Your *Tax Home*?

Since business travel counts only when you're away from your **tax home**, let's define that. Your tax home is the main place of your *business, or where you earn your income*. This can be a different location from where you live.[28] Take, for example, athlete Caitlin Clark. Clark, at the time of my writing, plays in the WNBA for the Indiana Fever, but she lives in Iowa. Her tax home is Indiana, where she plays, not Iowa, where she sleeps. The same could be true if you commute across state lines for your work. If you do branding work for biotech companies, you might rent an office on the Route 128 Tech Corridor in Massachusetts to be close to your target clients. If you commute from your home in Nashua, New Hampshire, that means your tax home is Massachusetts, not New Hampshire.

You can travel away from your tax home for up to a year. If your trip is longer than that, it's no longer business travel with travel deductions; it's a new tax home.[29]

Travel is fully deductible when it is 100% for business and does not include personal elements. You can deduct any "ordinary and necessary" expenses you incur, including baggage fees, shipping for getting materials to and from the temporary site, tips, laundry, airfare, taxis, etc.[30] Travel meals have special rules, which I covered earlier.

The rules get more complex when you mix business and pleasure, and they differ based on whether the travel is within the United States vs. outside it. For our purposes here, US travel includes only the 50 states and the District of Columbia.

US-Based Travel Rules

If your US-based trip is primarily for *business* but you take a personal side trip, extend the trip for a vacation, etc., then you may deduct only the business portion of the trip and the business expenses.[31] But you *may* deduct the entire cost of transportation to and from the travel location.

If your trip is primarily for *personal* reasons, but you do some business activities, you may deduct only the direct cost of those activities, not the cost of transportation to and from the travel location.[32] For example, if you're a professional drag performer and you visit LA to see friends, but you take one day of your trip to attend Ru Paul's DragCon, then you can deduct your DragCon ticket as a business expense but none of your other LA travel expenses.

If you travel on a cruise ship or to a resort, even if it's advertised as a business trip by the host, it is considered a vacation. Small amounts of time spent on business activities within this setting will not change this fact.

Rules for Foreign Travel: Airfare

When you travel outside the United States, your airfare (or other transportation cost) is fully deductible if entirely for business, or if it's *considered* entirely for business. This is true if you meet one of these four exceptions:[33]

- You have no substantial control over your trip. Self-employed people generally *do* have substantial control.
- Your travel is for less than seven days. This includes the day you return to the United States, but not the day you leave.
- If you're outside the United States more than five days but less than 25% of your time is spent on personal activities (by day), the trip is considered primarily business. For this purpose, you count both beginning and ending travel days. This is different from domestic travel rules.

For example, Mariana, an independent journalist, travels to Guinea to report on local people who've been displaced by a mining company, and a luxury car company that's in the area looking to clean up its aluminum supply chain, of which this bauxite mine is a key supplier. She works in Guinea for 14 days, and once this stressful reporting trip is over, she spends five days in Dakar, Senegal, relaxing at a nice hotel. Her travel takes a full day in each direction. Because the personal days in Dakar are less than 25% of her travel (5/21), her entire airfare is deductible. She may deduct 16 days of travel meals and accommodation.

- Vacation is not a major consideration.

One more wrinkle on deducting the *transportation* cost of foreign travel. If that foreign travel is primarily for business (meaning, "but not entirely, or not *considered* entirely"), then you can deduct only the proportion of that expense based on the number of days spent on personal vs. business activities. You determine this percentage by dividing your business days by your total days.

There are a number of noodley details about how to determine if a day was business vs. personal. The basics are that what counts as a business day are: travel days, days you spent on business, days your presence was required, and weekends and holidays if they are sandwiched between business days.[34] But look at this example for a neat trick.

For example, Alek, a model, lives in New York but goes to Paris for 10 days for fashion week, including travel days. She flies out Tuesday and lands in Paris on Wednesday. She goes to fittings at Hermès on Wednesday, Thursday, and Friday. Over the weekend, she visits museums and enjoys the city. On Monday, she has her final fitting and then has runway shows on Tuesday and Wednesday. She flies back to New York on Thursday. All of these days count as business days, because the transport days count, and *so does the weekend that fell between days where her presence was required*. Alek can deduct 10/10ths (aka 100%) of her airfare and eight days of travel meals and hotel. Note that while her personal weekend counts in this scenario as two business days because they were in-between days where her physical presence was required, that does not turn them into business days for the purpose of meals and accommodation. This rule strictly allows her the full airfare.

If we change the scenario and Alek flies to Paris on Friday, spends Saturday and Sunday enjoying Paris, works Monday through Friday, enjoys the following Saturday, and then flies home on Sunday, then three days of her trip are nonbusiness days (the first Saturday and Sunday and the following Saturday. Note that the second Sunday counts as business because it's a travel day), and she is allowed to deduct only 7/10 the cost of her airfare.

International Travel for Primarily Personal Reasons

Similar to US-based travel, if your international travel is primarily for personal reasons, then it's nondeductible. However, direct business expenses you incur are deductible.[35] If you are a fashion designer and you travel to Thailand for vacation but attend a Thai silk trade show to find a new silk supplier, you may deduct only the admission fee for that trade show.

Business Travel for Research

Travel for "education" (aka "general research"), whether domestic or international, is *never* allowed.[36] Tread carefully. A trip with a direct business purpose is fine, but simply going to a location to soak it in and learn about it (as many artists and writers do) will not make the trip deductible. Test this at your peril—I've seen novelists get nailed for it.

A deductible trip could look like this: you're contracted as a location scout for a mini-series about people at a luxury resort in Sicily. You travel to Palermo and set up meetings in advance with a hotel concierge, two craft services caterers, a "fixer" to help you navigate Italian red tape, and a list of locations to scout, according to a pre-arranged schedule. These include a grand outdoor stairway, an island villa, a beach location, and a luxury resort with a restaurant that meets the filmmakers' requirements. This is deductible business travel.

A counterexample: you're a novelist, setting your next novel in Palermo. You book a one-month trip to Sicily, where you stay in an Airbnb, take walks, meet people, soak in the local culture, and write every day. Despite writing while you're there, this is not deductible travel. It counts as travel for education, and that is not deductible.[37]

Final Thoughts on Business Travel

Business travel is a great deduction, often a necessary step to make contacts and gain business, and can be fun. Be aware that it's rightfully under IRS scrutiny, to prevent abuse, so keep it "businesslike." Arrange your meetings in advance, and save your receipts, correspondence, and calendar. If an IRS letter comes requesting all your travel documentation for the last three years, you'll breathe easier knowing you can show your business purpose and documentation for all of it. And absolutely, when you're in Tobago, after your business is done for the day, get a daiquiri, wink at the cute bartender, and put your toes in the sand.

The Home Office/Home Studio Deduction

When you work for yourself, you need a place to work. The home office/studio is one of the best deductions you can take for your business.

For all businesses, your dedicated workspace is deductible. But when you work from home, there are special rules. A deductible workspace must be used *exclusively* for business.[38] In other words, if it is also your dining room, your guest bedroom, or your garage, it's not deductible. It is okay to subdivide a space, however, so long as the demarcation is clear and the smaller subset *is* a dedicated workspace.

For example, let's say Latifah, a writer, lives in a large loft in Baltimore. The loft has an open floor plan, but Latifah has her writing desk, journaling chair, and reference books in one dedicated corner. She demarcates the exclusive-use writing space with two bookshelves at right angles, which create a visual barrier from the living space.

To take the deduction, measure the square footage of your home and that of your office to get a percentage.[39] For example, if Latifah's loft is 1,000 ft^2 and her office is 250 ft^2, then her home office ratio is 25%.

This percentage of your home costs—which would normally not be deductible, because they're personal—now becomes deductible as a dedicated work space expense. She'll calculate 25% of her total home costs (rent, utilities, renter's insurance) as her home office expense.[40]

If you live with roommates, their rooms don't count as part of *your* available personal space, so don't include that in your total square footage. If you work in an outbuilding like a garage or shed, you need to include the square footage of the shed in the total square footage of your home.

In addition, you may fully deduct *direct* expenses.[41] For example, if I have a home studio as a freelance sound engineer and I put soundproofing in my studio, that is 100% deductible.

To document your home office, take photos of the full space and keep them in your tax files.[42] Use this to illustrate what you use it for and to prove that it is a 100% business purpose. Audits happen retroactively, so if you don't document your space while you live there, and then you move, you'll lose your proof. You've probably got a phone with a camera on it with you right now. Go ahead and snap those pics now. Seriously, I'll wait.

While it's a fantastic deduction, you may take a home office expense only if you have a profit.[43]

Items Used for Business and Personal: "Listed Property"

It's normal to have certain items that are for both business and personal use. Examples include your car, your cell phone, or your computer. The tax term for this is **listed property**.[44]

The way to deduct these items is to make a reasonable calculation for your business usage and deduct only that percentage of the total.[45] For example, I have a high-end camera that I use to document my artwork.

But my husband also uses it to take family photos. Because of the personal use, I can't deduct the whole camera as an expense for my art business. So I assign a percentage to my business vs. personal use, and that percentage of the camera is deductible. In my case, it's about 60% business, 40% personal.

The spirit of this law is to allow you to deduct the legitimate business portion but not the personal portion. Understand that when it comes to deducting your home office, items like your Internet and phone are more accurately classified as listed property than lumped into your home office expense.[46] Think about it—if your home office is 11% of your home, that's no guarantee that your cell phone or Internet usage is 11% for business. It's better to calculate how much you use those things on their own merits.

Anytime you use a car or a laptop for business but you don't have a dedicated business car or business laptop, that's listed property. Never deduct 100% of it, because it's an easy lie for the IRS to spot. If you've got only one laptop, then at some point you are probably watching Netflix.

Depreciation: For Big Things That Get Deducted Over Time

Depreciation is for big-ticket items. In tax world, we call these **assets**.[47]

Assets have a long useful life and a high(ish) cost. You're generally required to spread out the deduction over the useful life of the asset, rather than deduct it all at once. This multiyear deduction is called **depreciation**.

Assets are different from **supplies**. Supplies are items that get used up, generally within a year. You get to deduct the full cost of supplies in the year that you purchase them.[48]

To track depreciable assets, you note the date you purchased the item, and if it's different from the purchase date, also the date you began using it,[49] plus the total cost to you, which includes *everything*—sales tax, installation fees, shipping, etc.[50]

When it's tax time, you look up the asset's useful life on an IRS table—your tax software will do this for you.[51] You don't get to choose this—you have to use the IRS-designated life span.

You spread the full cost of the asset out over the IRS's useful life for the asset and deduct a portion of it each year until the last year, when it's fully depreciated.[52] For a new desk (furniture = useful life: seven years), you deduct 1/7th the cost of the desk each year for seven years.

In practice, you don't need to do these calculations yourself. Your job is to track the purchase date/date placed in service and the total cost of the asset. If you're using tax software (and please do—software catches mistakes), the software will ask you to classify the type of asset, and that means it's looking up the asset life for you in the background. Likewise, it's a tax preparer's job to do this for you, if you're paying one.

Inexpensive Assets Expensed Like a Supply: The De Minimis Safe Harbor Rule

Small businesses often buy something that's technically an asset and yet is so inexpensive that it's silly (and an admin hassle) to depreciate it. My office printer, for example, was under $300, and is in this category. So there's a rule that allows you to deduct items that cost under $2,500 as a supply. It's called the **de minimis safe harbor rule**, and you'll want to read more in the document I cite[53] to apply it.

Getting the Whole Deduction: The Section §179 Expense

There's a special rule that often allows you to take the full deduction in year one despite the depreciation rules. This is called Section §179. Your accountant might say something like, "Don't worry about depreciation on that; we're just gonna take a 179 expense." And to translate that, it means you're taking advantage of this law and deducting the full expense in one year, rather than spreading it out. Rather than get into the nitty-gritty, understand that the spirit of the Section §179 expense is that Congress, to boost the economy, passed a generous law that allows small businesses to take a full deduction for assets most years.[54] Your software or your accountant will generally present the option for you and engage the mechanics of it by guiding you through some qualification questions to make sure you're eligible. You don't need to know every detail; you just need to know it exists and helps you.

Some states won't allow the §179 expense (hi, Ohio!), so you might see a difference in your expenses on your state income tax return vs. your federal one.[55] No biggie. Just making you aware of why those two things sometimes don't match.

Here are some pro tips when dealing with depreciation. First, your current depreciation schedule is important information that carries over from your last tax return and needs to be included in your current tax return, or else you lose a bunch of deductions. This is info your new accountant needs, and it's why they require you to give them last year's tax return (if it was prepared by someone else). If you DIY your taxes and switch software/preparation method, this is easy info to forget—so find your prior year depreciation schedule in last year's tax return, and carry it into the current year's return.

Pro tip 2: Even though the Section §179 expense often allows you to take the full cost in a single year, you may not want to, if you are struggling to show a profit in your business. It's okay to depreciate the asset if you prefer.

Pro tip 3: Track all your deductible expenses in your books (See Chapter 7: Bookkeeping). You don't need to decide until tax time whether you'll expense the whole amount in one year, using section §179, or if you'll depreciate the items over their IRS-designated useful life. You can decide at tax time which benefits you more.

Inventory, aka Cost of Goods Sold

Costs of goods sold (COGS) controls the deduction timing of the direct costs of materials and labor that go into your final product. Rather than deducting all the materials and labor costs in the year that you incur those expenses, the COGS rule says that you may deduct those expenses only when you sell the corresponding items.[56] Independent artists, writers, and performers who use NAICS code 711510 on their Schedule C are exempt from this requirement.[57] (See "Special Inventory Rule for Artists, Writers, and Performers" later in this chapter.)

For example, if you're a carpenter and you sell live-edged walnut tables and each table requires one walnut slab, your COGS tracking would look like this: You buy 20 walnut slabs this year for tables but sell only 9 tables. You may deduct the cost of only 9 slabs this year. The remaining 11 slabs will remain in your ongoing COGS inventory until you sell them, at which point you'll reduce your COGS by the amount of those slabs.

In spirit, it's meant to prevent accounting abuses that could potentially wipe out people's taxable income. If a jeweler wanted to avoid paying taxes and COGS rules didn't exist, she could buy 100 sapphires for her inventory at the end of the year and effectively eliminate her tax bill by stockpiling inventory. COGS rules prevent you from deducting a stockpile.

The Difference Between Inventory/COGS and Supplies

Expenses that you put into the COGS bucket are **direct costs**, both materials and labor costs (that you paid others' for, *never your own labor*) of producing your items for sale.[58] Direct costs in accounting are different from indirect costs. You might also hear these called **variable** vs. **fixed** costs. Indirect costs don't change when you sell more. Direct costs do. Indirect or fixed costs are your costs to keep the proverbial lights on—they're what you pay each month for the business simply to remain open, whether you're selling or not.[59]

For a product maker, direct costs are the materials that go into the product, plus any wages or contract labor to make each item.[60] In my tax education business, Sunlight Tax, my COGS expenses are very simple. This makes sense, because my direct costs of producing a knowledge service—teaching, writing, podcasting, and online courses—is minimal. Looking at my bookkeeping, my only COGS expense is my payment processing fees, specifically, credit card, Stripe, and PayPal fees. These are my only costs that vary in direct proportion to how much I sell. Most of my costs are fixed costs. Those are things like my software, my office, and my podcast editor. My friend Jessie, the founder of Asheville Tea Company, has much higher COGS because of her product-based business (I don't know her actual numbers and wouldn't share them if I did). Her COGS likely includes herbs from regional farmers, earth-friendly packaging, compostable tea bags, and labor costs for the workers who package and ship the tea.

COGS is a number that rolls over from last year's tax return to this year's—specifically, last year's "ending inventory" number (line 41 on your Schedule C) becomes this year's beginning inventory number (line 35 on your Schedule C).[61] And on your Schedule C each year, you start with your beginning inventory number; then add together your (direct cost) purchases, your direct labor costs, and your direct materials costs; and then you subtract your amount of inventory costs that remain unsold to get your ending inventory number.

On the Schedule C, it looks like this:

• Beginning inventory (expressed in wholesale/cost to you dollars) (line 35)
Plus
• Your (direct cost of) purchases (line 36) • Your (direct cost of) labor (never your own) (line 37) • Direct materials and supplies (line 38) • Other direct costs (line 39)
Equals
• Total inventory over the year (line 40)
Minus
• Ending inventory (line 41)
Equals
• Cost of goods sold (line 42)

Special Inventory Rule for Artists, Writers, and Performers

The COGS rules can feel tricky when you're a small business, and they're a frequent source of mistakes. For independent artists, writers, and performers, there is an exception in the tax code for tracking COGS. Artists, writers, and performers are not required to track COGS, because they successfully organized in the 1980s and pushed back against the inventory rules in the 1986 Reagan tax law change.[62] They argued that the value of art, writing, and performing is primarily in their labor (which is not deductible), and only to a minor degree in their materials. For this reason, tracking COGS is not just difficult but has little material effect on their taxes.

I know this is true from personal experience. As a painter, the cost of materials in any of my paintings is not only small but hard to track.

I might use 1/27th of a tube of cadmium red, ⅓ a tube of alizarin crimson, etc. (and I might use 70 different colors over the course of the painting, a little bit at a time), plus some canvas and some stretcher bars. These materials might add up to about $100 for a painting that sells for $14,000. Most of the price of my art is in my labor—the three to four months I spend painting it. Consider that every painting I make is unique, and I use different colors and materials for each, and I work on them all at the same time. Tracking COGS for me is downright silly. As the chef and cookbook author Julia Child, who was a part of this advocacy, said, "But how shall I allocate the oregano?"[63] And the courts found that she was right.[64] The cookbook's sales are a distant cousin to the amount of oregano in her test recipe.

The good news is that artists, writers, and performers won this fight. So if you identify as an "independent artist, writer, or performer" on your Schedule C (by choosing the North American Industry Classification System (NAICS) code—that's the six-digit industry identification code that goes on top of your Schedule C—711510, for Independent Artists, Writers, and Performers), then you qualify for this COGS-tracking exception.[65] In practice, this means you can deduct all materials as a supply in the year you incurred the expense, rather than separate out direct materials and labor cost into COGS.

Be sure that you use this exception only if the spirit of it applies to you. It's fine to track COGS if you don't have to. If you're already doing that and it's not a burden, keep doing it. But if you use materials that are a substantial expense in your product or service, then you *should* track COGS. For example, in 2007, visual artist Damien Hirst made a platinum cast of a skull, encrusted with 8,601 diamonds in a piece called *For the Love of God*, with an asking price of £50 million.[66] If Hirst was American (he's not) and filing a Schedule C, he definitely should be tracking COGS because the inventory cost of 8,601 diamonds is substantial.

Other Expenses: Where Every Other Expense Goes

Last on the Schedule C expenses is the catchall category, **other expenses**. If you can't find a home for a business expense in one of the designated categories, you can put it here. **Other expenses** works differently, in that you need to label the expenses you put in here. I recommend grouping things into reasonable categories, giving each a label, and putting the total amount of everything that falls under that label, rather than give each expense its own line. Your tax return is a summary document, not a laundry list.

Use professional labels. These can vary, depending on your field. They can be weird, because the purpose of this category is to capture what didn't fit elsewhere. These are suggestions, but you can use the ones that fit and make your own where you need to.

Next, I outline some common labels and best practices.

Research

Research has no home elsewhere on the Schedule C. Use it for expenses of staying current in your field, like journals, books, and courses you take to maintain your skills and industry knowledge. It should not be for personal pleasure. A musician can deduct the cost of her *Rolling Stone* subscription, concert tickets she bought to check out her new drummer's other band, and the paid apps she uses to help her with musical notation, tuning, and finding new music, whereas an accountant cannot deduct any of those things. But if you are that musician, don't deduct every concert ticket— surely you see music for pleasure! Just deduct the ones that served a business purpose.

Other examples of deductible research are a massage therapist who gets a massage from a competitor, to test the skills of a potential referral partner, or to learn about a new modality. But he can't deduct the massage expenses for getting the kink in his neck out—that's personal.

A filmmaker can deduct a portion of his Netflix/HBO/Apple TV+ subscriptions, but like all expenses that are partly business, partly personal, he needs to take only a percentage. Filmmakers Netflix and chill, too.

This category can look like "fun," so you must document it carefully and be reasonable with what you deduct. Unless you're an accountant. No one has ever subscribed to *Accounting Today* for fun.

Professional Development

Professional development doesn't have a Schedule C spot, so it goes here, in **other expenses**. You can include expenses for courses and coaching here. But be careful that this is only for business coaching and never life or wellness coaching. Unlike business coaching, life and wellness coaching are personal expenses.

Continuing Education Expenses vs. Student Expenses

Note the difference between professional development expenses and qualified tuition expenses for an eligible student.[67] You'll know that you're a qualified student if you receive a form called a **1098-T** Tuition Statement from your academic institution.[68] The qualified expenses paid for you are not a Schedule C expense. In fact, as a student, you are not running a business and don't file a Schedule C at all, unless you have a business separate from your schoolwork.

Education expenses that are deductible for a business are ones that maintain or improve skills you need for your present work, or your employer or the law requires to keep your present salary, status, or job.[69] For example, when I went back to school for accounting, to train in an entirely new line of work, my tuition was not deductible, nor were the prep courses I took to help me study for my licensing exams. Now that I have an established business as a tax educator, the costs of my continuing education courses, which are required to maintain my enrolled agent's license, *are* deductible.

Dues and Subscriptions

Dues and subscriptions belong in **other expenses**. These are straightforward and include membership fees you pay to professional organizations, or subscriptions to journals or periodicals that help to keep you current in your field.[70] This overlaps somewhat with research, and that's okay.

Shipping Expenses/Postage

Shipping is something that most businesses lump in with office expenses on the Schedule C.[71] That's fine. But I like to make shipping its own line when it's a large expense, as it is for, say, galleries or artists who ship large/fragile items. This is not strictly necessary, but I do it rather than overload the office expense category.

Business Gifts

Business gifts are a time-honored expense. However, the IRS has a strict $25 per gift limit.[72] Many people spend more than $25 on gifts for each client. But be clear; only the first $25 of each gift is deductible.

Startup Expenses

Startup expenses are a special category that you are eligible to use only in your first year of business. Indicate this by checking box H on your Schedule C, "Did you start or acquire this business this year."[73] Startup expenses are the one place where you may list expenses that you incurred *before* the current tax year. To be a startup expense, the expense must be something allowable as a business expense in any year, but it occurred before the business actually started.

Things that might go in this category are advertising, travel costs for securing distributors, suppliers, or customers, training costs of your own employees, contractors and their trainers, fees for consultants and advisors who help you start the business, such as a lawyer, accountant, or an expert in your industry.

If your startup costs are under $5,000, you may deduct all of them.[74] You list them as "startup costs" on your Other Expense line on the Schedule C. You must spread out your costs over $5,000 over a 180-month or 15-year period (this is called "amortizing" the cost).[75] If your costs exceed $50,000 (though if you're reading this book, you're probably not in this zone), then the $5,000 that you get to expense in year one is reduced dollar for dollar by the amount over $50,000 until it reaches zero. In other words, if you spend $57,000 on startup expenses, then you have to amortize the entire amount over a 15-year period, and you don't get the initial $5,000 deduction.

This may seem complicated, but this structure gives a bigger immediate benefit to the lowest-income taxpayer, while putting more restrictions on higher-income taxpayers, who have less need for the immediate benefit. This is tax equity at work.

To review the benefits of using a Schedule C and as a small business under US tax law, you get to take losses, which give you an immediate tax-reducing benefit that helps you through your startup phase or through a hardship beyond your control, and get to pay taxes on your *profit*, not on your gross income. To state that differently, you get to pay taxes only on what you *keep*, not your total earnings.

So now that you know about how losses benefit you and what deductions you are allowed to take, how do you do the math of figuring out what your profit is? The answer is bookkeeping.

CHAPTER SUMMARY

- US tax law is generous with business deductions. You may deduct business deductions for your self-employment. These are expenses that are both ordinary and necessary for your business.
- Keep your receipts and other documentation for every business expense for seven years, in case of audit.
- Some deductions have special rules, beyond keeping the receipt. These include your home office, business mileage, business meals, and business travel.
- Listed property are items used for both business and personal use, like your car or cell phone. These have special deduction rules.
- Depreciation means spreading out the deduction for big-ticket items over their useful life.
- Regarding inventory (COGS), deduct direct costs of materials and labor (other than your own) when you sell the corresponding items.
- Startup expenses are a special deduction for expenses incurred before your business started.

ENDNOTES

1. See Tax Guide for Small Businesses (For Individuals Who Use Schedule C), Pub. 334, 30.
2. "What kind of records should I keep," *U.S. Department of the Treasury, Internal Revenue Service*, last modified August 20, 2024, https://www.irs.gov/businesses/small-businesses-self-employed/what-kind-of-records-should-i-keep.
3. U.S. Department of the Treasury, Internal Revenue Service. *Travel, Gift, and Car Expenses*. 2023, Pub. 463, Washington, DC, 14.
4. *Travel, Gift, and Car Expenses*, Pub. 463, 15.

5. *Travel, Gift, and Car Expenses*, Pub. 463, 36.
6. *Travel, Gift, and Car Expenses*, Pub. 463, 16.
7. *Travel, Gift, and Car Expenses*, Pub. 463, 16.
8. *Travel, Gift, and Car Expenses*, Pub. 463, 16.
9. "Per diem rates," *U.S. General Services Administration*, accessed February 9, 2025, https://www.gsa.gov/travel/plan-book/per-diem-rates. See "Foreign Per Diem Rates by Location," *U.S. Department of State*, accessed February 9, 2025, https://www.gsa.gov/travel/plan-book/per-diem-rates.
10. *Travel, Gift, and Car Expenses*, Pub. 463, 16.
11. *Travel, Gift, and Car Expenses*, Pub. 463, 17.
12. *Travel, Gift, and Car Expenses*, Pub. 463, 17.
13. *Travel, Gift, and Car Expenses*, Pub. 463, 37.
14. *Travel, Gift, and Car Expenses*, Pub. 463, 21.
15. *Travel, Gift, and Car Expenses*, Pub. 463, 21.
16. *Travel, Gift, and Car Expenses*, Pub. 463, 21.
17. *Travel, Gift, and Car Expenses*, Pub. 463, 39.
18. *Travel, Gift, and Car Expenses*, Pub. 463, 22.
19. "Topic no. 510, Business use of car," *U.S. Department of the Treasury, Internal Revenue Service*, last modified November 22, 2024, https://www.irs.gov/taxtopics/tc510.
20. *Travel, Gift, and Car Expenses*, Pub. 463, 21.
21. *Travel, Gift, and Car Expenses*, Pub. 463, 22.
22. *Travel, Gift, and Car Expenses*, Pub. 463, 21.
23. "Standard mileage rates," *U.S. Department of the Treasury, Internal Revenue Service*, last modified February 12, 2024, https://www.irs.gov/instructions/i1040sc. See "2023 Standard Mileage Rates," *U.S. Department of the Treasury, Internal Revenue Service*, accessed May 22, 2024, https://www.irs.gov/pub/irs-drop/n-23-03.pdf.
24. *Travel, Gift, and Car Expenses*, Pub. 463, 6.
25. "Standard mileage rates."
26. *Travel, Gift, and Car Expenses*, Pub. 463, 22.
27. "Topic no. 511, Business travel expenses," *U.S. Department of the Treasury, Internal Revenue Service*, last modified December 3, 2024, https://www.irs.gov/taxtopics/tc511.
28. "Topic no. 511, Business travel expenses."
29. "Topic no. 511, Business travel expenses."
30. *Travel, Gift, and Car Expenses*, Pub. 463, 3.

31. *Travel, Gift, and Car Expenses*, Pub. 463, 9.
32. *Travel, Gift, and Car Expenses*, Pub. 463, 9.
33. *Travel, Gift, and Car Expenses*, Pub. 463, 22.
34. *Travel, Gift, and Car Expenses*, Pub. 463, 11.
35. *Travel, Gift, and Car Expenses*, Pub. 463, 9.
36. *Disallowance of certain entertainment, etc. expenses, U.S. Code* 26 (2020) § 274.
37. Tony Nitti, "Tax Court Holds That Family Vacations Are Not Deductible As Book-Writing Research," *Forbes*, March 10, 2016, https://www.forbes.com/sites/anthonynitti/2016/03/10/tax-court-holds-that-family-vacations-are-not-deductible-as-book-writing-research/?sh=37c5e3653b22.
38. U.S. Department of the Treasury, Internal Revenue Service, *Business Use of Your Home*, 2023, Pub. 587, Washington, DC, 3.
39. *Business Use of Your Home*, Pub. 587, 6.
40. *Business Use of Your Home*, Pub. 587, 7.
41. *Business Use of Your Home*, Pub. 587, 6.
42. *Business Use of Your Home*, Pub. 587, 17.
43. *Business Use of Your Home*, Pub. 587, 13.
44. *Business Use of Your Home*, Pub. 587, 16.
45. *Business Use of Your Home*, Pub. 587, 16.
46. *Business Use of Your Home*, Pub. 587, 16.
47. U.S. Department of the Treasury, Internal Revenue Service. *How To Depreciate Property*. 2023, Pub. 946, Washington, DC, 96.
48. U.S. Department of the Treasury, Internal Revenue Service. *Deducting Business Supply Expenses*. 2006, FS-2006-28, Washington, DC.
49. For most small businesses, the date of purchase and the date placed in service are one and the same. But if the item sits around waiting for the installation guy to hook it up (like a ceramic kiln, waiting for your electrician to put in a higher-amperage circuit) or is wildly expensive, like a 30-barrel brewing system for your brewery, at the cost of $1 million, you need to get even more specific about the exact difference between purchase date and the date the item was placed into service, because these might not line up, and a few months of depreciation can have a material effect on your taxes. The IRS has some special when-to-start-your-depreciation rules you'll need to check out. You can find those at https://www.irs.gov/publications/p946#en_US_2023_publink1000107328.
50. "Topic no. 704, Depreciation," *U.S. Department of the Treasury, Internal Revenue Service*, last modified February 13, 2024, https://www.irs.gov/taxtopics/tc704.

51. *How To Depreciate Property*, Pub. 946, 5.
52. *How To Depreciate Property*, Pub. 946, 32.
53. "Capital Expenditures; in general," *Code of Federal Regulations*, title 26 (2015): 550–558, https://www.govinfo.gov/content/pkg/CFR-2015-title26-vol4/pdf/ CFR-2015-title26-vol4-part1-subjectgroup-id149.pdf. See "Tangible Property Regulations - Frequently Asked Questions," *U.S. Department of the Treasury, Internal Revenue Service*, accessed December 3, 2024, https://www.irs .gov/businesses/small-businesses-self-employed/tangible-property-final-regulations#Ademinimis; U.S. Department of the Treasury, Internal Revenue Service. Instructions for Forms 1099-INT and 1099-OID. 2023, Washington, DC, 1.
54. *How To Depreciate Property*, Pub. 946, 15.
55. Jared Walczak, "Consistent and Predictable Business Deductions: State Conformity with Section 179 Deductions," *Tax Foundation*, January 28, 2015, https://taxfoundation.org/research/all/state/consistent-and-predictable-business-deductions-state-conformity-section-179-deductions/.
56. U.S. Department of the Treasury, Internal Revenue Service. *Accounting Periods and Methods*. 2022, Pub. 538, Washington, DC, 13.
57. "Adjusted gross income defined," *Code of Federal Regulations*, title 26 (1972): § 62(a)(2)(B), https://www.law.cornell.edu/uscode/text/26/62; "Joint Committee Report JCS-10-87: General Explanation of the Tax Reform Act of 1986," *Tax Notes*, May 4, 1987, https://www.taxnotes.com/research/federal/ legislative-documents/jct-blue-books/joint-committee-report-jcs-10-87-general-explanation-of-the/1r3py.
58. *Accounting Periods and Methods*, Pub. 538, 15.
59. *Accounting Periods and Methods*, Pub. 538, 15.
60. *Accounting Periods and Methods*, Pub. 538, 15.
61. U.S. Department of the Treasury, Internal Revenue Service. 2024 Instructions for Schedule C. 2024, Washington, DC, C-16.
62. Tax Reform Act of 1986, H.,R. 3838, 99th Cong. (1986). See Gary Klott, "I.R.S. Eases Rules on Deductions After Artists and Writers Protest," *The New York Times*, May 14, 1988.
63. Irvin Molotsky, "Tax Bill Is Lifting Curbs On Julia Child's Oregano," *The New York Times*, November 6, 1988.
64. Klott, "I.R.S. Eases Rules on Deductions After Artists and Writers Protest."
65. "Adjusted gross income defined," *Code of Federal Regulations*, title 26 (1972): § 62(a)(2)(B), https://www.law.cornell.edu/uscode/text/26/62; "Joint Committee Report JCS-10-87: General Explanation of the Tax Reform Act

of 1986," *Tax Notes*, May 4, 1987, https://www.taxnotes.com/research/federal/legislative-documents/jct-blue-books/joint-committee-report-jcs-10-87-general-explanation-of-the/1r3py.

66. Ciar Byrne, "Hirst's glittering price tag loses none of its shine," *The Independent*, last modified August 31, 2007, https://www.independent.co.uk/news/uk/this-britain/hirst-s-glittering-price-tag-loses-none-of-its-shine-463675.html.

67. "Topic no. 513, Work-related education expenses," *U.S. Department of the Treasury, Internal Revenue Service*, last modified October 3, 2024, https://www.irs.gov/taxtopics/tc513.

68. "Instructions for Forms 1098-E and 1098-T (2024)," *U.S. Department of the Treasury, Internal Revenue Service*, last modified April 3, 2024, https://www.irs.gov/instructions/i1098et.

69. "Topic no. 512, Work-related education expenses."

70. "2024 Instructions for Schedule C (2024)."

71. "2024 Instructions for Schedule C (2024)."

72. *Travel, Gift, and Car Expenses*, Pub. 463, 18.

73. Allen B. Ellentuck, "Deducting startup and expansion costs," *The Tax Adviser*, last modified September 1, 2017, https://www.thetaxadviser.com/issues/2017/sep/deducting-startup-expansion-costs.html.

74. Ellentuck, "Deducting startup and expansion costs."

75. "2024 Instructions for Schedule C (2024)," *U.S. Department of the Treasury, Internal Revenue Service*, last modified December 10, 2024, https://www.irs.gov/instructions/i1040sc.

THE ORGANIZATION: THE THREE SYSTEMS YOU NEED (TO STOP WASTING TIME ON THE WRONG THINGS)

Now that we've established that you report your freelance income on a Schedule C, the IRS considers you a business, you get a tax benefit for losses, and you get to deduct all "ordinary and necessary" expenses from your taxable income, let's examine the systems you need to be audit-ready and to calculate your profit.

I know this feels scary, but it's a fact. Audits are the only check in our system, and anything on your tax return can be checked for three years after you file your taxes (and up to six if you've substantially understated your income). Audits can happen to people who've done everything right. They are a checkup, not an accusation. The key is to follow the rules in the first place. (But if you need it, I cover audits in Chapter 19.)

THE THREE SYSTEMS YOU NEED AND WHY

There are three simple systems you need to streamline your taxes. And when you understand the *why* behind these three separate systems, you'll quit stressing needlessly.

- Receipt-tracking
- Tax documentation
- Bookkeeping

CHAPTER FIVE

RECEIPT TRACKING

I n the previous chapter, we established the importance of retaining your business receipts (for seven years), because they are the proof you need in case of an audit. You can receive an IRS examination letter (aka "audit") asking you to substantiate anything on your tax return going back three years, or six years if you've substantially understated your income.[1] It will often ask about expense items on your Schedule C. So think of your receipts the way you think of an insurance policy. You store them, but you need to refer to them only if the bad thing happens. Most years, you won't touch them. But if you get that love letter from the IRS, it's time to pull out your receipts.

In practice, when you show your receipts to the IRS, you'll need to mail copies. Digitizing receipts is absolutely fine, and many of your receipts are digital in the first place (like your email confirmations from online orders). Just know that if audited, you'll need to print them out and mail them.[2]

You also may be required, under audit, to match each receipt with your bank or credit card statement. This is no one's idea of fun. But two points: one, your bank and credit card statements are not sufficient proof of an expense. *Only a receipt is.* And two, if you're required to match your receipts with the bank statements, you'll really appreciate your receipts being in chronological order. Want a painless way to do that?

THE BEST RECEIPT-SORTING TIP YOU'LL EVER GET

For paper receipts, here's my number-one best receipt-sorting tip: don't. It's a waste of your time.

Put paper receipts in your wallet with the newest one *in front.* When your wallet gets full, dump the receipts into a physical file folder (make a new one for each calendar year) *in the front.* This way, they remain in chronological order *without you ever sorting them.*

You can scan them into software (QB self-employed, Xero Tax Touch, Scannable, Dropbox, etc.) so that all your records are digitized. The IRS allows you to destroy the original paper receipt so long as the digital version meets the record-keeping rules and is reliable to retrieve, complete, and legible.[3] Be sure you know exactly where to find them, especially given that you might be looking for them several years from now.[4]

Store your digital receipts for online purchases, too. I recommend creating a folder in your inbox for digital receipts, labeled by year.

You also need to keep supporting documents. Here's the word on that from the mothership (the IRS):

"Supporting documents include sales slips, paid bills, invoices, receipts, deposit slips, and canceled checks. These documents contain the information you need to record in your books. It is important to keep these documents because they support the entries in your books and on your tax return."[5]

Receipts Are for Storage

Your receipts are critical, but they go in deep storage. If you retain all of them and keep them in chronological order, by year, both paper receipts and electronic ones in your inbox, you've done everything you need to. Don't forget that for the special deduction categories that don't typically give you a receipt, you must also document those items the way the IRS requires—like keeping a mileage log to track your business mileage. I went over those requirements in the previous chapter.

There's no reason to touch your receipts at tax time. This is why, if you've ever attempted to bring receipts to an accountant, they gave you a dirty look. To do the work of preparing your taxes, you use the *next* two systems: tax documents and bookkeeping.

CHAPTER SUMMARY

- Keep your receipts for seven years. They are your proof of deductions in case of an audit, which can go back six years.
- Credit card and bank statements *do not count* as receipts.
- Digital receipts are still receipts. It's okay to digitize your paper receipts and ditch the paper, so long as all info is legible and you retain access to the digital file.
- There's a killer receipt-sorting tip in this chapter.
- Store digital receipts for online purchases in a folder in your inbox, labeled by year.
- Keep sales slips, paid bills, invoices, receipts, deposit slips, and canceled checks. These support the entries in your books and on your tax return.

- Store receipts in chronological order, by year, both paper and electronic. For special deduction categories without receipts, document as required by the IRS.
- Your receipts are for deep storage, not for bookkeeping. At tax time, your working documents are your tax documents and your bookkeeping.

ENDNOTES

1. "IRS Audits," *U.S. Department of the Treasury, Internal Revenue Service,* last modified September 9, 2024, https://www.irs.gov/businesses/small-businesses-self-employed/irs-audits#provide.
2. See Rev. Rul. 97-22, 1997-13 I.R.B. 9.
3. U.S. Department of the Treasury, Internal Revenue Service. Recordkeeping for Individuals. 2011, Pub. 552, Washington, DC, 2.
4. Recordkeeping for Individuals, Pub. 552, 6.
5. "What kind of records should I keep."

CHAPTER SIX

TAX DOCUMENTATION

The next system you need for your business is for tax documentation. This is quick.

Taxes are retroactive in the United States, so you won't receive your tax documents until the calendar year is over.[1] Starting in January, have a place ready to put your tax documents as you receive them. This sounds simple, and it is, but you need to take five minutes and actually do it. It will spare you the desperate April 14 panic attack where you rifle every stack of paper in a messy apartment looking for that one lost 1099. And yes, I've been there.

HOW TO ORGANIZE YOUR TAX DOCUMENTS

You'll need two places to store all your tax documents. One is digital, and the other is physical.

Digital Tax Documents

For the digital version, create a folder in your inbox (and if you're married, ask your spouse to do the same). Label it with the relevant tax year, and remember that taxes are retroactive, so if it's January now, that will be last year, not this year. So, "[insert last year] tax documents," for example. When your workplace, bank, brokerage, mortgage company, charity, or someone who paid you last year sends you a digital copy of your tax documents, put them into that folder. Most organizations are trying to go digital, so over time, this is the way that all of your tax documents will go.

Paper Tax Documents

For the tax documents you get in the mail, pick a location in your house where you will 100% put them without fail. For me, this is a hanging file folder marked by year, in a file cabinet. For you, it could be the lower-left drawer in your desk or your sock drawer. The key is that this is a rule that you follow every single time a document comes in the mail (usually marked on the outside with the words "important tax documents").

Setting up a place to put your paper and digital tax documents is a five-minute task that will save you hours of searching, stress, and headache. Once your last document is received, you need to get them all in the same place to do your taxes. If you're a die-hard paper lover, you'll print out the digital ones and add them to the folder with the ones you collected from snail mail. If you like trees, digitize the physical paper tax documents and upload them into a secure folder on your computer, like Dropbox. Remember that there's sensitive information in these, so don't email them or keep them anywhere they can be accessed by others without your permission. That's a path to identity theft. An app I like for digitizing my tax documents is GeniusScan. It turns photos into clean PDFs, and you can password protect the files and share them into your Dropbox account.

CHAPTER SUMMARY

- Set up a system to collect your tax documents into one place. This is quick and easy, but you have to do it.
- Starting in January, have a designated place ready to store your tax documents as you receive them. This will save you from an April 14 panic attack.
- You'll need two places to store your tax documents—one digital and one physical.
- Once you have all your documents, combine them in one place. Print digital ones if you prefer paper, or digitize physical ones and store them securely.
- There's sensitive information in your tax documents. Use secure storage methods like Dropbox and apps like GeniusScan to digitize and password-protect your files.

ENDNOTE

1. See *United States v. Darusmont*, 449 U.S. 292, 296–297 (1981) (giving Congress the ability to apply a retroactive effect to its tax laws, making them effective from the beginning of the tax year or from the date of the introduction of the bill that became the law).

CHAPTER SEVEN

BOOKKEEPING

B ookkeeping is whatever you use to track all the income and expenses of your business. It's how you know your taxable profit, by calculating what's left after your expenses.[1] This unlocks your ability to pay estimated quarterly taxes and stay out of tax debt and tax surprises.

Of the three systems you need to do your taxes, bookkeeping is the big one. It takes the most setup, and it requires the most ongoing maintenance.

You can do this using software, or you can do it on a spreadsheet.

The fact is, you can keep your bookkeeping really simple. You don't necessarily need to use software or pay monthly fees for it. Many of us take it for granted that we need to set up the full (and expensive) software system, as though we were running a Fortune 500 company, when in fact, we may just need some simple tracking.

First, decide if you need a simple spreadsheet system or the full software setup. After that, I'll teach you some of the universal bookkeeping things for everyone to know, and then, you can skip to the section that applies to spreadsheet bookkeeping or software, depending on your decision.

WHO NEEDS BOOKKEEPING SOFTWARE, AND WHO CAN KEEP A SIMPLE SPREADSHEET?

If you're operating in the zone of "side hustle" or if you just have a few 1099s each year and some expenses to track alongside that or if your sole reason for keeping books is to know your taxable income so you can pay estimated quarterly taxes, then you can do everything you need with a spreadsheet.

And if your business is growing, if you have more administrative complexity like running payroll, have more than 20 transactions per week, plan to grow your business substantially, plan to apply for a business loan, or need financial reporting statements, then you should do the work of setting up bookkeeping software that will track those things and that will grow with you.

Using software allows you to run reports—like the three key financial statements, which are the Profit and Loss statement, the Balance Sheet, and the Statement of Cash Flows.[2] If you need these, you need software. Good software also allows you to set up an automated bank feed, by connecting to your business bank account and pulling in your bank statements to reduce the work of bookkeeping.

You need to determine what your needs are and choose the option that fits you best (see Figure 7.1).

For my own work, I use a spreadsheet system for my painting practice, and I use software for my tax education business, Sunlight Tax. That's because the needs of these two operations are quite different.

Figure 7.1 Which bookkeeping is right for you?

Source: © Hannah Cole/Sunlight Tax.

Which bookkeeping is right for you?

Spreadsheet is good for:

- Fewer transactions, manual entry won't be overwhelming
- Side hustle or gig work
- Very part-time or simple
- Your business is small + not growing much/quickly
- Just have a few 1099s
- Just need to track expenses, calculate profit + pay quarterly taxes
- Don't have enough profit to warrant monthly fee for software

Software is good for:

- More transactions, need some automation
- Running reports, like a Profit + Loss statement, like to apply for a business loan, etc
- Growing your business and expecting more transactions/complexity
- Wanting to track equity/owner's draws
- Wanting to connect to your bank account/ an automated bank feed
- Wanting to analyze your finances each month by looking at financial statements
- Being prepared to pay a monthly software fee

For my painting practice, I'm lucky if I have 15 painting sales in one year. I do have expenses, but they usually come in a big lump as I prepare for a show, and they are pretty simple. So even with all the knowledge and experience that I have with accounting, my painting practice is small enough and simple enough to track manually on a spreadsheet. For that reason, I don't want to pay a monthly fee for software.

Sunlight Tax is completely different. I run payroll, I administer a 401k plan with automated withdrawals and matching, I pay a number of workers, and I analyze my financials every month. So I need software.

Feeling resistance to your numbers? Try out this thought: bookkeeping is self-care.

BOOKS ARE THE FULL STORY, TAXES ARE THE CLIFFS NOTES

It's important for you to know that bookkeeping and your taxes are two different things. They both tell the same story, but your bookkeeping is *War and Peace*, whereas your tax return is the *Cliffs Notes*.[3] Your bookkeeping is the true, complete, and accurate record of everything that happened in your business throughout the year. It's got every transaction, every nuance.

Your tax return is the summary. Your bookkeeping has every supply you bought throughout the year, on every date, from every supplier. Your taxes have one "supplies" number, which is the sum total of all of those supplies.

In practice, this means your living document is your bookkeeping. This is the place you do the work of tracking everything you need to in your business. So of course, your books should be accurate. At tax time, you will total up the categories in your bookkeeping and transfer those totals to your tax return.

What's also true is that the IRS cannot see every nuance of your books. They trust your summary, because you sign a legal document (your tax return) saying you're reporting it all accurately. But they reserve the right to ask to see the books, typically in the case of an audit, in case they want to clarify any questions they have about your return.[4] Think of your books as something the IRS *can* look at but usually doesn't.

SOMETIMES YOUR BOOKS AND TAXES DON'T MATCH

There are a few places where your books and your taxes won't match. This is legal and fine. But people freak out over it sometimes, so I want you to know that it's normal. There are places in the tax code[5] where what you deduct isn't exactly the same as what you spent, like spending more than $25 on a business gift, deducting only 50% of business meals, your home office, equipment that you depreciate, your business mileage, and when you have business expenses in your books that aren't deductible (like parking tickets or life coaching).

Likewise, you are not required to take every single deduction you are entitled to. Sometimes, if you have been struggling to show a profit in your business, you might choose to sacrifice a few expenses for the year to avoid a loss on your taxes. In reality, you already spent the money, and your books will show that.[6] So there is some decision-making and strategy that you can employ when taking numbers from your books to your tax return. Specifically, I'm talking about whether and how many deductions you take and in decisions about depreciation.

There's nothing wrong with your bookkeeping. These discrepancies are normal.

But do not get your wires crossed and think you've got any leeway on reporting your income. You don't. That's mandatory.

Remember, darling: you must report all your income. Underreporting your income by more than 25% is a felony.[7] You can go to jail for that.

FOR EVERYONE (SOFTWARE AND SPREADSHEET): FIRST STEPS TO BOOKKEEPING SETUP

First: Open a Separate Business Bank Account

You may be facing a cleanup project as you start your bookkeeping. Don't stress—that's normal. It's a rare human who set up the right accounts before they ever made their first transaction. The rest of us mortals clean up a mess after the fact.

But you can prevent future mess. Here's how: open a separate business bank account for all your business activity. This is a good idea for *absolutely everyone*. It doesn't even need to be what your bank technically calls a "business" account. The important thing is that the account is separate from your personal account and that you *use it as your business account*. Meaning, you deposit all your business income into that account, and you pay for all your business expenses out of that account.

The magic here is that by doing this, you create tracking. Your bank statement will show a record of all the money that came into and went out of your account, and this becomes the record for your bookkeeping.

This doesn't just make your bookkeeping easier. It gives you protection. The IRS expects you to have a business bank account and may question whether your business is a hobby if you don't have one (see Chapter 3, which discusses the IRS nine-point test to determine profit motive). And if you one day form an LLC for liability protection, you must uphold the separation between your business and personal assets by having separate accounts. If you don't, a court of law can invalidate your LLC's liability protection. This is called "piercing the liability veil."[8] It means not only that you've wasted all those filing and legal fees, but your legal protection vanishes.

Only pay for business items with your business bank account or dedicated business credit card, and pay for personal expenses out of your personal account.

How Do I Pay Myself?

If separating your business and personal accounts is so important, how do you pay yourself?

Good question. While it is definitely not okay to charge personal items to your business account, you do need to pay yourself, and you absolutely should. You do this by transferring the money between the accounts, as opposed to by charging personal items to the business account. When you make the transfer, if you have bookkeeping software, you label it as an "owner's draw."[9] If you want to make a transfer in the other direction, in other words, invest your personal money into your business, you transfer from personal to business. The label for your bookkeeping here is "owner's investment" or "owner's equity."[10]

Owner's draws are the rightful way to pay yourself when you're self-employed. They do not count as a deductible expense for your business, and an owner's investment likewise is not taxable income into your business.[11] Because this movement of money is not taxable, there's no need to report it on your taxes.[12] From the IRS perspective, you're just moving money from one pocket to the other. But from a legal perspective, you are maintaining the separation between your business and personal affairs that a business should.

SET UP SIMPLE SPREADSHEET BOOKKEEPING: THE QUICK AND DIRTY

Gather Your Bank Statements

First, gather your business bank statements and credit card statements. These are the core documents you will use to enter your business transactions into your books. Scan the other accounts/places you receive income/ spend money for the business (other bank accounts, PayPal, Etsy, Venmo, CashApp, other credit cards, cash transactions, etc.).

It's not always practical, but as much as you can find a way to make every bit of income and every expense transaction touch your business bank account, the easier it will be to do your books, because everything will appear on a single bank statement.

Once you've determined the places where other transactions happen for your business that you *cannot* consolidate into your business account, make a checklist of them for yourself. You'll want to scan that list every time you do your books to ensure you don't miss these.

Set Up Categories for Your Transactions

Now that you have the info in front of you (your business bank and credit card statements), you need to create categories in your books for each type of transaction.

On a spreadsheet, I recommend creating two tabs: one tab to track your income and the other to track your expenses. You'll want to break these categories down further into the types of income you receive and the types of expenses you incur. You'll find shifts over time in your income sources and spending categories, so you'll likely have to adjust them. That's fine. Bookkeeping is like a great partner—you want it to grow and change with you.

Income Categories

On your income tab, you'll want to set up categories that make sense for your business. The Schedule C, where you will ultimately report all the income you made in a calendar year, has just one line for income (line 1: Gross receipts or sales), where you'll lump everything together.[13] But your books are a living document, and they are meant to help you understand your business. So you will likely want to break down your income into meaningful categories by type. Keep it as simple as possible, but make a few key distinctions where it helps you understand your business. I recommend about one to five different categories of income, depending on your needs. Bookkeeping requires ongoing maintenance, so the simpler your setup, the simpler your maintenance.

Figure 7.2 shows a setup without separate income categories. This is how I do it for my art income:

For example, you may sell both a product and a service. Because you may owe sales tax on the product income, but not on the service income, it

Figure 7.2   Bookkeeping income categories.
Source: © Hannah Cole/Sunlight Tax.

	Item	Notes for your memory	Date	Amount
1	SUNLIGHT TAX			
2	Item	Notes for your memory	Date	Amount
3	Phillip/art sale hotel		1/4/2026	$2,700.00
4	print sale		1/7/2026	$280.00
5	Honorarium, UMMA		1/29/2026	$500.00
6	Slag Gallery, 4 paintings to corporate collection		3/18/2026	$4,717.00
7	Honorarium, Hampshire College		4/19/2026	$500.00

Figure 7.3   Bookkeeping income categories product/service.

Source: © Hannah Cole/Sunlight Tax.

	Item	Notes for your memory	Date	Service sales	Product sales
1	SUNLIGHT TAX				
2	Item	Notes for your memory	Date	Service sales	Product sales
3	reed sales		1/4/2026		$800.00
4	Club Cafe gig		1/7/2026	$280.00	
5	reed sales		1/29/2026		$500.00
6	Smith wedding		3/18/2026	$4,717.00	
7	reed sales		4/19/2026		$500.00
8	private lessons		4/20/2026	$1,080.00	
9	private lessons		10/4/2026	$1,000.00	

makes sense to break your income into product sales and service sales. You can use those generic names, something like "service income" and "product income," or you can customize your names.

For example, if you're a bassoonist and you earn your income through playing gigs for hire, weddings, private lessons, and your own band, plus you make your own double-reeds and sell them to your students and online, then you could set up your income categories like Figure 7.3.

But it might feel even more intuitive to you to label them as "Gigs & Teaching Income" and "Reed Sales." Whatever works for you.

Expense Categories

You'll probably have more expense categories than income categories. Your bookkeeping time will be mostly spent on tracking expenses, as they tend to be more frequent.

Set up expense categories that make sense for your work. I recommend matching your expenses closely with the Schedule C expense categories. This makes life simple at tax time, because you'll just total up all your expense columns and transfer them straight to the corresponding total on the Schedule C. In practice, this means you enter these totals into your software or in your accountant's tax organizer. (See Chapter 9 about reporting these for taxes.)

The Schedule C categories are as follows (these rarely change):

Line 8	Advertising
Line 9	Car and truck expenses
Line 10	Commissions and fees
Line 11	Contract labor
Line 12	Depletion
Line 13	Depreciation and Section 179 expenses
Line 14	Employee benefit programs (other than on line 19)
Line 15	Insurance (other than health)
Line 16	Interest a. Mortgage (paid to banks) b. Other
Line 17	Legal and professional services
Line 18	Office expense
Line 19	Pension and profit-sharing plans
Line 20	Rent or lease a. Vehicles, machinery, and equipment b. Other business property
Line 21	Repairs and maintenance
Line 22	Supplies (not included in Part III COGS)
Line 23	Taxes and licenses
Line 24	Travel and meals a. Travel b. Deductible meals
Line 25	Utilities
Line 26	Wages (less employment credits)
Line 27	a. Other expenses (from line 48) b. Energy-efficient commercial bldgs deduction (attach Form 7205)

I have a visual guide to tax deductions that I update every year, where I illustrate exactly what expenses go in each of these categories for a number of creative fields, with the tax rules for each category. This is a useful printable reference tool that you can get for free on my website at www.sunlighttax.com/deductionsguide.

I recommend looking at the categories on this guide and using them as your baseline for your expense tabs in your bookkeeping. You'll create a row of expenses at the top, with the leftmost column reserved for the item purchased and the next column for the date. I also put a third column after this, for notes (see Figure 7.4 for a partial look).

You'll enter each expense you see on your bank statement with the item in the leftmost column, then the date of transaction, and then the amount of the expense in the correct expense column. In the notes column, I note who I met with and the business purpose, to meet that extra-stringent IRS documentation requirement for business meals.[14]

Figure 7.4 Expense categories.
Source: © Hannah Cole/Sunlight Tax.

	SUNLIGHT TAX											
Item	Notes for your memory	Date	Advertising	Commissions + Fees	Contract Labor	Insurance (NOT health)	Interest	Legal + Profess son	Office/studio expense	Rent (property)
Twin Leaf	treated Tracey + collectors to drinks	5/10/2026								
Sarah D.	helped me install gallery show	9/16/2026			$397.50					
Moge Tea	tea to thank Tracey	9/19/2026								
French Broad Choc	Coffee to thank Mark for work pickup	9/30/2026								
Air BNB		10/2/2026								
Squarespace		10/16/2026	$96.00							
Apple Store, laptop		10/19/2026								
Creative Capital, contin. ed.		10/26/2026								
Cheap Joe's		10/28/2026								
Asheville Art Museum		11/29/2026								
Slideroom application		12/18/2026		$25.00						
Open Studios Press, entry fee		12/30/2026		$65.00						
Cheap Joe's		2/18/2027								
Neomonde Raleigh	install trip Raleigh	2/19/2027								
Hyatt, Raleigh	install trip Raleigh	2/19/2027								

If there are Schedule C expense categories that you will never use, it's okay to leave them off your spreadsheet. For example, if you're not logging timber, mining, or drilling for oil, you can forget Depletion. And if you don't have employees, then you won't have anything to report on line 26, Wages.

Make Your Spreadsheet Do the Math

If you're setting up bookkeeping on a spreadsheet, you're almost done. But taking 10 more minutes to add formulas into your spreadsheet so that you have an ongoing tally will make your life much easier.

Here's what you need. First, on the income tab, add a formula at the end of each income category column that adds up all the values in that column. Now you can see your running totals as you enter your income.

Next, if you have more than one column for income type, create a formula across the cells that tally the column totals to add those subtotals together. This number will now be your total income, aka gross income. You can keep track of it now, and watch it grow! It'll be the number you report on Part I line 1 of your Schedule C, **Gross receipts or sales**. Voilà!

Remember that this is your income *before* you deduct expenses—so it's not your taxable income just yet. We're about to get to that.

On your spreadsheet's expense tab, you will likewise add in formulas at the bottom of each expense column. This will give you a running total for expenses in each category.

What's even more delightful? If you set up each expense category to correspond with the Schedule C expenses (listed earlier), then your total for each category becomes the number you report in that line of the Schedule C. Simple and magical.

Then, create one more formula, across your expense totals row, that adds up all the expenses. Now you have the power to know your profit, which is what you'll owe tax on.

Let's pause here for just a second to notice that when you set up these expense totals, you will see that they are remarkably close to the numbers on your Schedule C in each category—but **not exactly**. A few of these numbers will be different from what you report on your tax return—for example, your meals expense will be half the amount here. Your depreciable assets column will be large, while your depreciation expense on the Schedule C will shrink down to only this year's portion(s). So take a breath and remind yourself that this is the core document for making the calculations on your tax return, but it is not your taxes.

From here, you can create one more formula (I like to do it on a new tab, called SUMMARY), where you pull the Total Income from your income tab, and subtract your Total Expense number from your expense tab. This gives you your net income, aka **profit**. This number is your answer to these questions: "How well am I doing?" and "Is this worth it?" and "How do I get the faintest clue how much tax I owe, especially midyear, before I ever sit down to do my taxes?"

And now that you have this magic number, you have the power to know your profit each quarter, calculate and pay what you owe in taxes (both the IRS and your state), and never pay a penalty again.

When you make a bookkeeping spreadsheet for yourself, the world is your oyster. I like to add tabs to track other things that I'll want nearby at tax time. I add a tab for mileage, where I note my January 1 odometer reading and might plug in a formula to multiply this year's business miles (so far) by this year's mileage rate to look at how much money I get to deduct for that, since it's not based on my actual car expenses.

I also make a tab to note what I paid each quarter for estimated quarterly taxes, because that's a number I need to report on my tax return. Remember, these are pre-payments of your tax bill, so you'll need to *report them* as paid, so they come off your tax bill. That's the whole idea. So why not make a place where I can quickly reference that info? The point of doing any of this setup, to me, is to make my life easier.

Last but not least, you can also make a summary tab with a few simple formulas to calculate what you owe in quarterly taxes, based on your profit each quarter, to make that calculation easier for yourself. The full estimated tax debrief is in Chapter 2, but the basic formula would be something like this:

Federal estimated tax payment:

Self-employment tax owed	= Net profit × 15.3%[15]
Plus	
Federal income tax owed	= Net profit × average Federal income tax rate[16]
= Total Federal estimated tax payment	

State estimated tax payment:

State income tax owed	= Net profit × average state income tax rate[17]

I have done all the work of setting this up on a spreadsheet and also added some bonuses that add more fine grain to the numbers. It's what I use myself for my painting practice. If you'd rather buy a copy of my premade spreadsheet than go through the work of setting up your own, you can find that at www.sunlighttax.com/taxesforhumans.

Or scan this QR code:

Once you've set up your spreadsheet, you can skip the next section and go straight to "Doing your bookkeeping (ongoing)," later in this chapter.

TO SET UP BOOKKEEPING SOFTWARE: HIRE A PRO (AND HOW TO DO THAT)

If you need bookkeeping software, hire a professional to do the setup. Of all the expenditures of your business, paying for competent bookkeeping setup is the most critical. If you spend money in one place in your business, this is the place to do it.

The ongoing work of bookkeeping is absolutely DIY-able. But the setup is technical, and it requires training in double-entry accounting.

I realize that this might feel disappointing to read. But it's important. Setting up your books incorrectly will give you errors that compound over time and cost you thousands of dollars to correct. It might feel cheap today, but it'll be very expensive tomorrow.

How to Hire a Bookkeeper

There's a huge range of abilities among bookkeepers, and no official licensing. For that reason, you should be looking for key technical, communication, and troubleshooting skills, as well as knowledge of your industry. These are some things to look for in a bookkeeper:

- They're careful about data security. They will never ask for your passwords or access to your actual bank account (only the statements/read-only access).
- They ask you questions to clarify, especially in the beginning. They get to know your business and your habits.
- They're curious about how your business works. A good bookkeeper is an ace in your hand. They can identify trends in your business, notice where you're overspending, or give you industry benchmarks about how you're doing. A bookkeeper with a sense

of curiosity, systems optimization, and critical analysis will be someone who is worth every penny and more.

Bookkeeper red flags

- They treat you disrespectfully.
- They ask for your bank passwords.
- They have no curiosity about the unique parts of your business.
- Your tax preparer complains about the quality of your books.

DOING YOUR BOOKKEEPING (ONGOING): SPREADSHEET AND SOFTWARE

Get Into a Rhythm

Doing your bookkeeping only once per year is five-alarm stressful. It's nearly as stressful as paying your taxes only once per year, in one heart-stoppingly large amount. For the same reason that paying quarterly taxes reduces your chances of a tax bill so high and surprising that you fall into tax debt, doing your bookkeeping more than once per year breaks it into chunks that feel better and require less work. Furthermore, it gives you the answer to those dreadful questions like "What am I making, and what will I owe for taxes?" at any point you decide you want to know.

So if your bookkeeping has been the full-year-at-the-last-minute-panic style, I highly recommend establishing a rhythm of doing your books once per quarter to start. And the very best timing is about two weeks before each of the quarterly tax deadlines.[18] This gives you the power to know your numbers, reduce your tax-time workload and stress, and also pay your estimated taxes accurately and on time. Never a penalty again! The dates to put in your calendar are:

April 3

June 3

September 3

January 3

And these are to meet the estimated quarterly tax deadlines of:

April 15

June 15

September 15

January 15[19]

I say the 3rd rather than the 1st, for the record, because your bank statements typically aren't available until a couple days after the end of the prior month.[20]

If your business has grown bigger, you will want to move to monthly bookkeeping. Once your business reaches a certain level of activity, doing three months of bookkeeping at a time gets too overwhelming. And more importantly, when your business is cooking, it's financially healthy to look at your numbers every month. You can use your books to make decisions about which expenses are paying off and which are not, which products or services are selling the best, and more. But if your business is smaller, quarterly bookkeeping is a good standard that will keep you from getting rocked by surprises that hid inside your numbers for too long.

DOING YOUR ACTUAL BOOKKEEPING

What are the actual tasks you need to do in your bookkeeping? At the most basic level, you do your books in order to know your profit, calculate and pay your estimated quarterly taxes, and track your expenses.

But there's a little more. The following is a breakdown of the tasks by the frequency with which you need to do them.

YOUR BOOKKEEPING TASKS BY FREQUENCY

The following are your bookkeeping tasks by frequency (used with permission from Marissa Domanski, MD Bookkeeping).

Daily

- Check your cash with a daily log into your bank (especially if your financial style is "avoidance").

Weekly

- Record your transactions in your spreadsheet or software if your business volume warrants it (large volume).
- File your receipts (the electronic ones and the paper ones) into your receipt folder for that year.
- Review any bills that will be due.
- Send Invoices.

Monthly

- Record your transactions in your spreadsheet or software, if your business volume warrants monthly recording (medium volume of transactions).
- If you use software, review your Profit & Loss report for the month. If you do monthly bookkeeping on a spreadsheet, calculate your profit for the month.
- Think about upcoming cash flow: how much will you spend; how much will you earn in the next month? Are there any tasks this brings up for you? Put those on your calendar.

Quarterly

- Record your transactions in your spreadsheet or software, if your business volume warrants quarterly recording (smaller volume).
- Calculate and pay your estimated quarterly taxes.
- File and remit your quarterly sales tax, if you're required (some may need to do this monthly, if your state assigned you a monthly filing frequency due to sales volume).

Yearly

- Finish bookkeeping for the prior year so that numbers are ready for your tax filing, or give summary data to your tax preparer.
- Send out any 1099s you owe.
- Review inventory: calculate items not sold.
- Pull annual reports for your tax preparer, if you use software.
- Review annual reports (if you use software) or your bookkeeping spreadsheet: Did you meet your goals for the year? Why or why not? What will you change in the next year?

BOOKKEEPING WILL TRACK YOUR BUSINESS INCOME, BUT NOT YOUR OTHER INCOME

If you've experienced the dread of not knowing if you're profitable at all, or not having any idea what your taxes are going to be, then setting up bookkeeping will end your fears. Going from total mystery, and the dread that accompanies that, to the power of knowing is amazing. It puts control back in your hands.

But your books are based on your business *only*. They *will* give you the numbers you need to know *what's taxable from your business income*.

But they won't tell you what unpaid taxes you have from other sources—real estate transactions, your spouse's business, your W2 or your partner's, farm income, your short-term rental property, etc. For most people who are self-employed, it's the business income that causes the tax stress. Your bookkeeping will solve that. But bookkeeping is only tracking your business and not everything in your life outside of that. If you sell some real estate, for example, you can still end up with a large tax bill. Your business books aren't going to speak to the other income you may have, so keep an eye on that, too.

This diagram you saw in Chapter 2 is a visual reminder that all your income gets pooled together into one income bucket, which generates one tax bucket (see Figure 7.5).

Figure 7.5   Taxes are based on all taxable income.

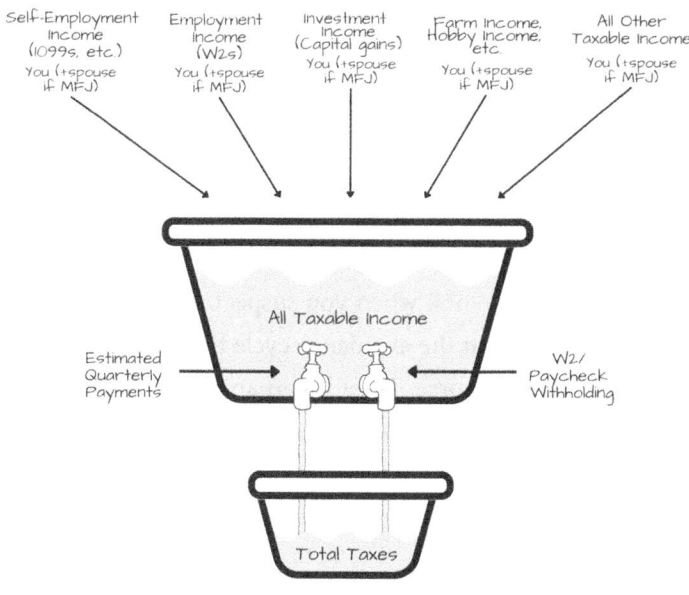

HOW IT'S ALL CONNECTED

Note the relationship between your taxes, your books, and your receipts/ documentation. Each is a summary of the one before it. Your taxes are the summary of your bookkeeping (with adjustments made for certain tax rules). And your receipts and documentation are the detailed proof that shows that each transaction in your bookkeeping is real. You never do your bookkeeping from your receipts—the papery mess of that makes me queasy. You do books from your bank and credit card statements. But your receipts are hanging out in your tax documentation folders on standby in case they are ever called on (aka "audited") to come out and say, "Yes. We're real. This transaction really happened."

If You're Avoiding Your Numbers, Read This

Does looking at your money feel scary as hell? I get it. No, really.

For years, I was barely making a profit as a professional painter, despite long hours in the studio, weekend grant-writing, and many evenings away from my family at openings and art fairs. Looking at my numbers felt like an assault. It seemed like they were whispering, "This isn't working. All your hard work and sacrifice is eating away at your marriage, and the prestige does nothing to pay this New York City rent."

I want you to approach your numbers with self-compassion. I know that it can feel painful to look when you suspect the numbers tell a story you don't want to hear. But the avoidance cycle this can lead to is a snowball that gets worse and worse. It leads to panic/stress-work, fights with your partner at tax time, disorganization, and tax bill surprises. This hole gets deeper.

Your power starts with knowing. So just as it's unpleasant to hop on a scale after an overindulgent holiday season, there's no way to pull the numbers into better shape until you do that hard thing and look for the first time. Try to see your numbers as information, without judgment. I know that's hard. But be as big-hearted toward yourself as you possibly can.

SET UP FOR SUCCESS AND REWARD YOURSELF

Make your bookkeeping sessions as pleasant as you can—with a glass of wine, good music, a clean desk, your kids at the neighbor's house, or whatever else it takes. Reward yourself for even the smallest progress in the beginning, when it's the hardest, so that coming back to them the next time becomes less hard. You'll see that this really works. Brain science says so.[21] And you will start to get a sense of control and power as you get into a rhythm of looking at your numbers, tracking your deductions, and knowing your status many months before tax time. The power is real.

CHAPTER SUMMARY

- Bookkeeping tracks all your business income and expenses, helping you know your taxable profit and plan for your tax payments.
- Of the three tax systems, bookkeeping is the most work and the most power. It requires setup and ongoing maintenance.

- Decide if your bookkeeping should be a simple spreadsheet or full bookkeeping software based on your business size and needs.
- Spreadsheet pros: simple, free, DIY-able. Spreadsheet cons: limited info, no financial reports, no automation.
- Software pros: financial reports, automated bank feeds, ability to handle complex accounting. Software cons: requires professional setup, complex, monthly fee.
- Bookkeeping is the detailed record of your business, like *War and Peace*. Your tax return is the Cliffs Notes.
- Your books and taxes will not match exactly; this is normal.
- Opening a separate business bank account is a good idea for everyone. It helps you track all business transactions, prevents future messes, and is protective for your business.
- Paying yourself is okay, but you need to do it right. Transfer money between business and personal accounts as "owner's draw" (money out) or "owner's investment" (money in) to maintain separation. Never pay for personal expenses through your business account.
- Spreadsheet setup: gather bank statements, set up income and expense categories, and use formulas to track totals and calculate profit.
- For software setup, hire a professional to avoid costly errors. Look for data security, curiosity, and good communication skills.
- Do your bookkeeping regularly, ideally quarterly or monthly, to avoid stress and stay on top of your money.
- Tasks by frequency: There are annual, quarterly, monthly, and weekly tasks to do for your bookkeeping.
- Your bookkeeping tracks your business income, not other income like real estate or your spouse's income. Keep an eye on all income sources for the full picture.
- Taxes summarize your bookkeeping. Receipts and tax documentation prove your transactions.

- Treat yourself with kindness as you approach your numbers. It can feel scary to even look. But knowing your numbers unlocks power.
- Make your bookkeeping sessions pleasant and reward yourself for small steps to build a habit that feels good.

ENDNOTES

1. See U.S. Department of the Treasury, Internal Revenue Service. Tax Guide for Small Businesses (For Individuals Who Use Schedule C). 2023, Pub. 334, Washington, DC.
2. "3 Financial Statements to Measure a Company's Strength," Charles Schwab, last modified February 13, 2023, https://www.schwab.com/learn/story/3-financial-statements-to-measure-companys-strength#:~:text=The%20income%20statement%2C%20balance%20sheet,financial%20health%20and%20underlying%20value.
3. See "War and Peace: Book Summary," CliffsNotes, accessed December 3, 2024, https://www.cliffsnotes.com/literature/w/war-and-peace/book-summary.
4. "IRS Audits: Records We Might Request," *U.S. Department of the Treasury, Internal Revenue Service*, last modified January 17, 2025, https://www.irs.gov/businesses/small-businesses-self-employed/audits-records-request.
5. Travel, Gift, and Car Expenses, Pub. 463, 14.
6. See U.S. Department of the Treasury, Internal Revenue Service. Tax Guide for Small Businesses (For Individuals Who Use Schedule C). 2023, Pub. 334, Washington, DC, 36.
7. "Failure to pay penalty," *U.S. Department of the Treasury, Internal Revenue Service*, last modified December 12, 2024, https://www.irs.gov/payments/failure-to-pay-penalty.
8. Nikki Nelson, "How to avoid piercing the corporate veil," Wolters Kluwer, last modified March 12, 2022, https://www.wolterskluwer.com/en/expert-insights/how-to-avoid-piercing-the-corporate-veil.
9. "How do I pay myself from my LLC," Wolters Kluwer, last modified March 12, 2023, https://www.wolterskluwer.com/en/expert-insights/how-do-i-pay-myself-from-my-llc.
10. "How do I pay myself from my LLC."
11. "How do I pay myself from my LLC."

12. "How do I pay myself from my LLC."

13. U.S. Department of the Treasury, Internal Revenue Service. 2024 Instructions for Schedule C. 2024, Washington, DC, C-12.

14. Travel, Gift, and Car Expenses, Pub. 463, 3.

15. Technically, ½ of this is deductible, so you're overshooting what you owe, but since your goal with estimates is to slightly overpay, rather than underpay, I'm not correcting for that, on purpose.

16. This number is damn hard to nail down, but it's called an estimate on purpose—it's ok to estimate. You may want to use an online income tax calculator to find the number, but keep in mind that your average income tax rate is much smaller than your marginal tax rate, and it needs to be calculated exclusive of your self-employment tax or else you're double-paying that part.

17. I recommend looking at last year's state income tax return and using your average state income tax rate for this number.

18. "When to Pay Estimated Tax," *U.S. Department of the Treasury, Internal Revenue Service*, last modified February 3, 2025, https://www.irs.gov/faqs/estimated-tax/individuals/individuals-2.

19. "When to Pay Estimated Tax."

20. Danielle Klimashousky, "How to Get a Bank Statement," SmartAsset, last modified September 13, 2023, https://smartasset.com/checking-account/how-to-get-a-bank-statement.

21. See Siegrid Löwel, Wolf Singer, Selection of Intrinsic Horizontal Connections in the Visual Cortex by Correlated Neuronal Activity, *Science 255*, vol. 5041, 209–212 (1992).

PART IV

DOING YOUR TAXES

Now that we've set the table, we'll get to the meat of this book: doing your taxes. But I want you to have the whole tax sandwich. So in this section, we'll start with understanding the actual tax forms themselves, and then we'll move to the input (aka the data entry of your taxes). Next, we'll do some tax triage, so you know when it's fine to DIY it and when you need to call in a pro. Lastly, we'll go over how to review your tax return. This part may feel less urgent to you, but it's your most powerful tool to understand your tax situation, catch mistakes, and head off trouble before it starts. Let's do this.

CHAPTER EIGHT

UNDERSTANDING YOUR TAX RETURN: THE ACTUAL DOCUMENT

There are two key pieces to doing your taxes: the tax information input and the actual forms that you send to the government. Tax professionals switch back and forth between "input mode" and "tax forms mode" as they work to check that the entries show up correctly on the final forms. That's how I'll break down the process of doing your taxes. In this chapter, we'll examine the end product—your final tax return—so you see how your data entry shows up. In the next chapter, I'll teach you how to do the data entry (aka "do your taxes"). And after that, I'll teach you how to review your tax return before you sign and submit it. It's a sandwich: tax form orientation, data entry, tax form review.

The first two pages of your tax return are a summary of everything else in your tax return. They're an answer key that helps you understand anything inside that year's taxes. Cool, right?

So let's break down the 1040. Use this to reference your info at any time.

THE INCOME GETS TALLIED

At the bottom of the first page of your 1040 is a summary of all the income from your tax household. Tallying this is the main job of the tax return. This includes your spouse if you file jointly and anything earned or received by other dependents,[1] from all sources, meaning freelance income, business income, wages, bank interest, rental income, farm income, stock and bond sales, property sales, jury duty pay, unemployment, Social Security, grants, cash prizes, gambling winnings or losses, etc.—the whole shebang.

You can see the total on line 15, taxable income (Figure 8.1).

Figure 8.1 1040—income section.

Source: Internal Revenue Service (IRS)/https://www.irs.gov/pub/irs-pdf/f1040sc.pdf./Public domain/ last accessed on March 21, 2025.

Income	1a	Total amount from Form(s) W-2, box 1 (see instructions)			1a
Attach Form(s) W-2 here. Also attach Forms W-2G and 1099-R if tax was withheld.	b	Household employee wages not reported on Form(s) W-2			1b
	c	Tip income not reported on line 1a (see instructions)			1c
	d	Medicaid waiver payments not reported on Form(s) W-2 (see instructions)			1d
	e	Taxable dependent care benefits from Form 2441, line 26			1e
	f	Employer-provided adoption benefits from Form 8839, line 29			1f
If you did not get a Form W-2, see instructions.	g	Wages from Form 8919, line 6			1g
	h	Other earned income (see instructions)			1h
	i	Nontaxable combat pay election (see instructions)	1i		
	z	Add lines 1a through 1h			1z
Attach Sch. B if required.	2a	Tax-exempt interest	2a	b Taxable interest	2b
	3a	Qualified dividends	3a	b Ordinary dividends	3b
	4a	IRA distributions	4a	b Taxable amount	4b
Standard Deduction for—	5a	Pensions and annuities	5a	b Taxable amount	5b
• Single or Married filing separately, $14,600	6a	Social security benefits	6a	b Taxable amount	6b
• Married filing jointly or Qualifying surviving spouse, $29,200	c	If you elect to use the lump-sum election method, check here (see instructions) ☐			
• Head of household, $21,900	7	Capital gain or (loss). Attach Schedule D if required. If not required, check here ☐			7
• If you checked any box under *Standard Deduction*, see instructions.	8	Additional income from Schedule 1, line 10			8
	9	Add lines 1z, 2b, 3b, 4b, 5b, 6b, 7, and 8. This is your **total income**			9
	10	Adjustments to income from Schedule 1, line 26			10
	11	Subtract line 10 from line 9. This is your **adjusted gross income**			11
	12	**Standard deduction or itemized deductions** (from Schedule A)			12
	13	Qualified business income deduction from Form 8995 or Form 8995-A			13
	14	Add lines 12 and 13			14
	15	Subtract line 14 from line 11. If zero or less, enter -0-. This is your **taxable income**			15

This section separates every type of income. This is a lovely tool you can use to reference how much of one type of income you made vs. another, like W2 income vs. self-employment income.

WHAT COUNTS/DOESN'T COUNT AS TAXABLE INCOME?

While you should assume that all income from earnings and investments is taxable, there are a few things that aren't.

Not taxable income:

- Gifts and inheritances
- Welfare payments
- Loans (because it isn't *your* money)
- Most healthcare benefits
- Cash rebates (on items you purchase from a retailer, manufacturer, or dealer)
- Alimony payments (only for divorce decrees finalized after 2018)
- Child support payments
- Reimbursements from qualifying adoptions

Income that is taxable:

- Grants
- Canceled debt
- Alimony (for divorce decrees finalized pre-2019)
- Barter income (for example, if you trade your work for dental care, then the price of that dental care is taxable; if you play music in a bar for drinks, the drinks are taxable)

Income that is partly taxable/sometimes taxable:

- Social Security benefits
- Money from qualified scholarships is not taxable unless you use it to pay for room and board or personal expenses.
- Money from a life insurance policy when someone dies isn't taxable. But cashing in a life insurance policy is likely taxable.

The Schedules Calculate Special Types of Income

Not all types of income are taxed the same way, which is why there are **schedules**. A schedule is a plug-and-play piece of a tax return whose purpose is to separate one type of income for special tax treatment. For example, freelance/sole proprietor income is calculated on a Schedule C. Why is that pulled out specifically? Because all income reported on your Schedule C is reduced by business deductions and then subject to self-employment tax. So the role of the Schedule C is to calculate what part of your total income you owe self-employment tax on. It's also where all your juicy business deductions go.

On my website (www.sunlighttax.com/taxesforhumans) there's an illustrated explainer of the different tax schedules, so you understand where to put what type of income and which schedules you do (and don't) need. The more schedules you have, typically the more complex your tax return and the more your tax software or accountant will charge you. So it's one way to understand how big your tax return is compared to others'.

TAX AND CREDITS: WHERE YOUR TOTAL TAX IS CALCULATED

Once your household income from all sources is listed—and the schedules have helped calculate the income for each category—the Taxes and Credits section on the 1040 page 2 shows the tax due on all of it.

Your different categories of taxable income times your various tax rates is your **total tax, line 24** (Figure 8.2). It's a number you'll want to reference later (see Chapter 2 on calculating your estimated quarterly taxes).

Identifying Your Tax Credits

Your **tax credits** show up in this section, because they are subtracted from the tax you owe. You may be eligible for a number of tax credits including (but not limited to) for child and dependent care, adoption, retirement savings, residential energy, a qualified clean vehicle, or education.

Tax Credits vs. Tax Deductions, Explained

Tax credits reduce your tax, dollar for dollar. They are powerful.[2] **Tax deductions**, on the other hand, reduce only your *taxable income*. So deductions also reduce the tax you pay but by less than tax credits.

Figure 8.2   1040 page 2—Tax and credits section.

Source: Internal Revenue Service (IRS)/https://www.irs.gov/pub/irs-pdf/f1040sc.pdf./Public domain/ last accessed on March 21, 2025.

Tax and Credits	16	Tax (see instructions). Check if any from Form(s): 1 ☐ 8814 2 ☐ 4972 3 ☐ _____		16	
	17	Amount from Schedule 2, line 3		17	
	18	Add lines 16 and 17		18	
	19	Child tax credit or credit for other dependents from Schedule 8812		19	
	20	Amount from Schedule 3, line 8		20	
	21	Add lines 19 and 20		21	
	22	Subtract line 21 from line 18. If zero or less, enter -0-		22	
	23	Other taxes, including self-employment tax, from Schedule 2, line 21		23	
	24	Add lines 22 and 23. This is your **total tax**		24	

PAYMENTS: SHOWS WHAT YOU'VE ALREADY PAID

The **Payments** section identifies what tax you've *already paid* (Figure 8.3). Any estimated quarterly tax payments you've made throughout the year show up here.[3] So do taxes withheld from you/your spouse's paycheck if you/they are a W2 employee. You may have additional withholding or tax prepayments from other sources, like applying last year's refund to this year's taxes or withholding on an IRA distribution. Your **total payments** (line 33) get subtracted from your total tax.

Let's pause. Calculating the tax you've prepaid is a key reason you get tax documents. If you're feeling unsure what was withheld on your paychecks, that info will be summarized on the W2 from your employer. Likewise, if you checked a box to have taxes withheld from an IRA distribution, you'll get a tax document (called a 1099-R) that shows you how much was withheld. These forms all become part of your tax reporting—you'll use them to tell your tax software (or accountant) what tax you've already paid.

If you pay estimated quarterly taxes, you need to track those payments and report them on your taxes.[4] This system is manual, so you *won't* get a tax document that reports that back to you. You have only your bank statements and possibly an email confirmation from the IRS or your state tax authority. Don't forget to report this info when you do your taxes.

Figure 8.3   1040—Payments section.

Source: Internal Revenue Service (IRS)/https://www.irs.gov/pub/irs-pdf/f1040sc.pdf./Public domain/ last accessed on March 21, 2025.

Payments	25	Federal income tax withheld from:	
	a	Form(s) W-2	25a
	b	Form(s) 1099	25b
	c	Other forms (see instructions)	25c
	d	Add lines 25a through 25c	25d
If you have a qualifying child, attach Sch. EIC.	26	2024 estimated tax payments and amount applied from 2023 return	26
	27	Earned income credit (EIC)	27
	28	Additional child tax credit from Schedule 8812	28
	29	American opportunity credit from Form 8863, line 8	29
	30	Reserved for future use	30
	31	Amount from Schedule 3, line 15	31
	32	Add lines 27, 28, 29, and 31. These are your **total other payments and refundable credits**	32
	33	Add lines 25d, 26, and 32. These are your **total payments**	33

REFUND/AMOUNT YOU OWE

Your payments (line 33) get subtracted from your total tax (line 24) to tell you what you get back (**refund**) or still owe (**tax bill**); see Figure 8.4.

You'll notice, if you look at the Amount You Owe section on page 2 of your 1040, that there are two lines.[5] The first is the **amount you owe** (line 37). The second (line 38) is your **estimated tax penalty**. If you have a penalty listed on line 38, it means your estimated tax payments weren't high enough. That's fixable. Let's make sure that line never has a penalty on it again. Deal?

Figure 8.4   1040—Refund and amount you owe sections.

Source: Internal Revenue Service (IRS)/https://www.irs.gov/pub/irs-pdf/f1040sc.pdf./Public domain/ last accessed on March 21, 2025.

Refund	34	If line 33 is more than line 24, subtract line 24 from line 33. This is the amount you **overpaid**	34
	35a	Amount of line 34 you want **refunded to you**. If Form 8888 is attached, check here	35a
Direct deposit? See instructions.	b	Routing number c Type: ☐ Checking ☐ Savings	
	d	Account number	
	36	Amount of line 34 you want **applied to your 2025 estimated tax**	36
Amount You Owe	37	Subtract line 33 from line 24. This is the **amount you owe**. For details on how to pay, go to *www.irs.gov/Payments* or see instructions	37
	38	Estimated tax penalty (see instructions)	38

147

PAYING YOUR TAXES

Paying your taxes, whether you like it or not, seems pretty straightforward. But there are a few things I want you to understand, because most people don't, and it gets them in trouble.

Filing your taxes and *paying* your taxes are separate things. You can do one without the other. This is very important. First, filing your taxes means the paperwork part *only*.

Getting an Extension Is for the Paperwork, Not the Payment

You can get an automatic extension of time to file. It's easy. You just have to submit form 4868 online or by mail postmarked to the IRS before the April 15 tax deadline. If you do this on time, you automatically get a six-month extension to *file your paperwork.*[6]

But **beware**. You do not get an extension—ever—of your time to *pay*.

The tax payment deadline is April 15 (or the Monday following if that date falls on a weekend), every year, no exceptions. If you pay after April 15, you're paying late. And you'll start accruing interest and penalties on your late payment.[7] So you can go ahead and file for an extension and get six extra months to fill out your tax return. But you still have to *pay your taxes* by April 15. The IRS requires you to make a guesstimate of what you owe and pay that with your request for an extension. You obviously aren't going to know exactly what you owe yet, because doing the paperwork is how you know, and you presumably filed for an extension because you needed more time for that. But you'll need to pay what you *think* you owe (yes, you guesstimate) and then settle up when you get your 1040 paperwork submitted.

If you overpay the amount that you owe, then you will get a refund. But if you underpay, then you will owe interest on the outstanding balance until you pay it.

Got that? I'm saying it because every year people get extensions and think they are getting more time to pay. But they are not. They are accruing interest.

Another reason that I want you to know that filing your taxes and paying your taxes are two separate items is that as a self-employed person, you should be paying taxes every quarter, but you're required to *file your tax return* (the paperwork) only once per year.

The third and final reason I want you to understand that *filing* tax and *paying* tax are separate things is because if you get in a heap of trouble and you can't pay your taxes, you can, and should, still file your tax return.

So go ahead and fill out your tax return, even if you can't pay. The reason here is that it's always better to be honest with the IRS than to avoid and deny. Generally speaking, if you come to the IRS, they treat you better. If they have to come after you, they tend to be less friendly. And that makes sense, right? If you file your taxes, even though you can't pay the amount you owe, you will avoid the Failure to File penalty. You'll still get the Failure to Pay penalty, but that is one less penalty, which is good. It also opens your options for a next step, which is payment plans (more on that in Part 6).

Avoid a tax snowball.

From my experience doing people's taxes, deciding not to file your tax return because you know you can't pay can start you into a very bad snowball situation. What I've witnessed is that people who do this become so fearful of facing up to that tax return that they get tempted not to file the next one. If you do this, pretty soon you are in an ugly back-taxes situation. So I highly recommend that when you have that hard year, you force yourself to file your paperwork anyway. If you stop yourself from getting into a back-taxes snowball by doing so, you will thank yourself later, even if it feels hard right now.

To recap, you file your tax return once per year. That filing can be extended six months if you need more time. You pay your tax due by April 15, every year. No extensions. Penalties start on April 16 if you haven't paid your tax bill. You also can and likely should be paying some form of tax payment all throughout the year—whether through payroll withholding because you're an employee or through making estimated tax payments every quarter because you're self-employed. If you get in trouble and can't pay your taxes, you should still file. And obviously you should get right with the IRS as soon as you can, not to mention get yourself on top of your quarterly tax payments so you don't continue to snowball your tax-paying problems.

CHAPTER SUMMARY

- Think of doing your taxes in two parts: inputting tax information (data entry) and checking the actual forms you send to the government to be sure the input came through accurately. Tax pros switch between these modes to check for accuracy.
- The first two pages of your tax return summarize everything inside your tax return. They are like an answer key for understanding your taxes.
- On the bottom of page one of your 1040, you'll find a summary of all your household income, including self-employment income, wages, rental income, capital gains, and more.
- Taxable vs. non-taxable income: Understand what counts as taxable income (e.g., grants, canceled debt) and what doesn't (e.g., gifts, inheritances).
- Schedules exist to separate certain types of income for special treatment. The Schedule C is for self-employment income, which

includes your gross income (all of it) and your business deductions, and calculates self-employment tax on your profit.

- Page 2 of the 1040 (the page with your signature) shows the tax due on all income, including tax credits that reduce your tax dollar for dollar.
- The payments section identifies taxes you've *already paid*, including your estimated quarterly payments and withholding from paychecks.
- Your payments are subtracted from your total tax to determine if you get a refund or owe more.
- Filing your taxes and paying your taxes are separate. You can get an extension to file the paperwork, but not to pay. Pay by April 15 to avoid penalties.
- Honesty with IRS: Always file your tax return, even if you can't pay. Avoid the Failure to File penalty and open options for payment plans.
- Not filing your taxes because you can't pay can lead to a back-taxes situation. File your paperwork to prevent this snowball effect, even if you can't pay. This saves you the Failure to File penalty and opens options for payment plans.

ENDNOTES

1. A dependent is a qualifying relative that you support financially, by paying more than half their living expenses. Not a spouse. There are IRS rules about who qualifies as your dependent. See U.S. Department of the Treasury, Internal Revenue Service. *Publication 4491, Rev. 10-2021.* 2024, Pub. 4491, Washington, DC.
2. "Tax credits for individuals: What they mean and how they can help refunds."
3. "Pay as you go, so you won't owe: A guide to withholding, estimated taxes and ways to avoid the estimated tax penalty," *U.S. Department of the Treasury, Internal Revenue Service,* last modified November 14, 2024, https://www.irs .gov/payments/pay-as-you-go-so-you-wont-owe-a-guide-to-withholding- estimated-taxes-and-ways-to-avoid-the-estimated-tax-penalty.

4. "Estimated taxes," *U.S. Department of the Treasury, Internal Revenue Service*, last modified August 22, 2024, https://www.irs.gov/businesses/small-businesses-self-employed/estimated-taxes.

5. "About Form 1040, U.S. Individual Income Tax Return," *U.S. Department of the Treasury, Internal Revenue Service*, last modified January 30, 2025, https://www.irs.gov/forms-pubs/about-form-1040.

6. "Get an extension to file your tax return," *U.S. Department of the Treasury, Internal Revenue Service*, last modified December 4, 2024, https://www.irs.gov/filing/get-an-extension-to-file-your-tax-return#:~:text=File%20Form%204868%2C%20Application%20for,paid%20for%20the%20filing%20year.

7. "Topic no. 756, Employment taxes for household employees," *U.S. Department of the Treasury, Internal Revenue Service*, last modified January 2, 2025, https://www.irs.gov/taxtopics/tc653.

CHAPTER NINE

HOW TO DO YOUR TAXES: THE INPUT

N ow we do your taxes. In the previous chapter, we looked at the two 1040 tax summary pages where this information ends up. In this one, we'll do the data entry to arrive at the final (accurate) tax forms.

The work of doing your taxes is largely in getting your numbers and documents into one place. The rest is just answering questions. Here's the breakdown:

- 90% answering info-gathering questions, mostly easy ones
- 10% nitpicky details that matter

From there, you either enter them into your tax software (commercial software, like TurboTax, or the IRS's Free file software, available at the IRS website) or hand them off to your tax preparer.[1]

As you info-gather, your own questions and concerns will surface, alongside the decisions and action items you need to make and take. Track these in a list as you work to capture all of your concerns, decisions, and to-do list items:

- **Your tax questions** (like if you're eligible for a certain tax credit).
- **Decisions** you need to make (like how much to fund your IRA).
- **Action items** (opening and funding the IRA account, conversations needed with your partner, setting up direct deposit or making your federal and state payments).
- **Note any life/income changes**, and make adjustments to withholding or estimated payments for the upcoming tax year. Because we tend to base estimated payments or paycheck withholding on the prior year, proactively adjusting your payments (up or down) is key to preventing tax stress next year. This might feel optional, but *it's your number-one tool for reducing your tax stress.*

I'm teaching you the *practical side* of doing your taxes—how to do the part you can do yourself, as well as you can, short of formal study in taxation. There may be scenarios that are too complex for a nonaccountant to handle. For that reason, I've included a chapter on triage (see Chapter 10 about when to call a tax professional).

Shouldn't Filing Taxes Be Free?

I think so. Paying taxes is our civic duty—isn't it bananas that we have to pay for the privilege?

US law says that taxpayers in the bottom 70% of US household incomes are entitled to a free tax return filing.[2] You heard that right. It's the law. Yet only about 2% of eligible taxpayers got free tax filing in 2023.[3] There's a scandalous history to this.[4]

Large tax prep companies profit off our tax fear and confusion. They lobby Congress to keep the tax code complex, prevent the IRS from

---

autofilling its own Direct File[5] software with numbers it *already has* from your tax documents, and hid "free file" search results from the US public.[6] There's great reporting on this that's worth reading.[7]

After years of tax companies deceiving taxpayers, the IRS finally took over the program, launching IRS Free File in 2024 for the 2023 tax filing season and expanding it in 2025.[8] As of the date of publication, you can go to the IRS Free File site here: https://www.irs.gov/filing/irs-free-file-do-your-taxes-for-free and file your tax return for free, so long as you qualify.[9] This program doesn't cover all states and often excludes taxpayers with a Schedule C, so it may or may not be available for you. You can use the lookup tool to see if you're eligible: https://apps.irs.gov/app/freeFile/.[10]

If you need help filing your taxes, find your local IRS Volunteer Income Tax Assistance (VITA) program. You can search here: https://irs.treasury.gov/freetaxprep/.[11]

PICK YOUR SOFTWARE

Please, use software. Never do your taxes directly onto the tax forms. Software, whether you're the one making the entries into it or your accountant is, catches many of your mistakes. Let your software do the complex calculations and catch when your brain transposes numbers (like writing $38,000 of income instead of $83,000).[12]

Speaking of dyslexic tendencies, transposing numbers on a tax return is so common that the IRS computers catch most instances of number transposition and send you an automatic correction letter.

Unless you're working with a tax preparer, you'll need to pick which software to use. I'm agnostic on this. Just pick one with transparent pricing, an interface that works for you, or the one you used last year.

DOWNLOAD A TAX ORGANIZER

Download a "tax organizer" for the current year (remember that "current" in taxes means the year that just ended). This is a list of questions, updated for the current tax year, to help guide you through your info-gathering. Most accountants provide one to their clients each year. But you can find one online for free. Do an Internet search for "[current year] tax organizer." Tax prep companies like TurboTax or TaxSlayer and some CPAs and EAs will have one available online for free.[13]

The organizer will serve as your checklist. Scan it before you get started to see if there are any irrelevant items, and cross those out. No organizer is perfect, and while the most "complete" organizer will ask you every conceivable question, that also makes it long, exhausting, and often irrelevant. So there's a balance to finding a good one. Once you do, bookmark it so you can get the updated version from the same place next year.

Let this tax organizer alert you to all the info you need to complete your taxes, and surface your answers for your tax software or your tax preparer. Nail down every detail that you can into one place. This will save you time when it comes to the data entry. And if you're working with an accountant, it will reduce your back-and-forth with that accountant, saving you money.

Details are kinda my thing. I was diagnosed with mild OCD when I was a kid, and if you look at my paintings, you can tell. This explains why tax work appeals to me. If you aren't a details person like me, this part may drive you bananas. If so, break up your info-gathering across multiple sessions. In taxes, the details really matter.

If you have an accountant and they have to email you multiple times to drill down on an answer you were vague about or didn't address, they will charge you for that time. If you're going DIY, a lack of detail will cause you confusion and wasted time. The more complete your info, the less work your tax return will be, whether you are paying someone to do it or doing it yourself.

GATHER YOUR TAX DOCUMENTS INTO ONE PLACE

Gather your physical (paper) and digital tax documents into one place, and get them all into one format (paper vs. digital) like we discussed in Chapter 6. Digital is best if you want to upload them to an accountant or your spouse, but remember to store and send them securely, since they contain sensitive info. Don't forget to gather the documents that your spouse received as well. And if that turns into a fight, perhaps on your tax checklist action items you might add "Book session with a couples counselor?" Kidding, but kind of not.

Don't email tax documents, ever, unless you have encrypted and password-protected them.[14] They've got your family's Social Security numbers and possibly your bank account numbers. Use data security best practices with your tax documents. All licensed tax professionals, whether it's an enrolled agent (EA) or a certified public accountant (CPA), are required by law to have a data security plan in place.[15] Sadly, this doesn't mean they do. If your accountant is casual about you emailing the documents with unencrypted Social Security numbers or bank account numbers on them, that's a red flag. It's increasingly common to get your identity stolen through a lax tax preparer.

An accountant following a data security plan will have a secure server where they want you to upload everything, and they'll never email you your tax return, unless it's field-masked or password-protected.

GET YOUR BOOKKEEPING DONE AND GRAB THE NUMBERS

For all of us self-employed folks, getting our bookkeeping done is usually the heaviest lift of getting our tax info ready.

You will be rewarded for doing your taxes early. How? Accountants get busier and busier with each passing day of tax season, and the earlier you get your documents in, the more responsive they will be to your questions. Many accountants (myself included) give a discount to clients who have their documents in before a certain date. Once it's March, it's peak season, and you're not getting a discount. Or quick email responses.

Your task is to get the numbers from your business into a usable format for tax preparation.

If you have bookkeeping *software*, there are two reports you'll need. You'll want to go into the reports section, and get a:

1. "Profit and Loss" statement for January 1 to December 31 of the prior year,
2. A "Balance Sheet" for 12/31

Note the dates on both—you will need those to run the right reports.

Your **profit and loss statement** tells you (or your tax preparer) how much taxable income, aka profit, you had last year.[16] It also tells you how much total, or gross income, you had.[17] You need to report both of these numbers. The profit and loss statement also gives most (but not all) of the info about your expenses in each category that you'll need to enter into your software.[18]

Your **balance sheet**, which in accounting is known as a "snapshot of your business," shows how much value exists in your business in a freeze-framed moment in time.[19] You need this at tax time because it has info about your **assets** (remember, these are the more valuable purchases, like equipment, you've made that have a useful life to you of more than a year, and may need to be depreciated).

If your books are on a *spreadsheet,* then you will need to refer to your up-to-date books for the year that just ended. You'll need to note the total amount of income you brought in (aka gross income), plus the total expenses you had in each of the Schedule C categories. Aren't you glad you organized this spreadsheet by Schedule C categories? It makes this part so *easy.* You don't need to calculate your profit from your spreadsheet books—you just need your gross income plus all your Schedule C expenses. This is because you'll do the calculation on the Schedule C itself, and because of a few differences in how you take the deductions on your tax return, your profit will come out a little bit differently on your Schedule C than in your books (and that's normal!). There will be a few key categories where you might use a different number from what's in your books. But we'll get to that in the "report your expenses" part of the Schedule C reporting section coming up at the end of this chapter.

90% CHECK-IN: YOU'VE DONE THE HARD PART

You've already gathered the bulk of your tax documents and finished your bookkeeping. That's about 90% of what you need ready to do your taxes. Celebrate it!

Of course, in tax, the details matter. So the rest of your tax preparation tasks are about answering basic questions, gathering additional info about what may have changed for you this year, and making some strategic decisions about putting money into tax-advantaged retirement accounts to lower your taxes (while of course also giving your future self some major financial security and freedom). A few of these questions may send you out hunting for another tax document.

What follows is a list of questions to start with and ask yourself every year once you've got your basic documents and bookkeeping ready. After that, I'll get into finer grain ("Details That Matter") with questions that come from the annual tax organizer that I make for my clients. Once you've gathered all of this and noted your answers to all the questions, you're ready to make your entries into your tax software or to hand over your tax documents to your accountant.

THE BIG-PICTURE QUESTIONS

Many of the following questions will seem obvious, be easy to answer, and yet have a huge impact on your taxes.

Filing Status: Who Do You File Taxes With?

You need to determine who you're filing taxes with. Your filing status affects your tax rate, your standard deduction amount, and the credits you're eligible for. If you're single and have no dependents, it's easy. You'll file as single.

If you're married, common-law married or recently stopped being married, or have dependents, determining your filing status can be trickier. I'll illustrate the broadest strokes here. But this surprisingly readable publication from the IRS will get into the nitty-gritty details that you might need: https://apps.irs.gov/app/vita/content/globalmedia/4491_filing_status.pdf.

Filing Status Options

You've got these options for filing:

- Single
- Married Filing Jointly (MFJ)
- Married Filing Separately (MFS)
- Head of Household (HOH)
- Qualifying Surviving Spouse (QSS)[20]

If you're not sure which filing status is best for you, there's a great tool at the IRS website to help you figure it out: https://www.irs.gov/help/ita/what-is-my-filing-status.

MARITAL STATUS FOR THE TAX YEAR: THE LAST DAY

Your marital status is a big deal when it comes to taxes. Whatever your marital status is *on the last day of the year* is your marital status to the IRS for that year's taxes. In cases of separation before a divorce is finalized, consult the website mentioned for more nuance.

COMMON LAW MARRIAGE

For people who are common law married, you are considered legally married for federal tax purposes if your common law marriage is recognized in the state where you live or in the state where your common law marriage first began.[21] Please note that this is for your federal income tax return only. You will also need to check the filing status rules for your state. It's possible that you'll need to file a state tax return with a different filing status than your federal return. This can be a little tricky, because most tax software will assume your status is the same for federal and state. If this is your situation, call in a tax professional.

FILING JOINTLY PUTS YOU ON THE HOOK, BUT GIVES YOU MORE CREDITS

If you are married and file a joint tax return, then you and your spouse become one single tax unit. You'll add both of your incomes and both sets of your dependents, if either of you have any. If you file this way, you will have one income total and one tax due amount on your tax return. Not two.

REAL-LIFE EXAMPLE

An example of a tax client of mine who chooses to file married filing separately (MFS) is Aisha (not her real name). Aisha is an artist with a lot of student loans, and filing MFS allows her access to an income-driven repayment plan on those loans that she wouldn't qualify for if her tax return was filed jointly with her husband and his income. So, even though Aisha has kids and misses out on the Child and Dependent Care Credit by filing this way, it's worth it to her for the lower student loan payments.

When you file jointly, both spouses sign a "joint and severable" legal document.[22] This means that if your spouse disappears from the face of the earth, you remain on the hook for all of their tax deeds and misdeeds for all of the tax years that you signed a joint return. This legal part is easy to gloss over, so make sure you understand it. If this actually happens to you, my condolences. I have help for you in Chapter 20. Also, married filing jointly is the one filing status you *cannot* undo. You're stuck with it for each year you file that way. No backsies.

Alternatively, you may file married filing separately.[23] This option limits some of the credits you're eligible for and may result in higher taxes, but it protects you from owing money for your spouse's debts if that spouse goes rogue. It also protects you from your spouses' creditors if your spouse is bringing debts to the marriage.

If you're single and have dependents, then you'll file as "Head of Household."[24] This is important, because you get a larger standard deduction (I'll explain that term in a minute—but basically a better deal) as well as more eligibility for various tax credits. The government recognizes that you've got a lot on your shoulders with people depending on you and gives you more benefits.

Lastly, if your spouse died last year, you have a few options. You're eligible to file jointly with your spouse for the tax year they died, so long as you don't remarry. If you have a child who lives with you and you support, then you may file as Qualified Surviving Spouse with dependent child for *two* years. This gives you a larger standard deduction than if you filed as Head of Household, so it's some extra help during a hard time.

Note that with the filing statuses Married Filing Separately, Head of Household, and Qualifying Surviving Spouse, your tax return is connected to someone else. When you provide that information (and you *must*), the IRS computers will connect your return to theirs, to make sure there are no conflicts. For example, if two divorced parents share custody of a kid and both claim the kid on that year's tax return, the second parent to file will be disallowed the claim. The kids' Social Security number on the tax returns is how the computer knows the mistake happened.

Consider which filing status is best for you. While it's stable for most people most years, it can change year to year, depending on your circumstances. Use the IRS tools I linked in this chapter if you need help.

Names and Identity Info

Your tax return is a legal document, which you and your spouse sign under penalty of perjury.[25] In case it's not clear, you need to put your legal name on it (and your spouse's and your dependents'). If you have a preferred name, and for that matter, pronouns that you'd like your accountant to address you by when you talk, I suggest you tell your accountant what those are, but clarify the legal name to go on the tax return. I had a mortifying experience once where I unintentionally dead-named a client, because I had only spoken to their wife up to that point and read the client's name off their tax return during the tax appointment. I felt awful. That experience prompted me to change my tax organizer to request preferred name and pronouns. But if that scenario applies to you, take note.

INFO ABOUT YOUR DEPENDENTS

You'll also need your Social Security number and the Social Security numbers of your spouse and children. If you produced a new human this year or adopted one, that's a significant tax event. Note it for your accountant, and be sure to gather up the full legal name and Social Security number for that tiny human. If you just had a baby and don't yet have their Social Security card, you'll need to contact the Social Security administration and possibly file for an extension while you wait. This is because you need a Social Security number to get the Earned Income

Credit (EIC) and child tax credit, if you're eligible, and you're no longer allowed to file an amended tax return after the fact to claim it.[26]

Identity PIN

If you've had an identity theft issue, for example, if someone fraudulently tried to file a tax return in your name (an increasingly common issue), the IRS will send you a PIN in the mail called an *identity PIN*.[27] You will not be able to file your tax return without it.[28] That's a security feature of having the PIN. It prevents an identity thief from filing another tax return in your name. But don't forget to tell your accountant the PIN or have your PIN handy as you complete your own tax return.

Did Your Mailing Address Change in the Last Year?

If your address changed in the past year, you might miss some of your tax documents. You'll need to contact any banks, employers, people, or organizations you or your spouse did contract work for and make sure they have your updated address. Ideally, you let them know this before mid-January, because by the end of January, they've already sent out your 1099 or W2, and now the IRS has their copy, but you don't.[29] By law, your employer or anyone you did work for who paid you over $600 must send you your tax form (W2 for employees and 1099-NEC for nonemployees/contractors) by 1/31.[30] So if you haven't received your documents by Groundhog's Day, something is wrong, and you should check.

While you also need to keep your address up-to-date with the IRS, this is not usually a big problem, because your tax return effectively gives the IRS your current address each time you file. Meaning, whatever address you list on your 1040 tax return becomes your address of record to the IRS, overriding the last address if there's a change.[31] This means the IRS sends correspondence to you at the address you list on your latest tax return.

Moving Expenses

Moving expenses are no longer deductible, unless you are active-duty military.[32] But if you moved, note the date of the move for your taxes. This can affect some calculations on your tax return like your home office (which presumably changed on your move date), your mortgage interest calculation, etc.

If you moved to a different state,[33] it's a big deal. Multistate tax returns present some of the trickier tax scenarios.[34] And you'll have one.

Disclose Foreign Bank Accounts

Obama-era legislation requires you to disclose if you have money in any offshore accounts and how much was there at the peak during the tax year. This is known as foreign bank account reporting (FBAR). The intent is to prevent hiding offshore bank accounts.[35] It's only a reporting requirement, not a tax. But the penalties for nonreporting are severe to the point of pain,[36] so don't miss this. It's worthwhile to close down accounts in other countries that you do not absolutely need. But, for those of you with dual citizenship or who have other reasons to need a foreign bank account, make sure this item is on your annual tax checklist.

At the time of writing, you do not need to file FinCEN form 114, aka FBAR, if (1) the aggregate value of all foreign accounts is $10,000 or less at all times during the year, or (2) the accounts are at a US military banking facility. Beware that FBAR rules may change or expand in the future to include virtual currency, although at the time of this writing, they do not include it yet.

State Tax Credits/Special Rules

State income tax law generally flows from federal income tax law, so while Wyoming flavor will tend to differ from Massachusetts flavor, it's all part of the same basic food group. One of the pleasures of modern-day tax software is that it allows you to input your tax info once but populates both your federal and state income tax returns at the same time.

That said, your state may have some special rules. Most of these you don't need to be aware of, because your tax software (or accountant) will account for them for you (like, in the case of your state having different depreciation allowances than federal). But there may be state tax credits you're entitled to, and you should do an Internet search and alert your tax preparer if you find one. A random sample that I've encountered that can get missed if you don't think to mention them are: the DC first-time homebuyer credit, the Massachusetts renter's deduction, and special state tax credits for clean energy improvements.[37] I've never located a comprehensive state tax credit lookup tool, but you can often find them by category; for example, North Carolina State University has a great state-by-state energy credit lookup tool.[38]

Give $3 to the Presidential Election Fund?

There's a checkbox on your tax return for this. This doesn't cost you anything; it just earmarks $3 for public campaign financing of elections and is the sole source of funds for this.[39] I check it, but you do you.

Digital Currency/Digital Assets/ Cryptocurrency?

This is a mandatory question, even if you answer "no." It puts you on notice that you need to report these transactions. The IRS language has evolved from "virtual currency" to "digital assets." Here's the latest version of this question, at the time of writing this book:

"At any time during [YEAR], did you: (1) receive (as a reward, award or payment for property or services); or (2) sell, exchange, or otherwise dispose of a digital asset (or a financial interest in a digital asset)?"[40]

To clarify what's included and reportable, here's the IRS definition:

- Convertible virtual currency and cryptocurrency
- Stablecoins
- Nonfungible tokens (NFTs)[41]

W2 Income

You get a W2 for income you earned as an employee. The lovely thing about W2s, as you know now, is that your taxes have already been taken out of these earnings. For this reason, it is critical that you not confuse any W2 income with freelance income. Your freelance/gig/1099/self-employment income has not had any tax withholding, so we'll carefully tally that income when we get to the Schedule C.

Note how many W2s you received. What about your spouse? Do a gut-check to make sure your W2s reflect about the amount of income you thought they did. If not, are you missing one? Is there an employer you need to check in with?

Mistakes occasionally happen on a W2 (but they are more common on 1099s), so it's worth checking them over to make sure your name and Social Security number are correct and that taxes were withheld for the right state. If you see something wrong, like your name, or SSN, contact your employer immediately to ask them to issue a corrected W2.

QUESTIONS TO ANSWER FOR YOUR SCHEDULE C/ SELF-EMPLOYMENT

If you earned self-employment income, the following section will guide you through the info you'll need to gather for your taxes. You already gathered your numbers from your bookkeeping. These are additional details. If you have no self-employment, you can skip this section.

If Your Spouse Is Also Self-Employed

If your spouse also had income from self-employment, then you'll have a second Schedule C. You should keep their self-employment income and expenses separate from yours. You will identify which spouse each Schedule C belongs to.

If You and Your Spouse Share a Business

If you and your spouse share a business/self-employment and you *do not* have an LLC and you *do not* file a partnership tax return (which is a separate tax return, for the partnership, due March 15), you have an option. You may elect to file as a "qualified joint venture."[42]

This option allows both spouses to receive proper credit for earnings toward their Medicare and Social Security benefits, without the accounting/ tax complexity and additional filing requirement of a partnership for federal taxes.[43] The qualified joint venture option allows this couple to effectively split one Schedule C in half, giving each spouse proper credit for their Medicare and Social Security.[44] If you want to make this election, make a note on your tax documents. You either need to tell your accountant or search for the term "qualified joint venture" in your DIY software and then follow the instructions to make the election. It should be as simple as checking a box.

Preliminary Identifying Info for Your Business

Was this your first year in business? Or did you acquire the business this year (by buying a pre-existing business)? If so, make sure to note that. This entitles you to the special deduction category of "startup expenses." It's juicy stuff and includes expenses you may have incurred before the year the business actually started, so don't miss it. See Chapter 4 for more detail. You may also check this box if you are restarting an old business. To do this, you must not have had a Schedule C for it the previous tax year.

Do you have an employee identification number (EIN) for this business? And is there a business name that's different from your name? You'll need to identify those at the top of your Schedule C. If you have a single-member LLC, then the answer to the EIN question is yes.[45] But you may also have obtained an EIN for sales tax collection reasons or because you registered a "doing business as" (DBA), even if you don't have an LLC.

This is a lot less complicated than people think. The IRS simply asks you to put that EIN onto your Schedule C. Remember, your Social Security number (or ITIN, if you don't have an SSN) is *already on your tax return*, so the IRS knows who owes the taxes on your business's money. My friend, it's you.

The LLC (if you're the sole owner/member) doesn't affect your income taxes. The only difference to the IRS between you having an LLC and not is that if you do, you'll put its EIN and name on top of your Schedule C.[46]

If you don't have an EIN, don't stress. Just leave it blank.

If your business operates at an address other than your home address, put that here. Your tax return already identifies your home address.[47]

Pick Your Industry Code

Next, you'll need to identify the field your business is in. If you're handing off your materials to an accountant, your business description helps them find the best category for your business.[48] Specifically, this informs the North American Industry Classification System (NAICS) code they pick for you. If you're doing taxes on your own, you'll need to make this determination.

Your NAICS code is somewhat important, but it won't be exact, and you don't need to freak out over that. Your goal here is to get into a category that fits what you do, in the broadest sense.

Most tax software will link you to a NAICS lookup tool.[49] But you can also use the link in the endnotes.

How Is the NAICS Code Used?

The IRS computers compare all the Schedule Cs within a single NAICS code to determine normal ranges for that type of business, at that income level.[50] And I don't know how finely they slice it—the IRS algorithm is secret—but they could also use data about your ZIP code and costs of living in your area—use your imagination.

So given that the IRS has all that data and knows the range of "normal" expenses for every category of every type of US business, they have a good sense of when the expenses are higher than normal on an individual tax return. If you have expenses that stand out from the norm in your field, your tax return will get flagged.[51] Getting flagged doesn't mean you get audited. But when tax returns are selected for audit, they are selected out of the pool of flagged returns.[52]

It's okay to be weird and unique, and sometimes that means you have an expense category that's unusually high. That's okay, so long as it is "ordinary and necessary" (remember those are IRS requirements) and that you've documented it properly. The IRS may ask to see your proof (yes, technically, that's an audit, and they have the right). But so long as you show that proof, you'll be fine.

For example, artist Dave Cole (no relation) makes large-scale sculptures about patriotism and masculinity. In his piece *The Knitting Machine*, two excavators each grasp a "knitting needle" fashioned from an aluminum utility pole and knit together a gigantic American flag.[53] If you make sculptures that large, you might have a warehouse rental expense that is astronomically high compared to any other artist. And yet, where are you going to house your utility poles and your John Deere excavators? In other words, a lot of creative work exists on the extreme edges. If your work has special requirements that make certain expenses extra high, that's okay. Just document the bejesus out of them, since you may need to show your receipts.

REPORT YOUR SCHEDULE C INCOME

Your most important task here is to report the correct amount of income that you received from your self-employment, because that's the law. You've already gathered this number (having set up a bookkeeping system and tallied your total income for the year). But now, you need to sort which part of this income is accounted for on your 1099s and which part is not.

A key check is to divide the total income you earned for the year into two categories: (1) income that was reported to you on a 1099 and (2) income that was not reported on a 1099. These two numbers should add up to the same total income number as your year-end bookkeeping. If they don't, then either you are missing income somewhere or you are double-counting some income. That's why this check is important.

Don't forget that you should *never* include any W2 income in this part of your tax return. A key role of your Schedule C is to calculate your tax due on the part of your income that hasn't had any tax withheld. Don't put income here that *has* had tax withheld.

Gather Your 1099s

As part of your tax organization and then as part of the previously mentioned check, gather all the 1099-NECs and 1099-Ks (in this section from now on, I will call these "1099s") you received for your self-employment.

There are many different types of 1099s, but these two are most common for reporting your self-employment income.

First, check that the information is correct on each 1099. Check your legal name and Social Security number (or ITIN) and that the amount you were paid is correct. Don't assume that it was. Many people who issue 1099s lack experience, and mistakes are rampant.[54] I've seen dozens of 1099s where the issuer mistyped the person's name or SSN, miscalculated the income, and even added an extra zero to the income amount. Do you want to be forced to report and pay tax on 10 times more money than you actually made? If the answer is no, then double-check.

What to Do If Your 1099 Is Wrong

If your 1099 is wrong, you can get it fixed. It's critical to do this correctly, though.

Here's how: contact the person/organization who issued the 1099 and ask them to issue you a **corrected** 1099.[55] Be explicit about what the mistake was and what the real answer is. It also pays to direct them, "You need to be sure you check the box marked 'corrected' when you fill out the form." *That checkbox is the override*—as long as they check it, the original (incorrect) 1099 is overridden in the IRS system by the "corrected" version. If they miss that checkbox, they've now issued you an *additional* 1099. Aka, they've given you more headache to deal with—multiple 1099s that will all be reported to the IRS. You'd then need them to issue you **two** corrected 1099s.

Yes, I've witnessed this nightmare.

Gather the Rest of Your Self-Employment Income Info

Whatever income you made that was not reported to you on a 1099 is still reportable income.[56] You want to be sure you're not getting any surprise late-issued 1099s (though this isn't always possible) and then tally up all your 1099 income and subtract that number from the "total income" you calculated in your books. This gives you your 1099 vs. non-1099 income that should add up to your total gross income.

How You Report the Two Types of Self-Employment Income

When you sit down to do your data entry, you'll enter each 1099 into your software and check the box/answer affirmatively that the income is from self-employment. That 1099 info will then populate into your Schedule C income total.

For the income that you didn't get a 1099 for, you'll tally it and report that as an addition to the number on line 1 of your Schedule C. Different software may ask you this question in different ways. The gist will be, "Was there any income you made from your self-employment that wasn't reported on a 1099?"

Especially if you're DIYing your taxes, you need to be 100% certain you're reporting the correct amount of income, so you need to triple-check that the amount being reported on line 1 of your Schedule C, "gross receipts or sales," is showing up accurately as the total amount you earned. Check this number before hitting "submit" on the final tax return.

REPORT YOUR SCHEDULE C EXPENSES

Once your self-employment income is reported, report your expenses.

Inventory, aka Cost of Goods Sold (COGS)

If you don't qualify for the inventory exception by using NAICS code 711510, Independent Writers, Artists, and Performers,[57] then you'll need to track COGS (see the business expense rules in Chapter 4). You'll need three numbers, expressed in dollars as the *cost to you*, not the retail amount you charge others.

First, you need this year's beginning inventory amount, expressed in dollars. This should be the same as last year's ending inventory amount. You can find this on last year's Schedule C, on line 41.

Second, you'll need to record your total inventory purchases for the year.[58] Remember that these are the amount you paid for labor and materials *that go into your product or service for sale* and not fixed costs (that don't vary whether sales are up or down). If you bake naughty bachelor/ette party cakes, for example, expenses that go into your COGS include sugar, cake boxes, little plastic genitalia, shipping, and payments to your baker and shipper. Your expenses for rent, web design, and your neon "Nastycakes" sign are fixed costs and therefore *not included* in COGS. See the rules in Chapter 4.

Lastly, determine the cost of all your "goods" still in inventory (aka this year's ending inventory).[59] This includes the cost of the products and the labor directly related to creating your product. Record your "Cost of goods sold" by adding your ending inventory plus "Total inventory purchases" minus your beginning inventory.

Expenses for Your Business

Now, you need your *total* expense for each Schedule C category. For the straightforward expenses that correspond directly to a Schedule C category, you'll record that total for your taxes. (See the expense categories in Chapter 7.) Those categories are listed next. After that, I'll discuss places where there's more complexity or an alternative calculation.

Expenses to Take Straight from Your Bookkeeping Totals

Put these expense totals straight from your bookkeeping categories into that place on the Schedule C.[60]

- Advertising/marketing/website hosting
- Commissions or fees
- Professional development
  - Dues or subscriptions (listed as "professional development" in the Other Expenses section)
- Interest (from business credit card or business loan)
- Insurance premiums (business-related, *not* health insurance)
- Legal and accounting services
- Office expenses, including:
  - Postage (unless you're separating it into **other expenses**)
  - Printing
- Repairs and maintenance

- Rents or leases
  - Vehicles, machinery, and equipment
  - Other business property (includes offices or studios)
- Supplies
- Taxes and licenses[61]

Expenses with Complexity or an Alternative Option

The following are the expense categories with more complex rules, or an alternative deduction option. What you list for your taxes here *may differ from your books.* Chapter 4 covers these rules, so refer to that chapter for details.

- Depreciation and Section 179 expense, for asset purchases (such as phones, computers, or equipment)
  - List each asset greater than $2,500 and the date purchased. Your accountant will determine how to depreciate it. If you're doing your own taxes, determine its depreciable life by looking up the IRS-assigned asset category.[62]
  - If the asset was less than $2,500, you may list it as a supply.[63]
  - If you have depreciating assets from prior years and your software (or accountant) from last year should automatically continue that depreciation. But if you switch software/accountant, locate the depreciation schedule from last year's taxes to carry over your depreciation into this year's taxes.
- Car and truck expense.[64]
  - See Chapter 4 for mileage deduction rules.
    - If using the **actual expense method**, total your vehicle expenses for the year. Determine your percentage of business miles to total miles, and multiply that percentage by your total vehicle expenses to get your actual expense deduction amount.

- If using the **standard mileage rate**, multiply your business miles by this year's standard mileage rate.
- Add parking and tolls to the number from your chosen method above, for your total car or truck expense.
- You'll also need to indicate the date you began using your vehicle in your business, and your total mileage for the year.
- Contract labor.
  - Report your total amount paid for contract labor.[65]
  - If you paid anyone over $600, make sure you've issued them the required 1099-NEC. You can't check this box on your taxes until you've done so. The deadline is 1/31. If you're late, file them ASAP, because penalties increase. If you need help, I have a mini-course available at www.sunlighttax.com/taxesforhumans about how to issue your 1099s.

Send Any 1099s You Need To

Before you can file your tax return, you need to issue any 1099s that you owe to anyone you paid for services (not products) over $600 for the year.[66] So if you hired anyone for your business, like a product photographer, a website designer, a social media manager, a snake wrangler, or a banana taster (hey, I don't know what kind of business you're in), you need to send out those forms by the deadline, January 31.[67] This is only for your business, not for personal things—so don't send 1099s to your cleaning person, house painter, or your hairdresser, for example.

Issuing your first 1099 can feel scary and technical. But it's mandatory. Your tax return contains two checkboxes, one asking if you made payments that would require you to file a 1099 and one asking if you filed those 1099s.[68] You. Are. On. The. Hook. For. This. Penalties for nonfiling begin accruing February 1.

One of the reasons that filing your 1099s is so critical, from a societal perspective, is that you're helping the IRS crack down on unreported income. Payments from people like us, micro-businesses, to other people like us are one of the key areas of unreported income. And that's not fair or right. So the IRS ensures that you're reporting all your income and all your payments in part by putting these checkboxes on your tax return to give you no fudgeability. If you use an accountant, they won't file your tax return until you're able to truthfully check both boxes. So you're not off the hook there, either.[69] That accountant is probably happy to charge you extra and file them for you, if you want that option.

- Meals.
  - Gather your total deductible meals expense. There are two parts:
    - For **meals with a business contact**, note the full amount (your software will cut this number in half, since only 50% is deductible).[70]
    - Add this to your **travel meals expense**. Compare your **actual travel meals expenses** with the **standard meals allowance** expense calculation (Chapter 4).[71] If you're handing off to an accountant, provide the actual travel meals expense, and also

report to them where you traveled and the days you were in each location, so they can calculate your deduction. If you're doing your own taxes, see Chapter 4 to calculate and compare your standard meals expense allowance, to your actual travel meals expense, and add the biggest one to client meals expense to get your total meals expense for line 24b.

- Travel.[72]
  - Record your deductible business travel expenses.
- Utilities (for your business only *not* for your home office).[73]
  - Telephone.
    - Record the deductible business use percentage of your phone expense.[74] Add this expense into the total utility expense.
  - Internet.
    - Record the deductible business use percentage of your Internet expense.[75] Add this to your utilities expense or to your office expense.
- For **home office** expense, provide:
  - Total square footage of your home.
  - Square footage of your office space.
  - Date you began using your home office for business.
  - Total cost of rent or mortgage interest for your home (for the year).
  - Total cost of utilities for your home (for the year).
  - Total cost of insurance for your home (for the year).
  - Total other costs of running your home, if applicable.
  - Total costs spent exclusively on the home office: **direct expenses** (list them). Note that direct expenses of your home office, like soundproofing or special lighting, for example, you'll get to take 100% of. The indirect expenses of running your entire home you will take as a percentage in proportion to your entire home.

- **Other expenses**. List other business expenses that don't fit in another category. Can include:
  - Professional development.
  - Research (books and periodicals).
  - Dues and subscriptions.
  - Start-up expenses (only if it's your first year in business).

That's everything you need for the Schedule C, which is the hardest part of your tax return. Put on some dance music and celebrate being past that section!

INCOME AND EXPENSES, *NOT* FROM SELF-EMPLOYMENT

Gather information for other parts of your tax return.

Health Insurance for Self-Employment

It may feel like this should go on your Schedule C, with your self-employment stuff, but it doesn't. It goes on Schedule 1, Part II, Adjustments to Income, line 17.

The rules for deducting your self-employed health insurance premiums are frustratingly narrow.[76] If you pay for your own health insurance in your name or your business's name and you are not covered *or eligible to be covered* by any employer-maintained, subsidized plan offered by your employer, your spouse's employer, your dependent's employer, or your children under age 27's employer, then you may deduct your health insurance premiums.[77] Your premiums may cover yourself and (if applicable) your spouse, your dependents, and any children under age 27 (even if they aren't dependents).[78] Qualified long-term health insurance premiums are included for this purpose, as are Medicare premiums (Parts A–D) that you pay as a self-employed person, and those for your spouse, dependents, and children under age 27.[79]

If eligible, gather the amount you paid for self-employed medical insurance premiums (not total healthcare costs).

Miscellaneous Income

Record any miscellaneous income received (not on a W2, and not from self-employment). That can include jury duty pay, unemployment compensation, cancellation of debt, hobby income, gambling winnings, prizes and awards, taxable refunds, alimony received (include the date of your original divorce or separation agreement), health savings account (HSA), scholarships, etc.[80]

RENTAL PROPERTY AND ROYALTY REPORTING

If you have income from royalties or a rental property, including short-term rentals (Airbnb, VRBO, etc.), record all the income, expenses, and property information for your Schedule E.[81] The Schedule E is extremely similar in structure to the Schedule C, so this might all look familiar.

Royalty income from your self-employment activity should be reported on your Schedule C.[82] That's confusing, since the word "royalty" is on the Schedule E. But if the income is due to self-employment, it's subject to self-employment tax on your Schedule C. So writers, playwrights, artists' licensing images or pattern design, musicians, etc.— your royalties most likely belong on your Schedule C.[83] That said, if your royalties are from, say, your grandfather inventing a piece of machinery, then yes, that's Schedule E.

Rental Property Basic Information

List the basic information for the rental property:[84]

- Physical address of the property
- Cost of the property
- Percentage of the property attributable to land vs. structure,[85] if known
- Is this your primary residence?
- Number of days you rented the property during the year
- Number of personal use days during the year
- Type of property (single-family residential, multifamily residential, vacation property, commercial property)

Rental Property or Royalty Income

List your gross receipts received (aka total rental income) or your royalties received.[86]

Rental Property Expenses

Then, you'll list your expenses for the rental property, which are deductible.[87] List (separately for each property):

- Advertising expense
- Auto and travel
- Cleaning and maintenance
- Commissions

- Insurance
- Legal and other professional fees
- Management fees (this includes VRBO or Airbnb fees)
- Mortgage interest paid to banks
- Other interest
- Repairs
- Supplies
- Taxes
- Utilities
- Depreciation expense (don't forget to look at last year's tax return for the depreciation that carries over, in addition to any assets you bought this year)
- Other expenses

PERSONAL EXPENSES FOR TAXES

In general, your personal expenses aren't deductible.[88] But the following items have either a tax credit, a deduction, or a tax implication associated with them, so you should gather this info to be sure you get any credits or deductions you may be eligible for and to avoid expensive back-and-forth with your accountant or wasted time if you're on your own.

Student Loan Interest Payment

If you paid any student loan interest, you'll receive a form called a 1098-E that reports that.[89] You will need to include this document with your reportable tax information.

Childcare Expenses

If you paid for childcare so that you could work or look for work, you may be eligible for a credit for childcare expenses.[90] The credit has a limit *per child*, so if you have more than one child, then you'll need to specify how much was paid for *each child* to each person or organization.[91] Summer camp counts, as long as it was day camp (not sleepaway camp) and as long as your child(ren) was enrolled so that you could work or look for work.

For each child, you'll need to provide:

- Name of the childcare provider (business name or the person's legal name).
- Person or organization's address.
- Amount you paid (person/organization).
- Person/organization's Federal tax ID number (either an EIN or a Social Security number). You may be able to look up the organization's EIN online, or you may have to ask for it.[92]

529 Plan Contribution

If you contributed to a 529 plan for education expenses,[93] provide the amount contributed and the name of the 529 plan. You may receive a tax document about this.

Medical Expense Questions

Was your entire family covered by medical insurance for the entire year? Note any gaps. If there were gaps in coverage and you had a medical insurance exemption, then list your exemption(s). The federal tax penalty for not having medical insurance ended in 2018, but many states still charge a penalty for gaps in coverage.[94] You may want to check with your state for those rules, to see if this applies to you.

Did you buy health insurance on the **marketplace**, aka Healthcare .gov? If so, you will need a tax form called a 1095A to complete your taxes. This is critical, as your tax return reconciles your marketplace health insurance subsidy, also known as your **advanced premium tax credit (PTC)**.[95]

The PTC is a subsidy you get on your monthly health insurance premiums, if you have household income below a certain threshold.[96] Apply at Healthcare.gov and fill out information about your household, including an estimate of your family's income.[97] The lower your household income, the higher your premium subsidy.[98]

Your estimated household income is the key to your subsidy. At tax time, you reconcile your estimated income with your actual income, and if your income was lower than expected, you may get an additional tax credit on your tax return. If your actual income was higher than expected, you'll be required to pay back some of your subsidy.

If you have marketplace insurance and you have an income change during the year, it's important that you update your information at Healthcare.gov (log into your marketplace account, go to "report a life change," and then to "update my application").

If you don't, you may end up with a surprise tax bill because you have to pay back your premium subsidy.

EXPENSES THAT YOU NEED TO TRACK ONLY IF YOU ITEMIZE

Figure 9.1 shows expenses that are **itemized deductions**. Here's what that means: all US taxpayers get an initial chunk of income tax-free. The options are a fixed amount, called the **standard deduction**, or a variable

Figure 9.1 Do you itemize chart.

Source: © Hannah Cole/Sunlight Tax.

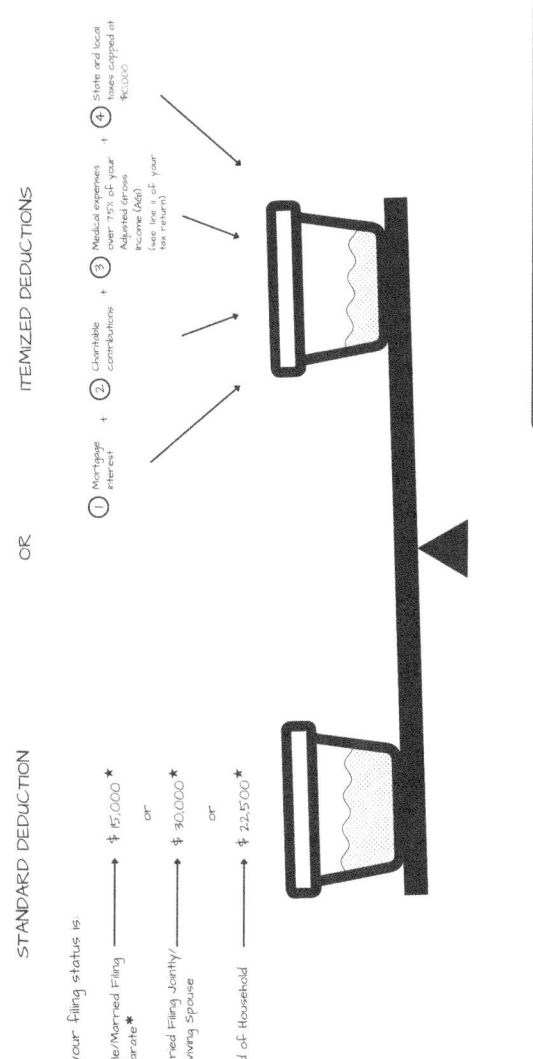

amount, called **itemized deductions**. You get to take the greater amount.[99] The standard deduction goes up each year but is around $15,000 if you're single and $30,000 if you're married.

This means that the only people who itemize deductions[100] have total itemizable expenses exceeding the standard deduction.[101] Itemizable deductions are these four things, added together: charitable contributions, mortgage interest, medical expenses that exceed 7.5% of your adjusted gross income (AGI), and state and local taxes capped at $10,000.[102] Note that these are *unrelated to your Schedule C business deductions* (you get those whether or not you itemize). Itemizing, because the expenses must be high, is generally for the well-heeled.

This means that itemized deductions are deductible only if you don't take the standard deduction. If you're in the 90% of US taxpayers who take the standard deduction, then gathering the following info would be a waste of your time.[103] So if you spent a lot (thousands) on charitable contributions, etc., and think you might be in the 10% of tax-payers who itemize, then you'll want to gather the following itemized deduction info. Otherwise, skip the items marked "itemizers only."

Medical Expenses Over 7.5% of Your Income: Itemizers Only

Your medical expenses need to be high compared to your income to get any deduction—typically young, healthy people can't. To do a gut-check on if it's worth gathering your medical expense info, do this calculation.

Pull out last year's tax return and look at line 11, AGI, on the first page of your 1040. Since you only get medical deductions once they exceed 7.5% of your AGI, multiply the AGI on line 11 by 7.5% to see what the medical expense threshold is for you before you get a deduction. Here's an example:

Line 11 adjusted gross income = $100,000

X 7.5%

—————

$7,500

So if my AGI was $100,000, I'd only get to deduct the amount I spent over $7,500. So if I spent $8,500 on medical expenses, then I would get a $1,000 medical expense deduction (because $8,500 − $7,500 = $1,000). It's only worth gathering my medical expenses in this scenario if my other itemized deductions (mortgage interest, charitable contributions, and $10,000 of state and local taxes) are close to exceeding the standard deduction amount for my filing status.

If you've done that math and determined it's worth your time, then record your:

- Insurance premiums paid.
- Physician and dental fees.
- Medicine and prescriptions.
- Miles driven for medical care.
- Any other medical expenses. You can find a complete list of allowable expenses for the medical deduction at www.irs.gov/help/ita/can-i-deduct-my-medical-and-dental-expenses.

Charitable Contributions: Itemizers Only

If you itemize, tally the amounts you donated to charitable organizations.

CASH CONTRIBUTIONS

Note that contributions are deductible only if made to a registered charitable organization and not to a friend or family member.[104] The IRS has a search tool that you can use to look up if the charitable organization is a valid one: https://www.irs.gov/charities-nonprofits/tax-exempt-organization-search.

NONCASH CONTRIBUTIONS

You may deduct noncash contributions at their fair market value. This means your deductible amount will be substantially less than what you originally paid—it's the amount the item could be sold for today. You need a receipt for any contribution over $500, and there are stringent requirements for donating a car (you must provide the receipt that the charity gave you for that donation).[105] If you donate an item valued over $5,000, for example, a family heirloom or an artwork, you're required to get an appraisal of that object for your tax records.[106] For everyday noncash donations, like clothes to Goodwill, you can find a noncash fair market value lookup chart on their website, like this one: https://satruck.org/Home/DonationValueGuide.[107] Record those amounts for your tax software or accountant.

While people wealthy enough to put their names on buildings get credited for charitable giving, people at the bottom of the income scale give the largest percentage of their income to charitable causes. This is likely because it's their own community who needs help—their friends and neighbors are living in poverty, so these folks know the need and help generously despite their limited means. If it were up to me, I would give a charitable tax benefit to the 90% of taxpayers who take the standard deduction, not just to itemizers.

Mortgage Interest: Itemizers Only

If you pay mortgage interest you should receive a tax form called a **Form 1098.**[108] It may include other information you need, such as points and real estate tax/property taxes paid through your escrow payment. If you pay a mortgage, also record any information you have about additional property taxes paid.

> If you didn't pay a mortgage, you don't generally need to worry about reporting property taxes on your taxes.

State and Local Taxes Capped at $10,000: Itemizers Only

Before the Tax Cuts and Jobs Act (TCJA) of 2018, there was no limit on how much state and local tax you could deduct.[109] But the TCJA put a $10,000 cap on this deduction.[110] If you itemize, you can stop collecting this info once you've hit $10,000—nothing over that amount will help you.

> In my opinion, this was the most partisan part of the TCJA, because it primarily affects blue states, which tend to have higher taxes. The citizens of those states, through their elections, chose representatives and policies that support those higher taxes—it was their decision to opt for more healthcare, public safety, and education, and the taxes that pair with that. By capping a deduction that used to give itemizers an average deduction around $36,000, the all-Republican Congress that passed this bill pressured those states to cut this spending, despite the will of those voters.

Note your **state and local income taxes paid** (do not repeat W2 info here—entering your W2 in your taxes will capture this). This includes taxes paid through estimated quarterly tax payments to your state.

Note your **real estate taxes paid**, and your **personal property taxes paid**, if they were paid on an annual basis, and based on the value of the property ("ad valorem"), like for a car or boat.

Health Savings Account (HSA)

For details on HSAs, see Chapter 14. If you/your spouse has an HSA, gather this info:

- Were you enrolled in a qualified high deductible health plan (HDHP) for all or part (list the months) of the tax year? Find this info on your health plan's website—they're required to tell you if your plan is a qualifying HDHP.
- Was your coverage just for you, or was it a family plan?
- Did you contribute to an HSA?
- What was the HSA contribution amount, and date?
- Did your spouse have a qualifying HDHP?
- Did they contribute to a HSA?
- What was the HSA contribution amount, and date?

ESTIMATED QUARTERLY TAX PAYMENTS

Did you or your spouse pay estimated quarterly taxes during the year? Those are prepayments of your taxes—you must report them in order to be credited.[111] This is easy to forget, because it's reported manually. Your software/accountant isn't telepathic. If you do forget, it ultimately gets worked out—the IRS will send you a letter after processing your return, saying you've overpaid your taxes by whatever amount of estimated payments you forgot to report and will send the money back to you. But it can feel scary to get a letter from the IRS, even when it's good news like this.

If you did pay estimates, report:

- The date and amount you paid each federal payment (you, and your spouse)
- The date and amount you paid each state payment (you, and your spouse)

OTHER IMPORTANT QUESTIONS TO ANSWER

Did you buy or sell a house this year? If so, be sure to include your HUD/settlement statement in your tax documents. You'll also need to list the:

- Sale price of the home you sold
- Date of sale
- Original price you paid for the home
- Date of your original home purchase

If you paid or received **alimony**, provide the payment amounts and date of your divorce agreement.[112]

If you **adopted a child**, provide adoption date, plus all costs associated with the adoption.[113]

If you **suffered a catastrophic loss** (like theft or natural disaster), provide details, including any insurance payments received.[114] If it was a natural disaster, was it in a federally declared disaster area? (This designation entitles you to bigger tax benefits.)

Max Out Retirement Plans, and Note Other Tax-Advantaged Activity

Please do. Not only is it a financial benefit for you, but not enough young people, creative people, or mission-driven people set money aside for themselves, their future, and their ability to rest. Money you put into an IRA is a future benefit to yourself, with a bonus tax subsidy from your government to help you do it. Don't let perfect be the enemy of the good. If you don't have a lot of money to contribute, put in as much as you can. Future you will be grateful.

In Chapter 14, I'll get into all the detail you need on using tax-advantaged accounts like retirement, education, and healthcare. Most of those decisions must be made by December 31. And that's why the process of looking over and maximizing those accounts is called *year-end* **tax planning**. But at tax time, do these two things:

1. Gather info about money into and out of any tax-advantaged accounts like retirement, education, or HSAs (IRA, SEP IRA, SIMPLE accounts, 401k/403b, 457b, Coverdell, HSAs, FSAs, 529 plans, etc.). Note if you made any qualified withdrawals or emergency withdrawals. For most of the ones you must report, you'll get a tax document.

2. If you're eligible to put money into an individual retirement arrangement (IRA), decide if and how much money you want to put in.[115] Decide if you'll put money into a pre-tax (known as a traditional IRA) or after-tax (known as Roth IRA) account. If you're eligible to put money into a SEP IRA, that is also a tax-time decision. For these three types of accounts[116] (traditional IRA, Roth IRA, or SEP IRA), you can make your contribution after December 31, all the way until April 15, to be counted for the

prior year's limit. For the SEP IRA, and only the SEP, you can make a contribution through the extension deadline, which is October 15. You and your spouse may both contribute up to the current-year maximum to an IRA.[117]

The SEP IRA contribution limit is up to 20% of your Schedule C business profit, as determined by your tax return. You can't determine your SEP contribution amount without doing your taxes, which is why the SEP, uniquely, allows contributions all the way to the extension deadline. There are *no extensions* for the Roth or traditional IRA.

Did You Contribute to Any Other Nonworkplace Retirement Plans?

If you or your spouse contributed to a Simplified Employee Pension (SEP) IRA, a Savings Incentive Match PLan for Employees (SIMPLE) IRA, or a solo 401k, list the amount you contributed and the date. If you're not sure if you can but want to learn more, check out Chapter 14. The SEP IRA, SIMPLE IRA, and solo 401k are additional tax-advantaged retirement accounts that help you save funds for your future while getting a tax benefit.[118]

Set Up Your Payment Info: Direct Deposit/Direct Debit

Your tax organizer should ask for your payment information so that you can direct debit your tax payment or receive your refund through direct deposit. Most people like receiving a direct deposit but feel nervous about a direct debit, before knowing if they owe money. The IRS is not permitted to withdraw any amount besides what is stated on your 1040 as the amount you owe.[119] They will not take out extra money, or past debts. This is safe.

Note the default withdrawal date for your payment is on tax day, April 15.[120] If you do your taxes in February, your payment won't get pulled until April 15, unless you specify an earlier withdrawal date. You do not need to hang onto your tax items or wait to answer your accountant's reminder email to sign your tax return until then. I highly recommend you set up an auto withdrawal of your tax payment. It leaves less room to forget to make the payment.

Triple-check which bank account you want to withdraw the money from, note the amount of the debit, and be sure to transfer the money into that account in time for the April 15 withdrawal. The IRS will charge you a penalty for insufficient funds.[121] Don't forget to set up payment info for your state tax payment as well—it is possible to do one and forget the other, so confirm both.

If you're getting a refund, the timing is *different*. The IRS will deposit your money into the account you specify as soon as your tax return is processed, which can be before or after tax day. There's a handy tool at the IRS website called "Where's my refund?" that gives you the current timing of IRS refund delivery.[122] The earlier you file your taxes, the quicker you get your refund. In early February, it might be a day or two after processing. Around April 15, it may take several months.

Checklist of Documents to Include in Your Tax Package

Your tax organizer should have a list of tax documents to double-check for, updated for the current tax year. I have a generic list of these, available at www.sunlighttax.com/taxesforhumans.

Be sure to look for the latest tax year changes. Save a great tax organizer in your tax files, and make it your starting point for next year.

Gather your list of tax questions that came up during this process, and do your best Internet research or ask your accountant for the answers. If your list of questions is long, that's a sign that you might need the help of a tax professional.

Make any decisions you need to—whether that involves talking to your spouse or gut-checking while looking at your bank balance.

And make sure to take action on all of the action items that you listed.

NOW CELEBRATE

Finishing your books and gathering all your tax documentation can feel exhausting. Often, the act of gathering your tax info reveals new errands, like calling a brokerage to open an IRA or chasing down a missing 1099. Congratulate yourself on getting it all gathered—it's a big job.

If you're working with an accountant, your next step is to hand this package off to them. Don't delay. The earlier your package arrives, the higher you are in their queue, and the more attention your tax return will get. If you send your materials past their stated deadline, or in the March 15 to April 15 crush, you're likely to have your taxes put on extension, potentially missing your IRA contribution window, and they may not communicate with you about it at all. If you're lucky enough to get your taxes done at that late date, they will not take much time to investigate ambiguous situations with you, guide you in any potential decision-making, or generally be available to answer your questions.

If you're doing your taxes yourself, then you are now ready to sit down with your documents and go through the software prompts to complete your tax return. This part is a lighter lift than the info gathering you just completed. So for real, raise a glass, or do a little hot girl boogie to some Megan Thee Stallion.

CHAPTER SUMMARY

- This chapter is about the "doing" part of your taxes: the data entry.
- The bulk of your work is getting your numbers and documents in one place. The rest is answering questions.
- Use tax software to catch mistakes and do calculations. Never do your taxes directly on the forms.
- Download a tax organizer, and use it as a checklist to guide your info-gathering. Nailing down these tiny details now saves you time, stress, and money, and reduces expensive back-and-forth with your accountant, if you have one.
- Collect all physical and digital tax documents into one place. Use data security best practices, because the info is sensitive.
- Get your bookkeeping done and grab the numbers. This is often the heaviest lift for self-employed folks.
- Determine who you're filing taxes with (aka your filing status). Your status affects your tax rate, standard deduction, and credits.

- Gather household names and identity info.
- Make sure all W2s and 1099s reflect the correct amount of income. Check for mistakes and request corrected forms if needed.
- Gather self-employment income and expenses from your books and report it accurately for the Schedule C. Separate income reported on 1099s from non-1099 income.
- Gather info for any personal expenses with tax implications, like student loan interest or childcare expenses.
- Be good to future you: Contribute to retirement plans (IRA, 401k, etc.) for financial security and tax benefits.
- Report any estimated quarterly tax payments you made during the year.
- Miscellaneous income: Record any miscellaneous income received, such as jury duty pay, unemployment compensation, cancellation of debt, hobby income, gambling winnings, prizes and awards, taxable refunds, alimony received, HSA distributions, and scholarships.
- For rental properties or royalties, record all income, expenses, and property information on Schedule E. Self-employment royalties go on Schedule C.
- Gather info on health savings account (HSA) contributions if enrolled in a qualified high deductible health plan (HDHP).
- Include details if you bought or sold a house (HUD/settlement statement), paid or received alimony (payment amounts and divorce agreement date), adopted a child (adoption date and costs), or suffered a catastrophic loss (details and insurance payments).
- Provide payment info for direct debit of tax payments or direct deposit of refunds. Ensure funds are available in the account by April 15.
- Celebrate!

ENDNOTES

1. "IRS Free File: Do your taxes for free," *U.S. Department of the Treasury, Internal Revenue Service*, last modified February 6, 2025, https://www.irs.gov/filing/irs-free-file-do-your-taxes-for-free.

2. Gary Guenther, "The Internal Revenue Service's Free File Program (FFP): Current Status and Policy Issues," *Congressional Research Service*, last modified May 30, 2024, https://crsreports.congress.gov/product/pdf/IF/IF11808.

3. Allie Volpe, "4 ways to file your taxes for free," *Vox*, last modified March 4, 2024, https://www.vox.com/even-better-guide-to-tax-season/24084590/file-your-taxes-for-free-file-direct-file-vita-cte-miltax.

4. Justin Elliott and Paul Kiel, "Inside TurboTax's 20-Year Fight to Stop Americans From Filing Their Taxes for Free," *ProPublica*, last modified October 17, 2019, https://www.propublica.org/article/inside-turbotax-20-year-fight-to-stop-americans-from-filing-their-taxes-for-free.

5. The Direct File program is run directly through the IRS, at no cost to taxpayers, and is different from the Free File program, which is administered through private tax prep companies. In early 2025, as part of the Department of Government Efficiency (DOGE) cuts, IRS workers were told to stop work on the 2026 Direct File program, effectively ending it, according to the Associated Press. Fatima Hussein, "Trump administration plans to end the IRS Direct File program for free tax filing, AP sources say," Associated Press, last modified April 17, 2025, accessed May 13, 2025, https://apnews.com/article/irs-direct-file-tax-returns-free-trump-4bb0bca02fab9b3d06ae6f45ac67b7ab.

6. Volpe, "4 ways to file your taxes for free."

7. Ann Carrns, "I.R.S. to Begin Trial of Its Own Free Tax-Filing System," *New York Times*, last modified March 14, 2024, https://www.nytimes.com/2024/01/05/your-money/irs-tax-filing-free-online.html. See also Netflix Is A Joke, "Why Doing Taxes Is So Hard | Patriot Act with Hasan Minhaj | Netflix," YouTube Video, 25:25, June 29, 2020, https://www.youtube.com/watch?v=7xQQkzWhMOc.

8. Carrns, "I.R.S. to Begin Trial of Its Own Free Tax-Filing System."

9. "IRS Free File: Do your taxes for free," *U.S. Department of the Treasury, Internal Revenue Service*, last modified February 6, 2025, https://www.irs.gov/filing/irs-free-file-do-your-taxes-for-free.

10. "Choose a trusted partner to file your taxes," *U.S. Department of the Treasury, Internal Revenue Service*, accessed February 20, 2025, https://apps.irs.gov/app/freeFile/general/.

11. "Get Free Tax Prep Help," *U.S. Department of the Treasury, Internal Revenue Service*, accessed December 3, 2024, https://irs.treasury.gov/freetaxprep/.

12. "What you need to know about filing an amended tax return," *U.S. Department of the Treasury, Internal Revenue Service*, last modified June 17, 2017, https://www.irs.gov/pub/irs-tipss/oc-amended-returns.pdf.

13. See "Tax Preparation Checklist," *TurboTax*, last modified May 15, 2024, https://turbotax.intuit.com/tax-tips/tax-planning-and-checklists/tax-preparation-checklist/L7LHiDqGJ.

14. Dan Moisand, "How can I get my tax information to my preparer safely?," *Moisand Fitzgerald Tomayo*, February 15, 2024, https://moisandfitzgerald.com/how-can-i-get-my-tax-information-to-my-preparer-securely/#:~:text=Repeat%20%E2%80%93%20DO%20NOT%20email%20tax,a%20password%2Dprotected%20ZIP%20file.

15. See U.S. Department of the Treasury, Internal Revenue Service. *Creating a Written Information Security Plan for your Tax & Accounting Practice*. 2022, Pub. 5708, Washington, DC.

16. Jason Fernando, "Profit and Loss Statement Meaning, Importance, Types, and Examples," *Investopedia*, last modified June 29, 2024, https://www.investopedia.com/terms/p/plstatement.asp.

17. Fernando, "Profit and Loss Statement Meaning, Importance, Types, and Examples."

18. Fernando, "Profit and Loss Statement Meaning, Importance, Types, and Examples."

19. Jason Fernando, "Balance Sheet: Explanation, Components, and Examples," *Investopedia*, last modified June 19, 2024, https://www.investopedia.com/terms/b/balancesheet.asp.

20. Kagan, "Filing Status: What it Means on Your Taxes, Types."

21. Rev. Rul. 58–66, 1958-1 C.B. 60.

22. Mary Recor, "Innocent or Not: Let the Factors Decide," *The Tax Adviser*, June 1, 2011, https://www.thetaxadviser.com/issues/2011/jun/recor-jun11.html.

23. U.S. Department of the Treasury, Internal Revenue Service. *Dependents, Standard Deduction, and Filing Information*. 2024, Pub. 535, Washington, DC, 7.

24. *Dependents, Standard Deduction, and Filing Information*, 2.

25. See *Beard v. Commissioner*, 82 T.C. 766 (1984), aff'd 793 F.2d 139. (6th Cir. 1986) ("A valid return is a document that: (1) purports to be a return, (2) is executed under penalties of perjury, (3) reports sufficient data to calculate the tax liability, and (4) most importantly, constitutes an honest and reasonable attempt to satisfy the requirements of the law.").

26. "Who Qualifies for the Earned Income Tax Credit (EITC)," *U.S. Department of the Treasury, Internal Revenue Service*, last modified December 20, 2024, https://www.irs.gov/credits-deductions/individuals/earned-income-tax-credit/who-qualifies-for-the-earned-income-tax-credit-eitc.

27. "Get An Identity Protection PIN (IP PIN)," *U.S. Department of the Treasury, Internal Revenue Service*, last modified January 27, 2025, https://www.irs.gov/identity-theft-fraud-scams/get-an-identity-protection-pin#:~:text=If%20you%20are%20a%20confirmed,from%20tax%2Drelated%20identity%20theft.

28. "Get An Identity Protection PIN (IP PIN)."

29. "What to do when a W-2 or Form 1099 is missing or incorrect," *U.S. Department of Treasury, Internal Revenue Service*, last modified December 5, 2024, https://www.irs.gov/newsroom/what-to-do-when-a-w-2-or-form-1099-is-missing-or-incorrect.

30. "1099 vs. W-2 Tax Forms: When Do Employers Use Them and Why?," *Paychex*, last modified October 31, 2024, https://www.paychex.com/articles/payroll-taxes/1099-vs-w2-when-should-employers-use-these-tax-forms.

31. "Topic no. 157, Change your address—How to notify the IRS," *U.S. Department of the Treasury, Internal Revenue Service*, last modified August 28, 2024, https://www.irs.gov/taxtopics/tc157.

32. "Moving expenses to and from the United States," *U.S. Department of the Treasury, Internal Revenue Service*, last modified August 20, 2024, https://www.irs.gov/individuals/international-taxpayers/moving-expenses-to-and-from-the-united-states#:~:text=Moving%20expense%20deduction%20eliminated%2C%20except,a%20permanent%20change%20of%20station.

33. Or in a few cases, even moving within the same state but to a different city could affect your taxes. For example, if you moved into or out of New York City, which has a city tax.

34. Kemberley Washington, "When Do I Need To File Taxes In Multiple States?," *Forbes*, last modified April 5, 2024, https://www.forbes.com/advisor/taxes/when-should-i-file-taxes-in-multiple-states/.

35. "How to report foreign bank and financial accounts," *U.S. Department of the Treasury, Internal Revenue Service*, last modified November 5, 2024, https://www.irs.gov/newsroom/how-to-report-foreign-bank-and-financial-accounts#:~:text=The%20FBAR%20is%20also%20a,income%20maintained%20%20or%20generated%20abroad.

36. The "nonwillfulness" penalty ("Whoops! I genuinely didn't realize I was required to report this!") is up to $10,000, but the "willfulness" penalty ("I was trying to hide the fact that I have an overseas bank account by not reporting it!")

has a ceiling of $100,000 or 50% of the balance in the account at the time of the violation, whichever is greater. See 31 U.S.C. § 5321(a)(5)(B)(i); 31 C.F.R. § 1010.821. 2 31 U.S.C. §§ 5321(a)(5)(C), (D)(ii) ("The maximum penalty for a nonwillful violation is $10,000 (adjusted for inflation). The maximum civil penalty for a willful violation is 50% of the maximum account balance during the year (or, if greater, $100,000 [adjusted for inflation] per violation.)").

37. Taylor Freitas, "Washington, D.C. first-time homebuyer assistance programs," *Bankrate*, last modified February 23, 2024, https://www.bankrate.com/mortgages/washington-dc-first-time-homebuyer-assistance-programs/. "Deductions on Rent Paid in Massachusetts," Mass.gov, last modified May 29, 2024, https://www.mass.gov/info-details/deductions-on-rent-paid-in-massachusetts#overview.

38. See "DSIRE," Database of State Incentives for Renewables & Efficiency, NC Clean Energy Technology Center, last accessed February 6, 2025, https://www.dsireusa.org/.

39. Janet Nguyen, "How the $3 campaign contribution check box on your tax form works," *Marketplace*, last modified November 4, 2021, https://www.marketplace.org/2021/11/04/how-the-3-campaign-contribution-check-box-on-your-tax-form-works/.

40. "Digital assets," *U.S. Department of the Treasury, Internal Revenue Service*, last modified January 23, 2025, https://www.irs.gov/businesses/small-businesses-self-employed/digital-assets.

41. "Digital assets."

42. "Election for Married Couples Unincorporated Businesses," *U.S. Department of the Treasury, Internal Revenue Service*, last modified August 26, 2024, https://www.irs.gov/businesses/small-businesses-self-employed/election-for-married-couples-unincorporated-businesses.

43. Kevin R. Sell, "Qualified joint ventures for spouses," *The Tax Adviser*, October 1, 2018, https://www.journalofaccountancy.com/issues/2018/oct/irs-qualified-joint-ventures-for-spouses.html.

44. "Election for Married Couples Unincorporated Businesses."

45. See "Employer ID numbers," *U.S. Department of the Treasury, Internal Revenue Service*, last modified January 15, 2025, https://www.irs.gov/businesses/small-businesses-self-employed/employer-id-numbers.

46. Rachel Smith, "How To File Schedule C Form 1040," *Bench*, last modified January 26, 2024, https://www.bench.co/blog/tax-tips/schedule-c.

47. Smith, "How To File Schedule C Form 1040."

48. Geri Detweiler, "Small Business Owners Guide to IRS Business Codes and NAICS Codes for Financing Success in 2024," *Nav*, last modified September 12, 2024, https://www.nav.com/blog/irs-business-codes-and-naics-codes-1890584/.

49. "NAICS Code & SIC Identification Tools," *NAICS Association*, accessed February 7, 2025, https://www.naics.com/search/.

50. Detweiler, "Small Business Owners Guide to IRS Business Codes and NAICS Codes for Financing Success in 2024."

51. Joy Taylor, "19 IRS Red Flags: What Are Your Chances of Being Audited?," *Kiplinger*, last modified January 26, 2025, https://www.kiplinger.com/taxes/tax-returns/602068/irs-audit-red-flags.

52. Tim Owens, "An Inside Look at How Tax Audits Work, From a Former IRS Auditor," *Keeper Tax*, June 21, 2023, https://www.keepertax.com/posts/irs-audits.

53. "Dave Cole: The Knitting Machine," *Massachusetts Museum of Contemporary Art*, accessed July 2024, https://massmoca.org/event/dave-cole-the-knitting-machine/.

54. "The Most Common Form 1099 Filing Mistakes (and how to correct them)," *Eide Bailly LLP*, last accessed February 5, 2025, https://www.eidebailly.com/insights/articles/2020/1/what-you-need-to-know-to-correct-form-1099.

55. "What to do when a W-2 or Form 1099 is missing or incorrect," *U.S. Department of the Treasury, Internal Revenue Service*, last modified December 4, 2024, https://www.irs.gov/newsroom/what-to-do-when-a-w-2-or-form-1099-is-missing-or-incorrect.

56. Robby Nelson, "How To Report Cash Income Without a 1099," *Keeper Tax*, last modified September 12, 2023, https://www.keepertax.com/posts/how-to-report-cash-income-without-1099.

57. See U.S. Department of the Treasury, Internal Revenue Service. Tax Guide for Small Businesses (For Individuals Who Use Schedule C). 2023, Pub. 334, Washington, DC, 15.

58. U.S. Department of the Treasury, Internal Revenue Service. Accounting Periods and Methods. 2022, Pub. 538, Washington, DC, 14.

59. Accounting Periods and Methods, Pub. 538, 14.

60. I haven't listed every category, because some feel irrelevant to this book's audience. But so you're aware, I've skipped these categories: Mortgage interest (for business property, not personal), energy-efficient commercial buildings deduction, depletion, employee benefits programs, wages, pension and profit-sharing plans. See "Instructions for Form 1040-C (Rev. January 2025)," *U.S.*

Department of the Treasury, Internal Revenue Service, last modified January 2025, https://www.irs.gov/pub/irs-pdf/i1040c.pdf.

61. I haven't listed every category, because some feel irrelevant to this book's audience. But so you know, I've skipped: Mortgage interest (for business property, not personal), energy-efficient commercial buildings deduction, depletion, employee benefits programs, wages, pension and profit-sharing plans.

62. "Instructions for Form 1040-C (Rev. January 2025)." See U.S. Department of the Treasury, Internal Revenue Service. Instructions for Forms 1099-INT and 1099-OID. 2023, Washington, DC, 1.

63. "Tangible property regulations—Frequently asked questions," *U.S. Department of the Treasury, Internal Revenue*, last modified October 2, 2024, https://www.irs.gov/businesses/small-businesses-self-employed/tangible-property-final-regulations.

64. "Instructions for Form 1040-C (Rev. January 2025)."

65. "Instructions for Form 1040-C (Rev. January 2025)."

66. "Reporting Payments to Independent Contractors," *U.S. Department of the Treasury, Internal Revenue Service*, last modified October 2, 2024, https://www.irs.gov/businesses/small-businesses-self-employed/reporting-payments-to-independent-contractors.

67. Robert W. Wood, "What Are 10 Things You Should Know About 1099s?", *Investopedia*, last modified February 18, 2024, https://www.investopedia.com/financial-edge/0110/10-things-you-should-know-about-1099s.aspx#:~:text=Usually%2C%20anyone%20who%20was%20paid,income%20during%20the%20tax%20year.

68. "Instructions for Forms 1099-MISC and 1099-NEC," *U.S. Department of the Treasury, Internal Revenue*, last modified January 2024, https://www.irs.gov/pub/irs-pdf/i1099mec.pdf.

69. American Institute of Certified Public Accountants, Code of Professional Conduct 1.130.010.

70. "Instructions for Form 1040-C (Rev. January 2025)."

71. "Instructions for Form 1040-C (Rev. January 2025)."

72. "Instructions for Form 1040-C (Rev. January 2025)."

73. "Instructions for Form 1040-C (Rev. January 2025)."

74. "Instructions for Form 1040-C (Rev. January 2025)."

75. "Instructions for Form 1040-C (Rev. January 2025)."

76. See U.S. Department of the Treasury, Internal Revenue Service. Health Savings Accounts and Other Tax-Favored Health Plans. 2024, Pub. 969, Washington, DC, 13.

77. Health Savings Accounts and Other Tax-Favored Health Plans. Pub. 969, 17.
78. Health Savings Accounts and Other Tax-Favored Health Plans. Pub. 969, 17.
79. Health Savings Accounts and Other Tax-Favored Health Plans. Pub. 969, 9.
80. See "About Form 1099-MISC, Miscellaneous Information," *U.S. Department of the Treasury, Internal Revenue Service*, last modified December 10, 2024, https://www.irs.gov/instructions/i1040sc.
81. See "2024 Instructions for Schedule E (2024)," *U.S. Department of the Treasury, Internal Revenue Service*, last modified December 2, 2024, https://www.irs.gov/pub/irs-pdf/i1040se.pdf.
82. "2024 Instructions for Schedule E (2024)."
83. "2024 Instructions for Schedule E (2024)."
84. "2024 Instructions for Schedule E (2024)."
85. This gets weedy, but land is not depreciable, while physical structures like buildings are. An accountant or real estate broker may be able to help you determine this percentage.
86. "2024 Instructions for Schedule C (2024)."
87. "2024 Instructions for Schedule C (2024)."
88. See "Income & expenses," *U.S. Department of the Treasury, Internal Revenue Service*, last modified August 20, 2024, https://www.irs.gov/faqs/small-business-self-employed-other-business/income-expenses#:~:text=You%20wouldn't%20write%20off,it%20easier%20to%20keep%20records.
89. "Topic no. 456, Student loan interest deduction," *U.S. Department of the Treasury, Internal Revenue Service*, last modified January 2, 2025, https://www.irs.gov/taxtopics/tc456.
90. "Topic no. 602, Child and Dependent Care Credit," *U.S. Department of the Treasury, Internal Revenue Service*, last modified January 2, 2025, https://www.irs.gov/taxtopics/tc602.
91. "Topic no. 602, Child and dependent care credit."
92. See "Instructions for Form 2441 (2024)," *U.S. Department of the Treasury, Internal Revenue Service*, last modified December 12, 2024, https://www.irs.gov/instructions/i2441.
93. "Topic no. 313, Qualified tuition programs (QTPs)," *U.S. Department of the Treasury*, last modified January 2, 2025, https://www.irs.gov/taxtopics/tc313.
94. "Health coverage exemptions: Forms & how to apply," Healthcare.gov, accessed November 24, 2024, https://www.healthcare.gov/health-coverage-exemptions/exemptions-from-the-fee/.

95. "Health Insurance Marketplace Statements," *U.S. Department of the Treasury, Internal Revenue Service*, last modified December 18, 2024, https://www.irs.gov/affordable-care-act/individuals-and-families/health-insurance-marketplace-statements.

96. "The Premium Tax Credit - The Basics," *U.S. Department of the Treasury, Internal Revenue Service*, last modified September 13, 2024, https://www.irs.gov/affordable-care-act/individuals-and-families/the-premium-tax-credit-the-basics.

97. "The Premium Tax Credit - The Basics."

98. "The Premium Tax Credit - The Basics."

99. Unless you're married filing separate, in which case you must itemize if your spouse itemizes regardless of benefit.

100. Unless they're married filing separate.

101. "Topic no. 503, Deductible taxes," *U.S. Department of the Treasury, Internal Revenue Service*, last modified January 27, 2025, https://www.irs.gov/taxtopics/tc503.

102. "Topic no. 503, Deductible taxes."

103. Internal Revenue Service. 2022. Statistics of Income. Table 1.3. "All Returns: Sources of Income, Adjustments, Deductions, Credits, and Tax Items, by Marital Status, Tax Year 2020 (Filing Year 2021)." Washington, DC.

104. See U.S. Department of the Treasury, Internal Revenue Service. Charitable Contributions. 2023, Pub. 526, 2, Washington, DC.

105. Charitable Contributions, Pub. 526, 21.

106. Charitable Contributions, Pub. 526, 22.

107. "Donation Value Guide," *The Salvation Army Thrift Stores*, last accessed February 6, 2025, https://satruck.org/Home/DonationValueGuide.

108. "Instructions for Form 1098," *U.S. Department of the Treasury, Internal Revenue Service*, last modified January 5, 2022, https://www.irs.gov/instructions/i1098.

109. Aaron Lorenzo, "Tax Bill Whacks Liberal Big Cities," *Politico*, December 19, 2017, https://www.politico.com/story/2017/12/19/cities-republican-tax-bill-304123.

110. Aaron Lorenzo, "Tax Bill Whacks Liberal Big Cities."

111. "Estimated taxes."

112. "Topic no. 452, Alimony and separate maintenance," *U.S. Department of the Treasury, Internal Revenue Service*, last modified September 17, 2024, https://www.irs.gov/taxtopics/tc452#:~:text=You%20can't%20deduct%20alimony,payments%20applies%20to%20the%20modification.

113. "Topic no. 607, Adoption credit and adoption assistance programs," *U.S. Department of the Treasury, Internal Revenue Service*, last modified February 14, 2024, https://www.irs.gov/taxtopics/tc607.

114. U.S. Department of the Treasury, Internal Revenue Service. Casualties, Disasters, and Thefts. 2024, Pub. 547, Washington, DC, 3.

115. See U.S. Department of the Treasury, Internal Revenue Service. Contributions to Individual Retirement Arrangements (IRAs). 2024, Pub. 590-A, Washington, DC.

116. "Retirement topics—IRA contribution limits," *U.S. Department of the Treasury, Internal Revenue Service*, last modified August 20, 2024, https://www.irs.gov/retirement-plans/plan-participant-employee/retirement-topics-ira-contribution-limits.

117. "Retirement topics—IRA contribution limits," *U.S. Department of the Treasury, Internal Revenue Service*, last modified June 25, 2024, https://www.irs.gov/retirement-plans/plan-participant-employee/retirement-topics-ira-contribution-limits.

118. Trenton Reed, "Comparing retirement plans: 401(k) vs. SIMPLE IRA vs. SEP IRA," *Human Interest*, last modified April 26, 2024, https://humaninterest.com/learn/articles/retirement-plan-comparison-401k-vs-solo-401k-vs-simple-ira-vs-sep-ira/.

119. "Pay taxes by Electronic Funds Withdrawal," *U.S. Department of the Treasury, Internal Revenue Service*, last modified September 27, 2024, https://www.irs.gov/payments/pay-taxes-by-electronic-funds-withdrawal.

120. "Direct deposit is the best way to get a federal tax refund," *U.S. Department of the Treasury, Internal Revenue Service*, last modified December 18, 2024, https://www.irs.gov/newsroom/direct-deposit-is-the-best-way-to-get-a-federal-tax-refund#:~:text=Direct%20deposit%20is%20the%20best%20way%20to%20receive%20a%20tax,refund%20they%20may%20be%20owed.

121. "Dishonored Check or Other Form of Payment Penalty," *U.S. Department of the Treasury, Internal Revenue Service*, last modified November 8, 2024, https://www.irs.gov/payments/dishonored-check-or-other-form-of-payment-penalty.

122. "IRS Where's My Refund," *U.S. Department of the Treasury, Internal Revenue Service*, accessed February 7, 2025, https://sa.www4.irs.gov/wmr/.

CHAPTER TEN

TAX TRIAGE: WHEN TO DIY YOUR TAXES VS. WHEN TO CALL IN A PRO

Some tax stuff is DIY-able. And some tax stuff will trigger special tax laws, and you should be aware when you're in one of those areas. In this section, I'll lay out some tax situations that are sticky enough that you should consult an expert rather than tough it out on your own.

One of the tricky things about taxes is that every now and then, a complex problem arises without warning, opening a tax research rabbit hole. For example, a friend who prepares taxes in Massachusetts had a client who sold a home that had been passed down for generations since colonial times. If there was ever a deed to the house, it was from 400+ years ago, and it was gone now. And yet, the tax return required an original value of the house. It was not just unclear whether the house had been built by the family or purchased, but the currency in colonial Massachusetts was not even the US dollar (it was the Massachusetts pound). This presented an unexpected challenge about how to value the house to calculate capital gains on the sale.

Be aware of the following situations, but also understand that complexity can sneak up on you from behind.

> If you're doing your own taxes and an issue arises where you need help, file for a tax extension to give yourself more time and then seek the help you need.

TAX SITUATIONS FOR A PRO

A Big Transition or Change in Financial Circumstance

When your taxes remain similar from one year to the next, doing your own taxes is not only easier, but your last tax return can help guide you in handling this year's taxes. Don't go full autopilot, but you can lean heavily on last year (tax pros have an acronym for this, called SALY, same as last year). Furthermore, if your income and tax situation remain stable relative to the prior year, you aren't likely to have a large overpayment or underpayment of tax or need to make adjustments to your withholding or estimated tax payments for the coming year. You're less likely to face a large tax bill and the destabilizing fallout that that can bring you.

The corollary is that if you have a change in your financial situation, it's good to bring in a pro. Transitioning from one financial circumstance to another can bring you a tax hiccup, and that's a time when you want guidance. The following scenarios can shift your tax picture.

Marriage

An accountant can run tax scenarios to show you whether it's financially better for you to file jointly or separately (though you'll have to ask). They can also help you understand your tax change now that you're married. Here's an example I encounter often: a self-employed person and a W2 employee get married. The employee is used to a simple tax return, usually files early, and gets a refund. The self-employed person is behind on their bookkeeping and waits too long to contact their accountant. They feel ashamed of their disorganization and not paying quarterly taxes and suspect they have a big tax bill coming. To the employee, filing taxes jointly for the first time may come as a shock. The refund they are used to will probably be eaten up by the tax bill owed from their new spouse's unpaid taxes. It's not a great first-taxes-together experience.

A good accountant can help each party understand why this is happening, whose income is generating what tax obligation, and how to mitigate it for next year. Hint: the self-employed person can make bookkeeping a regular habit to be less surprised by their numbers and pay quarterly taxes to avoid the tax day mega-bill. Consider your accountant's fee an investment in your marital health. Regular bookkeeping and paying quarterly taxes are a path to less fighting with your partner. If that sounds like a ghost from my past, trust your instincts.

I've seen a surprising number of people ask their accountant if they should get married. To which I say, "Do you love them? Are they a good partner?" If tax is the deciding factor on your marriage, something else is wrong.

Divorce

This is the marriage scenario in reverse. Money may be a source of pain, and the tax return is a tender experience. Don't hire an accountant who's an insensitive jerk, if you can help it. You may want help knowing your rights and making sure you get what you're entitled to, such as claiming your dependent children, if that's part of your divorce settlement. You should be aware that a licensed tax professional, meaning an enrolled agent (EA) or a certified public accountant (CPA), is legally required to alert you to conflicts of interest. If you're using the same accountant after the divorce that you did while married, they should have you sign a conflict of interest disclosure and agreement if they do your taxes as well as your ex's. Many professionals who should do this don't. There are tax positions that favor one ex-spouse over the other, so it may be in your best interest to seek a new accountant after a divorce. You should at least make your accountant aware that you know the rules and you expect fairness.

Recent or Upcoming Retirement

There's tax planning that you may need as you approach retirement. For example, understanding the potential taxability of your Social Security payments and the tax implications of withdrawals from your retirement accounts, including setting up your required minimum distributions (RMDs), once you turn 73. Penalties can be stiff if you don't take your RMDs.[1] The IRS's Tax Counseling for the Elderly (TCE) program offers free counseling for taxpayers over age 60 and specializes in pension and retirement-related issues. You can find a TCE program near you at irs.treasury.gov/freetaxprep/.

The RMD age has shifted in recent years and may increase again. Be sure to check the age requirements if you're close to retirement.

A Loss of Income

The good news: you probably won't face a tax bill. You're more likely to have a refund or to owe less than last year if your income drops. But you may want to seek help in case you're eligible for tax credits for lower-income taxpayers or tax deductions that you may not previously have qualified for.

Complex Household

The complexity surrounding members of your household, who claims who, and who your dependents are, for example, if you care for elderly parents, is a reason to seek help. While anyone can face these questions, lower-income taxpayers tend to face them most often and at greatest personal cost, due to housing instability, family members moving in and out, custody issues, and caring for dependents you may or may not be related to. The Volunteer Income Tax Assistance (VITA) program can help. VITA volunteers encounter these challenges frequently, can help you make the right determination, and do it for free. You can locate your nearest VITA program at irs.treasury.gov/freetaxprep.

Income Threshold Concerns

If you receive benefits subject to an income threshold, for example, disability payments, the advance premium tax credit, or income-dependent subsidized housing, exceeding the allowable threshold can have dire consequences. A tax professional can run various scenarios through their software to see how your taxes may change. They can help you take advantage of tax-lowering deductions available to you. The VITA program is a good source of help if price is a concern.

SCENARIOS THAT CAN SPIKE YOUR TAXES

Big influxes of income can spike your taxes. If you wait until tax time to deal with an event like the sale of a business, a windfall grant, or a large real estate purchase, you may be too late to mitigate the tax bill. The following scenarios are good reasons to reach out to a tax professional *before* the end of the tax year and, preferably, before the transaction itself. Year-end tax planning can help you reduce the taxes by maximizing every available tax-advantaged account and strategy. Tax planning in advance of a significant event is key, because there may be rules that help you manage the tax impact.

Buying or Selling Real Estate or a Business

Generally in taxes, you are taxed when the income becomes available to you. If you're expecting a big payout, expect a tax bill. But there are some rules that can help you manage or defer the tax impact of a large sale. Don't sell real estate or a business without consulting a tax expert for tax planning.

A windfall grant or inheritance is another reason to do tax planning. While you may have less control over the timing of a windfall or inheritance than the sale of a business, timing is still important, and it pays to think ahead. Tax planning can help you spread out the taxes and lessen the dollar amount by maximizing your available tax-advantaged accounts.

Large Gain in Income

A large gain in income is similar to a windfall or inheritance but may be a permanent change, rather than a one-time event. For this reason, talk to a professional about updating your W4 to increase your withholding, changing your estimated payment amounts or establishing better tax-saving habits, like regular year-end tax planning, or establishing a solo 401k.

HIGH-COMPLEXITY TAX SITUATIONS

Some tax situations are complex and require the specialty tax knowledge of an accountant. Having one of the following scenarios doesn't *necessarily* mean you need a pro. But be aware that these are times to proceed with caution.

Multiple States

International Tax Situations

Complex Real Estate Transactions

Complex Investments[2]

Complex Depreciation/Capital Expenditures

> This may apply if you build a house or renovate a studio.

Inheritance

> You may need to file a **trust or estate tax return**,[3] and there may be additional financial implications for you.

Crypto or Digital Asset Trades

> Digital asset transactions are not the same as equity transactions (like stocks and bonds), and they are not currency under US law (yes, despite the name).[4]

> Crypto is closer to gambling than investing. You don't get the investor protections of Securities and Exchange Commission (SEC) oversight that you do with stocks and bonds. You're in the Wild West. Maybe you strike gold, but maybe you're the greater fool at the wrong end of a pump-and-dump scheme. Buyer beware.

Corporate Tax Returns

This book teaches you to do your Schedule C, and that's how you report your self-employed income *by default*.

But you can *elect* a different type of tax entity. See Chapter 12. If you have a separate tax entity, you have a corporate tax return, with a March 15 deadline. And if so, hire a tax professional. For clarity, these are the possible separate tax entities (see Chapter 12 for details):

- **S Corporation**, files an **1120 S**
- **Partnership** (excluding a married couple who file a **qualified joint venture**—see Chapter 9), files a **1065**
- **C Corporation**, files an **1120**

Tax Entity Formation

See Chapter 12 for more, but if you're choosing a new tax entity, consult a tax expert. If you want an LLC, that's a *legal* entity, and you need a lawyer.

Complex Decisions/ Expert Guidance

For tax resolution issues, like letters from the IRS, tax payment plans, past unfiled tax returns, or complex decisions, a tax professional can help.

But know that a tax preparation fee doesn't include walking you through the tax return (though a good tax pro should give you the highlights), educating you on tax rules, helping you adjust your quarterly tax payments, checking in each quarter, tax planning to save you money, or guiding you to choose tax-advantaged retirement accounts. These are generally additional paid services (and can be worthwhile). I have opinions on this, and if you want to know more, check out my article on tax preparation vs. tax advisory services at www.sunlighttax.com/taxesforhumans.

CHAPTER SUMMARY

- When to DIY your taxes and when to call in a pro. Some tax situations can trigger special tax laws, open a research rabbit hole, or require expert help to weigh options. Consult a tax pro for:
- Big transitions or changes in financial circumstances.
  - Marriage or divorce.
  - Approaching retirement. Understand the tax implications of Social Security payments and retirement account withdrawals. The IRS's Tax Counseling for the Elderly (TCE) program offers free help.

- Loss of income: You might be eligible for tax credits or deductions for lower-income taxpayers.
- Seek help for complexity around household members and dependents. The Volunteer Income Tax Assistance (VITA) program can help.
- If you receive benefits subject to an income threshold, a tax professional can help manage your taxes to avoid exceeding limits.
- Big influxes of income can spike your taxes. Consult a tax professional before the end of the tax year for planning to manage the tax impact.
  - Buying or Selling Real Estate or a Business.
  - Windfall Grant or Inheritance: Timing is important.
  - Large Gain in Income: Update your W4, change estimated payments, and establish tax-saving habits.
- High-complexity tax situations:
  - Multiple states, international tax situations, or digital asset transactions.
  - Complex real estate transactions, investments or capital expenditures (like building a house or studio).
  - Corporate tax returns: If you have or want to form a separate tax entity, hire a tax professional. Possible entities are S Corporation, Partnership, or C Corporation.
  - For tax resolution issues, payment plans, past unfiled returns, or complex decisions, a tax professional can help.
- Tax preparation fees don't include educating you on tax rules, year-end tax planning, or helping with quarterly payments. These are additional services that can be worthwhile.

ENDNOTES

1. "Retirement plan and IRA required minimum distributions FAQs," *U.S. Department of the Treasury, Internal Revenue Service*, accessed January 29, 2025, https://www.irs.gov/retirement-plans/retirement-plan-and-ira-required-minimum-distributions-faqs.
2. "Topic no. 409, Capital gains and losses," *U.S. Department of the Treasury, Internal Revenue Service*, last modified January 2, 2025, https://www.irs.gov/taxtopics/tc409.
3. "File an estate tax income tax return," *U.S. Department of the Treasury, Internal Revenue Service*, accessed August 22, 2024, https://www.irs.gov/retirement-plans/retirement-plan-and-ira-required-minimum-distributions-faqs.
4. "Digital assets," *U.S. Department of the Treasury, Internal Revenue Service*, last modified January 23, 2025, https://www.irs.gov/businesses/small-businesses-self-employed/digital-assets.

CHAPTER ELEVEN

HOW TO REVIEW YOUR TAX RETURN

O f all the chapters in this book, this one is the biggest bang for your buck. This is the final review part of the tax sandwich we started in Chapter 8: tax form orientation, data entry, tax form review. Get ready for more tax knowledge and control.

You *must* review your tax return before you file it. This also goes for your spouse, if you file jointly. You're signing a legal document that says you know and take responsibility for what's in it—even if you hire a tax preparer.

This is your chance to make corrections and save yourself headaches before a mistake turns into a drawn-out pen-pal relationship with the IRS. Speak up if you see a mistake. This chapter will give you the power to spot an error and make sure your income and payments are reported correctly.

THE FIRST TWO PAGES SUMMARIZE EVERYTHING

No matter how ginormous your tax return is, the first two pages summarize everything in it. Reviewing them will outline all the information contained inside. If needed, you can refer to areas deeper within the document. How do you know where to look? That line on the 1040 will actually *tell you*. There may be specific parts of your return you want to review, like, for example, your Schedule C, to see that your business income and deductions are reported correctly. Or, you can see how various calculations were made by examining those forms. I like looking at the calculation page for my SEP IRA, for example.

Every year, I want your minimum baseline habit to be reviewing those first two pages. This will give you a sense of whether it's all correct or something is off.

The form 1040 starts with your basic identifying information. Then there's a section for **Income** that summarizes all your reported income totals, by income type (W2, self-employed, investment income, etc.).

Next is the section **Taxes and Credits**, which shows you how much tax you owe, subtracts any credits you're getting, and adds back any additional taxes you owe, most notably self-employment tax. The last line in this section delivers your **total tax**.

The next section, **Payments**, lays out all the taxes you've already paid, and subtracts those from your total tax.

The result appears in one of the next two sections, either **Refund** or **Amount You Owe**. The basic math here is that if you've overpaid your taxes for the year, you'll see an amount listed in the refund section, and you get that amount back. If you've underpaid taxes for the year, you'll see your remaining balance listed in the **Amount You Owe** section. If you didn't pay or underpaid estimated tax payments, you'll also see a penalty calculated here, which is added to your total amount due.

Lastly, there's info about who prepared your tax return, whether you authorize them (or anyone else) to discuss it with the IRS, and then your signature (or signatures, if you're married filing jointly).

That's pretty straightforward, right? Let's dig in.

REVIEW THE IDENTIFYING INFO

This is easy. Review the top part of your return (see Figure 11.1) to make sure your name and your spouse's are spelled correctly and are the same as on last year's return. Make sure your Social Security numbers and your address are correct. Remember that the address written here will become the IRS's address of record for you, until you file a tax return with a new address. So be sure it's a place you can receive mail.[1]

Check that the filing status on the return is correct. If it's not, it needs to be corrected. If you had your taxes prepared by someone and they messed up the filing status, that's a bad sign.

Lastly, double-check that all your dependents are listed and check their names and Social Security or ITIN numbers.

Figure 11.1 1040 form top ID info.

Source: Internal Revenue Service (IRS)/https://www.irs.gov/pub/irs-pdf/f1040sc.pdf./Public domain/ last accessed on March 21, 2025.

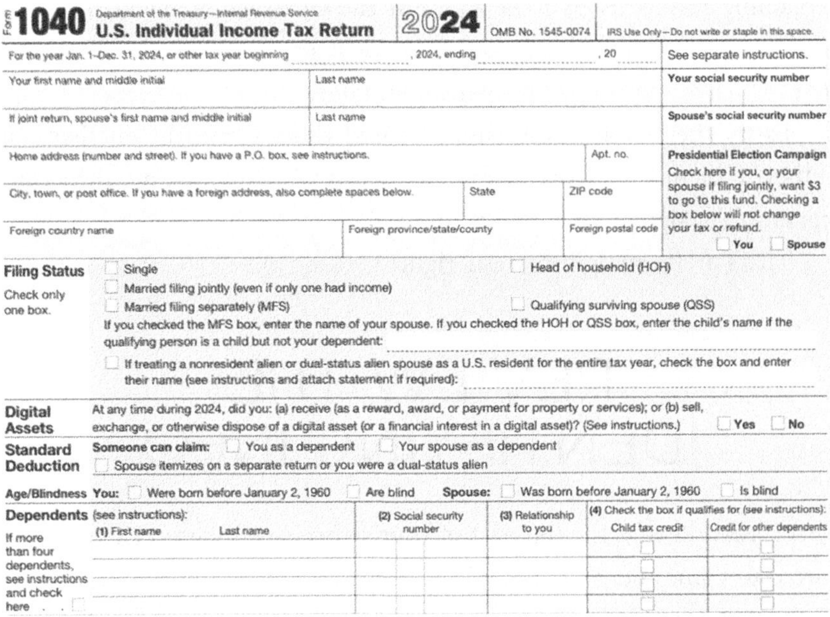

Form 1040 Department of the Treasury—Internal Revenue Service U.S. Individual Income Tax Return 2024 OMB No. 1545-0074 IRS Use Only—Do not write or staple in this space.

For the year Jan. 1–Dec. 31, 2024, or other tax year beginning , 2024, ending , 20 See separate instructions.

Your first name and middle initial | Last name | Your social security number

If joint return, spouse's first name and middle initial | Last name | Spouse's social security number

Home address (number and street). If you have a P.O. box, see instructions. | Apt. no. | Presidential Election Campaign Check here if you, or your spouse if filing jointly, want $3 to go to this fund. Checking a box below will not change your tax or refund. ☐ You ☐ Spouse

City, town, or post office. If you have a foreign address, also complete spaces below. | State | ZIP code

Foreign country name | Foreign province/state/county | Foreign postal code

Filing Status Check only one box.
☐ Single
☐ Married filing jointly (even if only one had income)
☐ Married filing separately (MFS)
☐ Head of household (HOH)
☐ Qualifying surviving spouse (QSS)
If you checked the MFS box, enter the name of your spouse. If you checked the HOH or QSS box, enter the child's name if the qualifying person is a child but not your dependent:
☐ If treating a nonresident alien or dual-status alien spouse as a U.S. resident for the entire tax year, check the box and enter their name (see instructions and attach statement if required):

Digital Assets At any time during 2024, did you: (a) receive (as a reward, award, or payment for property or services); or (b) sell, exchange, or otherwise dispose of a digital asset (or a financial interest in a digital asset)? (See instructions.) ☐ Yes ☐ No

Standard Deduction Someone can claim: ☐ You as a dependent ☐ Your spouse as a dependent
☐ Spouse itemizes on a separate return or you were a dual-status alien

Age/Blindness You: ☐ Were born before January 2, 1960 ☐ Are blind **Spouse:** ☐ Was born before January 2, 1960 ☐ Is blind

Dependents (see instructions): If more than four dependents, see instructions and check here . . ☐

(1) First name Last name	(2) Social security number	(3) Relationship to you	(4) Check the box if qualifies for (see instructions): Child tax credit	Credit for other dependents
			☐	☐
			☐	☐
			☐	☐
			☐	☐

THE INCOME SECTION: YOUR ANSWER KEY

I consider the Income section on page 1 of the 1040 (see Figure 11.2) to be the least utilized resource in America. Also, your accountant is charging you $100–$400/hour to answer your questions, and you can find a lot of the answers for yourself, right here, for free. So next time you wonder what your **adjusted gross income** (AGI) is, because you're filling out a FAFSA, just look at line 11, and then take that $100 accounting fee you saved and treat yourself to a nice dinner.

Figure 11.2 1040—income section.

Source: Internal Revenue Service (IRS)/https://www.irs.gov/pub/irs-pdf/f1040sc.pdf./Public domain/ last accessed on March 21, 2025.

Income	1a	Total amount from Form(s) W-2, box 1 (see instructions)	1a	
Attach Form(s) W-2 here. Also attach Forms W-2G and 1099-R if tax was withheld.	b	Household employee wages not reported on Form(s) W-2	1b	
	c	Tip income not reported on line 1a (see instructions)	1c	
	d	Medicaid waiver payments not reported on Form(s) W-2 (see instructions)	1d	
	e	Taxable dependent care benefits from Form 2441, line 26	1e	
	f	Employer-provided adoption benefits from Form 8839, line 29	1f	
If you did not get a Form W-2, see instructions.	g	Wages from Form 8919, line 6	1g	
	h	Other earned income (see instructions)	1h	
	i	Nontaxable combat pay election (see instructions) 1i		
	z	Add lines 1a through 1h	1z	
Attach Sch. B if required.	2a	Tax-exempt interest 2a	b Taxable interest	2b
	3a	Qualified dividends 3a	b Ordinary dividends	3b
	4a	IRA distributions 4a	b Taxable amount	4b
Standard Deduction for—	5a	Pensions and annuities 5a	b Taxable amount	5b
• Single or Married filing separately, $14,600	6a	Social security benefits 6a	b Taxable amount	6b
• Married filing jointly or Qualifying surviving spouse, $29,200	c	If you elect to use the lump-sum election method, check here (see instructions) ☐		
• Head of household, $21,900	7	Capital gain or (loss). Attach Schedule D if required. If not required, check here ☐	7	
• If you checked any box under *Standard Deduction*, see instructions.	8	Additional income from Schedule 1, line 10	8	
	9	Add lines 1z, 2b, 3b, 4b, 5b, 6b, 7, and 8. This is your **total income**	9	
	10	Adjustments to income from Schedule 1, line 26	10	
	11	Subtract line 10 from line 9. This is your **adjusted gross income**	11	
	12	**Standard deduction or itemized deductions** (from Schedule A)	12	
	13	Qualified business income deduction from Form 8995 or Form 8995-A	13	
	14	Add lines 12 and 13	14	
	15	Subtract line 14 from line 11. If zero or less, enter -0-. This is your **taxable income**	15	

In addition to summarizing the totals for each income type you had (wages, self-employment, capital gains, etc.), this section of your 1040 gives you three important totals, all bolded for your convenience:

1. Your **total income**, on **line 9**
2. Your **adjusted gross income (AGI)**, (important for a lot of tax calculations), **line 11** and
3. Your **taxable income, line 15**

Have you ever wondered how much of each type of income you made last year (employee vs. self-employed vs. investments)? Here's a tidy summary of each type of income you made for the year. If you find yourself wondering what your ratio of employee to self-employed income is so you can fill out your next W4 accurately, that info is right here.

Schedules 1, 2, and 3 are part of every taxpayer's tax return, right at the front, after your 1040 summary pages. They are different from the Schedules that have letters, like the Schedule C and Schedule E. Schedule 1 is "Additional Income and Adjustments to Income," Schedule 2 is "Additional Taxes," and Schedule 3 is "Additional Credits and Payments."

Line 8 summarizes *additional* income, from the Schedule 1, "Additional Income and Adjustments to Income."[2] This will mostly be your business income, but you can check to see on the Schedule 1, Part I,[3] **line 3** (your business income). You may want to look at this schedule to see what other income sources apply to you, like taxable unemployment compensation, jury duty pay, hobby income, or rental income. These items add to your total taxable income.

Items that reduce your taxable income are listed on Part II of the Schedule 1, and **line 10** of your 1040 summarizes that total. These are things like your self-employed SEP contribution deduction, your deductible IRA contribution and other tax-advantaged contributions, and a bunch of other items, some of which won't apply to you. If you're using tax-advantaged accounts to save money (see Chapters 14 and 15), this is where you'll see those results.

DO YOU ITEMIZE?
THE ANSWER IS ON LINE 12

Lastly, the important tax question that many people shockingly don't know the answer to is whether you itemize or take the standard deduction. Mystery, begone! **Line 12** has your answer. You'll see a convenient sidebar on line 12 listing that year's standard deduction amounts for each filing status. If that number (for your status) is listed on line 12, *then you take the standard deduction.* Your answer to the question "Do you itemize?" will be "no." On the other hand, if you see a different number from the ones listed in that sidebar, you're itemizing. Generally this number should be bigger than the standard deduction amount for your filing status, because you get to take the bigger deduction. The exception is if you're married filing separately, in which case you're stuck itemizing if your spouse itemizes, even when it's lower.

YOUR TAX AND TAX CREDITS

In the next section, at the top of page two, you'll find all the summary info about your tax and tax credits (see Figure 11.3).

Most of this is self-explanatory, but let's look at a few things.

Line 17 refers to the Schedule 2, "Additional Taxes." You can refer to your Schedule 2 to see a breakdown of all the different types of taxes that you owe and their precise amounts. The Schedule 2 comes in the beginning part of your full tax documentation, so you won't have to flip through more than a couple pages to find it.

Figure 11.3   1040 tax and credits section.

Source: Internal Revenue Service (IRS)/https://www.irs.gov/pub/irs-pdf/f1040sc.pdf./Public domain/ last accessed on March 21, 2025.

Tax and Credits			
	16	**Tax** (see instructions). Check if any from Form(s): 1 ☐ 8814 2 ☐ 4972 3 ☐ _____	16
	17	Amount from Schedule 2, line 3	17
	18	Add lines 16 and 17	18
	19	Child tax credit or credit for other dependents from Schedule 8812	19
	20	Amount from Schedule 3, line 8	20
	21	Add lines 19 and 20	21
	22	Subtract line 21 from line 18. If zero or less, enter -0-	22
	23	Other taxes, including self-employment tax, from Schedule 2, line 21	23
	24	Add lines 22 and 23. This is your **total tax**	24

Line 20 refers to the Schedule 3, "Additional Credits and Payments." This is another part you may want to peek at to see all the tax credits you're getting.

When you're self-employed, your self-employment tax is a big factor in your total tax, so to see what that amount is, look at Schedule 2, "Additional Taxes," line 4. Line 23 in the Tax and Credits section includes this amount but may lump in other stuff.

USE LINE 24 FOR YOUR ESTIMATED QUARTERLY PAYMENTS

Your total tax is on line 24, and it's super important. This is all your federal taxes combined from all sources. Remember that if you're married filing jointly, then this number includes you and your spouse together. This is the number you can use to meet the first of the two safe harbor thresholds for paying your estimated quarterly taxes.

LOOKING DEEPER

If you want to see the calculations for any of the other numbers on your tax return, or if you want to see the various other schedules and what was determined by them, you may flip to the calculation form that is referred to on any given line of the two-page 1040 or to the appropriate schedule. I recommend that you glance through Schedules 1, 2, and 3, which are right at the beginning of your tax return, behind the two-page summary, because these tell you the specifics of any additional taxes you're paying (like your total self-employment tax), and every little thing that is increasing your tax (like extra income) or decreasing it (like special tax credits or your contributions to tax-advantaged accounts).

PAYMENTS

The next section (Figure 11.4) is where the taxes you've already paid, whether from your estimated tax payments or through W2 payroll withholding, get subtracted from your total tax. It's nice to see each part broken out, because it helps you understand if, for example, your W2 withholding is high enough or if you need to file a new W4 to increase it.

If you look at this and instantly see that it's not, go to the free Paycheck Checkup tool on the IRS website with this info, and fill out a new W4 to increase your withholding. Go ahead and do it now: https://apps.irs.gov/app/tax-withholding-estimator.

Figure 11.4   Payments section.
Source: Internal Revenue Service (IRS)/https://www.irs.gov/pub/irs-pdf/f1040sc.pdf./Public domain/ last accessed on March 21, 2025.

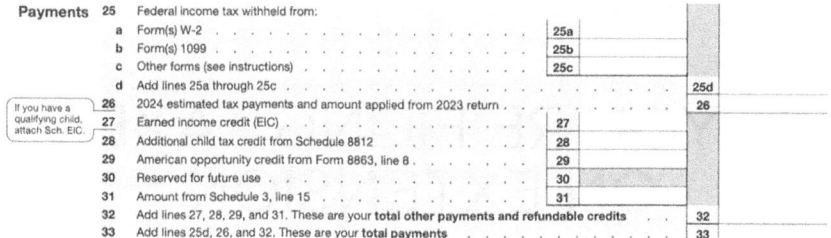

MAKE SURE YOUR ESTIMATED TAX PAYMENTS ARE REPORTED

Note here the **total estimated tax payments** you've made for the year, on **line 26**. How closely have they reduced your tax bill to near zero?

There's no automatic reporting of your estimates, so you need to report them when doing your taxes and then check that they are showing up here, on **line 26**, before you sign and submit your tax return.

The Point of Taxes: Getting "Taxes Paid" Line 33 as Close as Possible to "Total Tax" Line 24

Your goal each year is to adjust your combined estimated tax payments and W2 withholding so that the **total payments, line 33** is roughly equal to **line 24, total tax**. Think that through with me. This means you're aiming to have paid, through all payment sources (withholding and estimates, mostly), all the tax you owe for that year by this time. Make sense?

IF YOU'RE FILING TAXES ON EXTENSION

In case you're filing on extension or if you ever intend to, note that **line 10** of your Schedule 3 lists any amount you may have paid with your extension request. You are supposed to make a payment of what you think you owe when you file for an extension. And this is where that amount shows up and gets credited toward your eventual tax bill.

WHAT'S LEFT: REFUND/ AMOUNT YOU OWE

This (Figure 11.5) is the last of the numbers sections in the 1040 summary. It answers the basic equation that taxes set up:

What's the total tax you owed for the year

– What amount of that did you already pay + any tax credits that reduce your tax

= What you overpaid/what's left to pay

So if you **overpaid**, then you will see a number listed in the **Refund** section, **on line 34.** You can, and I recommend that you do, include your bank information here to receive your refund as a direct deposit. This is faster and more secure than a check in the mail. Double-check your account info to make sure it's correct.

Note that you can apply your refund to next year's estimated tax payment. If you want to do that, you can control the amount (it doesn't have to be all of it), and you'll see that amount listed on **line 36, "Amount of line 34 you want applied to your [insert next year] estimated tax."**

Figure 11.5 1040—refund and amount you owe sections.

Source: Internal Revenue Service (IRS)/https://www.irs.gov/pub/irs-pdf/f1040sc.pdf./Public domain/ last accessed on March 21, 2025.

Refund	34	If line 33 is more than line 24, subtract line 24 from line 33. This is the amount you **overpaid**		34
	35a	Amount of line 34 you want **refunded to you.** If Form 8888 is attached, check here ☐		35a
Direct deposit? See instructions.	b	Routing number	c Type: ☐ Checking ☐ Savings	
	d	Account number		
	36	Amount of line 34 you want **applied to your 2025 estimated tax**	36	
Amount You Owe	37	Subtract line 33 from line 24. This is the **amount you owe.** For details on how to pay, go to *www.irs.gov/Payments* or see instructions		37
	38	Estimated tax penalty (see instructions)	38	

If you've underpaid your taxes, you'll see a number in the other part of this section, **Amount You Owe**. That number, **what you owe,** aka **your tax bill, appears on line 37**. If you were required to pay estimated taxes but didn't or if you underpaid them, you'll also see a number on **line 38,** which is your **estimated tax penalty**.[4]

YOUR SIGNATURE(S), TAX PREPARER, AND THIRD-PARTY INFO

This last section has no numbers, but you need to check it (Figure 11.6). If you don't sign your tax return, it isn't valid. In this era of electronic filing, you won't be able to submit your tax return without the proper signatures. Also, please note that your signature is your consent to file. If you work with an accountant, that's their signal to submit it. Don't sign your tax return until you've reviewed it.

Note that if you are married filing jointly, both of you must sign and date the return. You are not allowed to sign for your spouse. Here's a reminder that each spouse has full responsibility for everything on a joint

Figure 11.6 1040 third-party designee.

Source: Internal Revenue Service (IRS)/https://www.irs.gov/pub/irs-pdf/f1040sc.pdf/Public domain/ last accessed on March 21, 2025.

Third Party Designee	Do you want to allow another person to discuss this return with the IRS? See instructions ☐ **Yes.** Complete below. ☐ **No**					
	Designee's name		Phone no.		Personal identification number (PIN)	
Sign Here	Under penalties of perjury, I declare that I have examined this return and accompanying schedules and statements, and to the best of my knowledge and belief, they are true, correct, and complete. Declaration of preparer (other than taxpayer) is based on all information of which preparer has any knowledge.					
	Your signature		Date	Your occupation	If the IRS sent you an Identity Protection PIN, enter it here (see inst.)	
Joint return? See instructions. Keep a copy for your records.	Spouse's signature. If a joint return, **both** must sign.		Date	Spouse's occupation	If the IRS sent your spouse an Identity Protection PIN, enter it here (see inst.)	
	Phone no.		Email address			
Paid Preparer Use Only	Preparer's name	Preparer's signature		Date	PTIN	Check if: ☐ Self-employed
	Firm's name				Phone no.	
	Firm's address				Firm's EIN	

tax return. Each spouse should review the return and ask any questions that it brings up. It's very important, you're on the hook, and now is the time.

This is also the place to put your IRS-provided identity protection PIN, if you've been sent one because of a past identity theft issue/ID security concern.[5] You will not be able to submit your return or have the IRS accept it without this PIN. That's a good thing. This mechanism prevents a fraudster from filing a fake return in your name.

If someone besides you prepared your tax return, then their info goes in the Paid Preparer Use Only section. Just because someone prepared your return does not give the IRS the right to talk to them about your return.[6] If you want to grant them that permission, you'll need to specify that at the top, in the Third Party Designee section. Feel no pressure to authorize this. But if you want this tax preparer to be able to discuss your return with the IRS should you receive any letters or need to communicate about your return, this is where to do it.

REVIEW YOUR SCHEDULE C

We've talked a lot about the Schedule C to this point, but there are a few numbers to review each year, before filing your completed tax return (see Figure 11.7).

The most important number to check is **gross receipts or sales; Part I, line 1** of your **Schedule C**.[7] This number should accurately state how much total income you received from your self-employment. If this number doesn't match your bookkeeping, then you may have missed reporting a 1099 or are double-counting some of your income. This is your chance to go back and see if your 1099s were all properly attributed to your Schedule C, that they are all accounted for, and no income is double-counted. You also need to make sure that whatever additional

Figure 11.7 HERE—Schedule C, Part 1.

Source: Internal Revenue Service (IRS)/https://www.irs.gov/pub/irs-pdf/f1040sc.pdf./Public domain/ last accessed on March 21, 2025.

SCHEDULE C (Form 1040)	Profit or Loss From Business	OMB No. 1545-0074
	(Sole Proprietorship)	2024
Department of the Treasury Internal Revenue Service	Attach to Form 1040, 1040-SR, 1040-SS, 1040-NR, or 1041; partnerships must generally file Form 1065. Go to *www.irs.gov/ScheduleC* for instructions and the latest information.	Attachment Sequence No. 09
Name of proprietor		Social security number (SSN)

A Principal business or profession, including product or service (see instructions)   **B Enter code from instructions**

C Business name. If no separate business name, leave blank.   **D Employer ID number (EIN) (see instr.)**

E Business address (including suite or room no.)
City, town or post office, state, and ZIP code
F Accounting method: (1) ☐ Cash (2) ☐ Accrual (3) ☐ Other (specify)
G Did you "materially participate" in the operation of this business during 2024? If "No," see instructions for limit on losses ☐ Yes ☐ No
H If you started or acquired this business during 2024, check here ☐
I Did you make any payments in 2024 that would require you to file Form(s) 1099? See instructions ☐ Yes ☐ No
J If "Yes," did you or will you file required Form(s) 1099? ☐ Yes ☐ No

Part I   Income

1	Gross receipts or sales. See instructions for line 1 and check the box if this income was reported to you on Form W-2 and the "Statutory employee" box on that form was checked ☐	1
2	Returns and allowances	2
3	Subtract line 2 from line 1	3
4	Cost of goods sold (from line 42)	4
5	**Gross profit.** Subtract line 4 from line 3	5
6	Other income, including federal and state gasoline or fuel tax credit or refund (see instructions)	6
7	**Gross income.** Add lines 5 and 6	7

self-employment income you had (that wasn't reported on a 1099) is accurately reflected in this total.

Sometimes your software or accountant will misattribute a 1099 to "other income" when it's rightfully self-employment income that belongs on your Schedule C. If this happens, you'll see that 1099 amount appear on line 8 of your Schedule 1. Now's the time to correct it.

Next, take a look at your expenses in part II of Schedule C (see Figure 11.8).[8] If you realize there's a blank area where you know you had expenses, now is your chance to go dig up that last business expense. I recommend comparing your current year's Schedule C expenses to the prior year's, as that will prompt you about a missed category.

Next, note your **total expenses** on **line 28**.[9] Remember that unlike your income, your expenses will differ a little bit from the total in your books, so that is not a concern here. But it might be interesting to see the difference between your expenses allowed on your tax return vs. those in your books. Note that line 28 shows you expenses before any

Figure 11.8 HERE—Schedule C, Part 2.

Source: Internal Revenue Service (IRS)/https://www.irs.gov/pub/irs-pdf/f1040sc.pdf./Public domain/ last accessed on March 21, 2025.

Part II **Expenses.** Enter expenses for business use of your home **only** on line 30.

8	Advertising	8		18	Office expense (see instructions)	18	
9	Car and truck expenses (see instructions)	9		19	Pension and profit-sharing plans	19	
				20	Rent or lease (see instructions):		
10	Commissions and fees	10		a	Vehicles, machinery, and equipment	20a	
11	Contract labor (see instructions)	11		b	Other business property	20b	
12	Depletion	12		21	Repairs and maintenance	21	
13	Depreciation and section 179 expense deduction (not included in Part III) (see instructions)	13		22	Supplies (not included in Part III)	22	
				23	Taxes and licenses	23	
				24	Travel and meals:		
14	Employee benefit programs (other than on line 19)	14		a	Travel	24a	
				b	Deductible meals (see instructions)	24b	
15	Insurance (other than health)	15		25	Utilities	25	
16	Interest (see instructions):			26	Wages (less employment credits)	26	
a	Mortgage (paid to banks, etc.)	16a		27a	Other expenses (from line 48)	27a	
b	Other	16b		b	Energy efficient commercial bldgs deduction (attach Form 7205)	27b	
17	Legal and professional services	17					

28	**Total expenses** before expenses for business use of home. Add lines 8 through 27b	28	
29	Tentative profit or (loss). Subtract line 28 from line 7	29	
30	Expenses for business use of your home. Do not report these expenses elsewhere. Attach Form 8829 unless using the simplified method. See instructions. **Simplified method filers only:** Enter the total square footage of (a) your home: ______ and (b) the part of your home used for business: ______. Use the Simplified Method Worksheet in the instructions to figure the amount to enter on line 30	30	
31	**Net profit or (loss).** Subtract line 30 from line 29. • If a profit, enter on both **Schedule 1 (Form 1040), line 3,** and on **Schedule SE, line 2.** (If you checked the box on line 1, see instructions.) Estates and trusts, enter on **Form 1041, line 3.** • If a loss, you **must** go to line 32.	31	
32	If you have a loss, check the box that describes your investment in this activity. See instructions. • If you checked 32a, enter the loss on both **Schedule 1 (Form 1040), line 3,** and on **Schedule SE, line 2.** (If you checked the box on line 1, see the line 31 instructions.) Estates and trusts, enter on **Form 1041, line 3.** • If you checked 32b, you **must** attach **Form 6198.** Your loss may be limited.	32a ☐ All investment is at risk. 32b ☐ Some investment is not at risk.	

calculation is made for your home office/studio. This is because you only get to take a home office deduction if you have a profit. **Line 30** tells you what your **home office deduction** is.[10]

Lastly, note **line 31**, where your **profit** (or **loss**) is listed.[11] It's good to have a sense of what this number is each year. Also, if you have a loss, you want to keep an eye on your numbers and aim to increase your profit so you don't continue to have a series of losses on your Schedule C. This will put you on the wrong side of the Hobby Loss Rule.

If you find that you're almost profitable, but not quite, it can be worth sacrificing a few of your deductions to be able to have a profit on your Schedule C that will count toward the three out of five-year Hobby Loss threshold. You are allowed to not take every deduction you're entitled to. But don't get confused; you still have a legal obligation to report every dollar of income.[12]

Figure 11.9 HERE—Schedule C, Part 3.

Source: Internal Revenue Service (IRS)/https://www.irs.gov/pub/irs-pdf/f1040sc.pdf./Public domain/
last accessed on March 21, 2025.

Part III	**Cost of Goods Sold** (see instructions)

33	Method(s) used to value closing inventory: a ☐ Cost b ☐ Lower of cost or market c ☐ Other (attach explanation)	
34	Was there any change in determining quantities, costs, or valuations between opening and closing inventory? If "Yes," attach explanation	☐ Yes ☐ No
35	Inventory at beginning of year. If different from last year's closing inventory, attach explanation . . .	35
36	Purchases less cost of items withdrawn for personal use	36
37	Cost of labor. Do not include any amounts paid to yourself	37
38	Materials and supplies	38
39	Other costs	39
40	Add lines 35 through 39	40
41	Inventory at end of year	41
42	**Cost of goods sold.** Subtract line 41 from line 40. Enter the result here and on line 4	42

Finally, on the second page of your Schedule C, you'll find Part III, the Cost of Goods Sold calculation (see Figure 11.9).[13] You may want to note **line 41**, your **inventory at end of year,** because you will need this number on next year's tax return, where it will become your new **line 35, inventory at beginning of year.**[14] And note **line 42**, which is your actual **cost of goods sold.**[15]

If you're an Independent Artist, Writer, or Performer using the NAICS code 711510, you're allowed to take advantage of the COGS exception,[16] in which case this section will be blank. You're done with the numbers!

YOUR SIGNATURE IS YOUR CONSENT TO FILE

Once you're satisfied that you understand the basic numbers and you've checked the ID and bank account info, you're done reviewing your tax return. Your signature on your tax return is the signal to your accountant, if you have one, that you've reviewed it and consent to file. Don't sign it until this is true. If you're using tax software, you can now sign it and hit the "submit" button.

Remember that this document is yours. It's a tool you can use at any time of year, when you need to reference various income types and taxes paid. All tax software and all tax preparers are required to give you a copy of your signed return.[17] Have it, review it, save it (for seven years), and refer to it whenever you need to.

You're done!

CHAPTER SUMMARY

- Always review your tax return before filing. This applies to your spouse too if you file jointly. You're each signing a legal document, so make sure everything is correct.
- The first two pages summarize everything in your tax return. Reviewing them gives you an overview and helps you spot errors before they become headaches.
- Check all ID info for your household members: names, Social Security numbers, and addresses. Check that your filing status is the one you chose.
- The income section summarizes all your reported income by type (W2, self-employed, investment, etc.). It includes your total income, adjusted gross income (AGI), and taxable income.
- Do you itemize? Line 12 will tell you if you take the standard deduction or itemize.
- Tax and Credits: This section summarizes your total tax and any credits you receive. Check Schedule 2 for additional taxes and Schedule 3 for additional credits and payments.

- Your total tax is on line 24. Use this number to meet safe harbor threshold number one for your estimated quarterly taxes.
- Payments Section: This section shows the taxes you've already paid. Ensure your estimated tax payments are reported correctly on line 26.
- Refund/amount you owe: This section shows if you overpaid or underpaid your taxes. If you overpaid, you'll see a refund amount. If you underpaid, you'll see the amount you still owe.
- Signature and preparer info: Ensure you and your spouse (if filing jointly) sign the return. If you have an IRS-provided identity protection PIN, include it here.
- Review Your Schedule C: Check your gross receipts or sales on line 1. Ensure all income is reported accurately. Review your expenses in Part II and compare them to the prior year. Note your total expenses on line 28 and your profit or loss on line 31.
- Cost of goods sold: If applicable, review Part III for the cost of goods sold calculation. Note your inventory at the end of the year on line 41 and your actual cost of goods sold on line 42.
- Once you're satisfied with your review, sign your tax return. This signals your consent to file. Keep a copy of your signed return for your records.
- Let that relief wash over you.

ENDNOTES

1. The 1040 instructions, which you can get from the blank 1040 form available on the IRS website, give you info if you need to list a PO box. Note that these instructions will answer almost any question you have about whether you entered something correctly, so definitely note those as a resource. Find them right here: https://www.irs.gov/instructions/i1040gi.
2. Form 1040-X.
3. Form 1040-X.

4. Form 1040-X.
5. See "Get an Identity Protection Pin (IP PIN)," *U.S. Department of the Treasury, Internal Revenue Service*, last modified January 27, 2025, https://www.irs.gov/identity-theft-fraud-scams/get-an-identity-protection-pin#:~:text=If%20you%20are%20a%20confirmed,from%20tax%2Drelated%20identity%20theft.
6. "Topic no. 312, Disclosure authorizations," *U.S. Department of the Treasury, Internal Revenue Service*, last modified August 29, 2024, https://www.irs.gov/taxtopics/tc312.
7. "2024 Instructions for Schedule C (2024)," C-6.
8. "2024 Instructions for Schedule C (2024)," C-15.
9. "2024 Instructions for Schedule C (2024)," C-12.
10. "2024 Instructions for Schedule C (2024)," C-11.
11. "2024 Instructions for Schedule C (2024)," C-15.
12. See "The Truth about Frivolous Arguments—Section 1 (A to C)," *U.S. Department of the Treasury, Internal Revenue Service*, last modified December 11, 2024, https://www.irs.gov/privacy-disclosure/the-truth-about-frivolous-arguments-section-i-a-to-c#voluntary ("Any taxpayer who has received more than a statutorily determined amount of gross income in a given tax year is obligated to file a return for that tax year. Failure to file a tax return could subject the non-compliant individual to civil and/or criminal penalties, including fines and imprisonment.")
13. "2024 Instructions for Schedule C (2024)," C-16.
14. "2024 Instructions for Schedule C (2024)," C-17.
15. "2024 Instructions for Schedule C (2024)," C-15.
16. "Adjusted gross income defined," *Code of Federal Regulations*, title 26 (1972): Section 62(a)(2)(B), https://www.law.cornell.edu/uscode/text/26/62; "Joint Committee Report JCS-10-87: General Explanation of the Tax Reform Act of 1986," *Tax Notes*, May 4, 1987, https://www.taxnotes.com/research/federal/legislative-documents/jct-blue-books/joint-committee-report-jcs-10-87-general-explanation-of-the/1r3py.
17. "Tax return preparer must furnish copy of return to taxpayer and must retain a copy or list," *Code of Federal Regulations*, title 26 (1972): Section 6107(a), https://www.law.cornell.edu/uscode/text/26/6107 ("Any person who is a tax return preparer with respect to any return or claim for refund shall furnish a completed copy of such return or claim to the taxpayer not later than the time such return or claim is presented for such taxpayer's signature.")

PART V

THE LEVEL-UP: SMARTER TAXES TO GET YOU MORE MONEY

T his is where you learn all the tax-related benefits that can help you save more and grow your money. The best part about using tax benefits is that it's the ultimate "work smarter, not harder." This is not about hustling more; it's about squeezing the most out of every dollar.

CHAPTER TWELVE

WHAT'S A TAX ENTITY, AND DO I NEED ONE?

A t a certain point in your business, you might decide to choose a "tax entity" that is different from a Schedule C (the default). Generally, you will do this because you have grown your income to a point where you will save money by forming a different tax entity, because you plan to take on investment from shareholders (aka sell equity in your business) or because you have multiple owners or are changing the ownership structure. Separately, you may also decide to form a "legal entity" (that's something different) for liability protection.

But what I see way too often is that people form a legal or tax entity because a friend did it, because an Instagram ad told them they would save tons of money by forming an S Corp, or because someone "businessy" said so.

Your business is unique, and not all legal and tax entities make sense for you. And some things, like an S Corp, can and should be done *later*, when you have the profit to support it and the administrative capacity to maintain it. A legal or tax entity comes with a cost and some legal and tax obligations.

LLCs[1] and S Corps can give you great benefits. But they can also cause you nightmares if you form them when they're not a good fit for your unique situation.

I never want you to form an entity without understanding what it means for your business. So let's get into it.

FIRST, ASK THESE QUESTIONS

Before you form a business entity, I want you to answer these very basic questions for yourself:

- Is this a *legal* entity or a *tax* entity?
- What is the purpose of forming this entity for my business?
- What new administrative tasks will having this entity require of me, and can I commit to those?
- How much will forming this entity cost, and what is the annual cost of maintaining it? Does that make sense for the size and income of my business?
- Does this entity give me an additional tax return to complete, and am I prepared to pay the additional cost of that, keep the tidy books required for that (either myself or by paying a bookkeeper), and get that tax return completed timely, which is one month earlier (March 15) than the personal income tax deadline (April 15)?
- Does having this entity make sense for my business?

If you answer all of these questions before you form your new entity, you'll never have to pay an accountant like me to help you navigate a nightmare mess. That's a great start.

TAX ENTITY VS. LEGAL ENTITY

The first confusing thing to sort out is that a **tax entity** and a **legal entity** are two different things.[2]

Let me warn you now: if you want tax advice, I recommend you stick to a tax professional. I know from years of confused clients that there are a lot of lawyers out there giving incorrect tax information. I don't give legal advice, because I'm not a lawyer. And of course, it's possible your lawyer is a tax lawyer or actually has some tax training. But don't assume they know taxes just because they're a smarty-pants with contracts.

What Is a Tax Entity?

In layperson's terms, your **tax entity** refers to the way you are taxed. If you are a sole proprietor or a single-member LLC (that hasn't elected a tax entity), you do not have a separate tax entity. You simply report your business income and expenses on your Schedule C on your personal income tax return (the 1040).

You may **elect** to form a separate tax entity.[3] You do this (and we're about to get into the details) either because it saves you money, because you plan to take on investors/sell equity in your company, or because you have or want a different ownership structure, like multiple owners. You cannot do it by accident or in your sleep. So if you aren't sure if you have a separate tax entity, *you probably don't*.

Having a **separate tax entity** means you have an additional tax return on top of your personal income tax return (aka your 1040). These are the possible tax entity types and the corresponding tax return they require:[4]

Nonseparate entities:	report their income on:	pay tax on that income on:
Sole proprietor	Schedule C on the 1040	1040, at their personal rate
Single-member LLC[5]	Schedule C on the 1040	1040, at their personal rate

Separate tax entities:	report their income on:	pay tax on that income on:
S Corporation	Form 1120 S	1040, at their personal rate
Partnership	Form 1065	1040, at their personal rate
C Corporation	Form 1120	Form 1120
Non-profit [501(c)(3)]	Form 990	Trick question! Exempt!

What Is a Legal Entity?

A **limited liability company (LLC)** is a **legal entity**, but not a tax entity. A legal entity is a legal structure that separates the business from the individual who owns it.[6] The purpose of forming an LLC is for *liability protection.*

How Does an LLC Work?

So how does that work? When you form an LLC, you place a legal shield in between your personal assets and your business assets. It's easier to understand this function by comparing it to what happens when you don't have an LLC. When you operate a business and don't have an LLC, you're called a **sole proprietor.**[7] As a sole proprietor, you and your business are one and the same. If you hurt someone and they sue you for it, 100% of your assets are open to being claimed for damages.[8] If you have to pay damages, your available assets will include not just your business assets but also everything you own personally, like your home, your car, your 401(k), and your kids' college funds.

When you form an LLC, you create a liability shield—literally you limit your liability.[9] This means if you get sued for something you do in your business (or one of your employees does, etc.), then of course you still have to pay damages if you're found at fault. But the lawsuit stops at the door to your home. None of your personal assets can be touched—only your business assets. Most people's wealth is held in personal assets, not business assets. If you were to sue my business, Sunlight Tax LLC (please don't), anything I might owe in damages would be limited to what Sunlight Tax owns. And since I run an online business, that's not much more than a laptop and a bunch of software subscriptions.

But there is a flipside to that. When you create this liability shield in between you and your business, essentially saying that the two things are separate, you need to act in a way that upholds that separation. A dedicated business bank account is a good idea for everyone, but it is *mandatory* when you have an LLC. Furthermore, it is mandatory that you maintain the separation of your business and personal assets by only using your business account and business credit card to pay for business expenses.[10]

In the worst-case scenario, if you use your business debit card to pay for personal expenses like rent, clothing, and groceries, and then you get sued, your bank records can be subpoenaed, and the fuzziness between your business and personal accounts comes to light, and the judge can invalidate your LLC protection.[11] Now those lawsuit damages can include your house, your savings, etc. This is called "piercing the liability veil." In other words, you can pay good money to have a lawyer set up an LLC for you and good money to maintain that LLC each year. And you can find yourself completely without the protection you thought you had if you get sloppy with your accounting.

How Does the IRS See My LLC?

The IRS ignores it.

Many people assume that an LLC changes their taxes. It doesn't. As long as you are a *single-member* LLC (that means you are one owner), then your taxes are totally the same as they were before you formed the LLC. No tax change.

Here's your proof: the IRS calls single-member LLCs "disregarded entities."[12]

Any guesses why?

Because the IRS *disregards* them. Yes, really. An LLC is irrelevant to how you file your taxes. If you had a Schedule C yesterday and then you form an LLC, you still have a Schedule C today. No change in your taxes.

This is different if you are a *multi*member LLC. If you are multimember, meaning there's more than one owner of the LLC, then the IRS needs more info.

Why? Because while it's easy for them to know who to send the tax bill to when the LLC has a single member (you), with multiple members, you're sharing income. The IRS doesn't know who to send that tax bill to without you doing some paperwork to tell them. Like, do you and your partner split profits 50/50? Or is it 90/10? You have to tell them so you can each pay the right amount of tax.

An LLC Can Layer on Top of *Any* Tax Entity

So in the case of a multimember LLC, you will be taxed as a partnership by *default*. However, if you prefer, you can elect to be taxed as something different instead, like an S Corporation or a C Corporation. In either case, the income from your business will no longer be reported on a Schedule C.

When you're a single-member LLC, there's still only one person to send the tax bill to. And believe me, the IRS has your number on that. And by "has your number," I mean they have your Social Security number, which is legally attached to your LLC's Employer Identification Number (EIN). If you don't remember or a lawyer did it for you, you got a new EIN when you filed your LLC formation paperwork on your Secretary of State's website.[13] So yes, literally, they have your number. Both of them, actually.

Single-member LLCs have a default tax filing, too.[14] Just as a multi-member LLC defaults to being taxed as a partnership, but can elect to be taxed as something different, a single-member LLC defaults to being taxed on a Schedule C, but can also elect to be taxed as something different. You can start out as a single-member LLC, taxed on a Schedule C, and then later decide you want to form an S Corp and do your tax filing on an 1120 S.

To use myself as an example, my company, Sunlight Tax, is owned solely by me. When I first started Sunlight Tax, I reported my business profits on a Schedule C. Then I formed an LLC, and I still filed a Schedule C. No change. Then, several years later, once it made sense (that is, once I was making enough money to break even on it, and I had the administrative capacity to run payroll), I filed the paperwork with the IRS to elect to be taxed as an S Corporation. Once the IRS approved my S Corp, I then started filing a separate corporate return (an 1120 S) for Sunlight Tax. But I kept the LLC, because I still want liability protection for my personal assets. In my art practice, I started out with a Schedule C, I still have a Schedule C, and until the day I hang up my smock, I will continue to have a Schedule C. Nothing there has changed.

How Do You Form an LLC?

To form an LLC, you file paperwork with the Secretary of State in your state. Officially, what happens is that your name and Social Security number get legally tied to a business name and, if you choose to get one, an EIN. You generally want the help of an attorney, so you can be sure you're dotting all your i's. An attorney will help you draw up your Articles of Organization, which tell the state your business's name, purpose, location, and management structure.[15] They might offer to do a name search to be sure you're not trying to use a name that is already claimed by another business.

GET A PO BOX IF YOU DON'T WANT YOUR ADDRESS MADE PUBLIC

All LLCs in each state are searchable and public.[16] You will be required to list a business address, and this information is publicly available. If you have threatening people in your life or from your past, then this is the time to get yourself a PO box.

NEW RULES FOR LLCS

In 2024, a new law, called the Corporate Transparency Act, was passed that required all LLCs[17] to file a simple information report to identify the "beneficial owner(s)" of your LLC.[18] The report is called a Beneficial Ownership Information Report (BOIR).[19] This was a good law—its purpose was to prevent financial crimes that are enabled by unidentified owners of LLCs. There was confusing back and forth due to litigation challenging the law, and ultimately, it was ended. But while the BOI report is no longer required at the federal level, similar state laws, like the New York LLC Transparency Act, are still in effect. Note that at the time of my writing, if you have a New York–based LLC, you will need to comply with that law. Since other states may pass similar laws between the time of my writing and you reading this, it's a good idea to check with your state for any new LLC laws.

How Do You Maintain Your LLC?

After the initial formation paperwork, which will be the most expensive part of forming your LLC (specifically, your lawyer's fee), you will need to do some simple maintenance each year to keep your LLC in good standing.[20] This varies by state, but in general, you'll need to pay a fee to your Secretary of State and affirmatively check that your articles of incorporation are up-to-date.[21] Be aware that if your LLC is not up-to-date, that is also publicly available information.

Do You Need an LLC?

Not necessarily. Remember that an LLC is for liability protection. If you're not particularly concerned with liability, then what are you doing getting an LLC?

You do not need an LLC to get an EIN. You can grab one of those off the IRS website in less than five minutes and for free, if you need it, say, for sales tax purposes.

You don't need an LLC to operate under a different business name. You can do that by filing **Doing Business As (DBA)** paperwork with your state.[22]

You don't need an LLC to be "official." Do a quick Internet search or check the Secretary of State's website for your state to see what local registration requirements you are subject to in your area and for your field.[23] Some groups, like health and beauty practitioners, will need to register their business because they are subject to health and safety laws. You may or may not need to register your business, but you should definitely check to see what your state, county, and city requires.

You don't need an LLC to collect sales tax. To collect sales tax, you need to register your business with the Department of Revenue/Tax[24] for your state. This is important because it's illegal to collect sales tax before you are registered with your state. It's also illegal to not collect the sales tax that you are required to. So the key here is to get thee to your Department of Revenue, scan their sales tax FAQs to see if your sales are subject to sales tax, and get yourself registered. I also like the Tax Jar blog for good info on determining if you have what is called **sales tax nexus** in a given state or municipality.[25] Having nexus is the key determining factor of whether you owe sales tax and where.

Another Protection Option: Business Liability Insurance

You don't need an LLC as your only option for liability protection. However, liability protection is the job of the LLC, so if that's the concern, you are in the right zone. Another option is **business liability insurance**. This can be cheaper than forming and maintaining an LLC. But be aware that liability insurance and an LLC do slightly different things.[26] The LLC shields your personal assets from a lawsuit. That's great, and you may want that. I do! That's why I have one. But you may want money to help get you through various business disaster scenarios, and that is the role of insurance. Your LLC isn't going to give you a car rental if your delivery van is out of service for a time or pay for legal counsel if you need it. Insurance can do those things. So you may choose one, both, or neither. Your liability is something you should carefully assess and determine what your needs and budget are.

You definitely don't need an LLC to save you money on taxes. It won't. Choosing a tax entity is a separate decision from forming an LLC. You don't need to do it at the same time, and the reason for doing it is totally different: tax structure vs. liability protection.

The Word Corporation Is Super Confusing

I've noticed that the word *corporation* is used very differently by accountants vs. lawyers vs. the IRS. And I believe this is a big source of confusion.

Here's my take. When the IRS uses the word *corporation*, it's usually referring to only C Corporations.[27] To the IRS, this makes sense because C Corporations are the only corporations that pay corporate tax. All Schedule C businesses, S Corporations, and Partnerships *pay taxes* on their business profit on their personal income tax returns (that is the definition of a "pass-through" entity).[28] C Corporations are the only businesses that *pay taxes on their own corporate tax return, at the corporate tax rate*. That's what the IRS cares about.

Likewise, when politicians talk about corporations, they are also usually referring to C Corporations. Why? Because they are interacting with the IRS and changes to tax law. So they are often aligning with the IRS way of using the word corporation.

When accountants talk about corporations, they are usually referring to *all* of the separate tax entities.[29] So that isn't just C Corporations, but also S Corporations and Partnerships. The reason accountants think of it this way is because accountants are busy preparing the *corporate* tax returns of those entities and are under a March 15 deadline to get it all done (vs. *personal* tax returns, which are due on April 15). Your accountant will usually go out for a round of beers on March 16 to celebrate making it to the "corporate" tax deadline. This is a huge part of their workload, which is why they orient to that definition of corporation.

Lastly, although it's incorrect, you may hear people use the word *corporation* to refer to LLCs.[30] LLC stands for Limited Liability *Company*, not corporation. An LLC actually *isn't* a corporation.[31] But you'd be surprised how common this mistake is even among lawyers and accountants.

Keep in mind that this is my own personal assessment of these groups. But I hope you find it sheds some light on the confusing word *corporation*. Now you'll understand that when you Google a question about corporations, the organization that's behind the answer is going to determine which kind of corporation they are even talking about.

WHEN TO FORM AN S CORPORATION?

A **tax entity** is the tax structure of a business.[32] It generally dictates how you'll be taxed, how many parties are being taxed, and for what portion of the business profits. It can also dictate additional financial structures, like the number and type of shareholders that are allowed and how those shareholders will be taxed.

If you have multiple owners of your business or you plan to sell equity in the business or register with the Securities and Exchange Commission and get listed on a stock exchange, then deciding what tax entity to be is a key decision, with many factors to consider.

But if you're a solo business owner (no other owners), not planning to sell equity, then the primary reason to form a different tax entity is to save money on self-employment tax. When the time is right, and that means when you have a high enough profit that you will break even on the expenses of doing so, it might make sense for you to elect to form an S Corporation.

Figure 12.1 shows you when it might be time for you to consider forming an S Corporation and when it isn't.

If you're a good candidate for forming an S Corporation, forming one can save you money on taxes. But it is important to know what your obligations are and if the math of tax savings will work *for you*. I've seen a lot of people get bogged down in accounting fees and admin they aren't prepared to handle, as well as seen some nightmare scenarios that are even worse. So don't jump into an S Corporation formation without understanding how it affects you first.

I have an article on my website to give you all the information you need about how an S Corp works, what money it can save you, and what your new obligations will be, once you form it. I include info on the other types of tax entities as well. That's at www.sunlighttax.com/taxesforhumans.

Figure 12.1   When to consider forming an S Corp.
Source: © Hannah Cole/Sunlight Tax.

When to consider forming an S Corporation

- You're consistently making over $60k in <u>profit</u>

- You are set up on bookkeeping software and consistently keeping books, or are ready to do so

- You are not in New York City. These states also have rules that can lessen the S Corp savings: California, Illinois, New Jersey, Minnesota, and Tennessee.

- You're starting to have more money than time, and are ready to pay for professional bookkeeping <u>and</u> accounting

- You have the administrative capacity to set up (or pay to have set up) and run payroll and stay compliant with state employment law

- You have enough consistent profit to pay yourself a salary each month, with money left over

- You can afford the effort and expense of an additional tax return (1120S) with an earlier deadline (3/15)

CHAPTER SUMMARY

- When to form a tax entity other than a Schedule C: if your income has grown, you plan to take on investors, or you have multiple owners.
- Always consider your unique needs before forming an LLC or an S Corp. Don't get stuck with an entity you can't handle or afford, or that is a bad choice for your situation. Only you know the inside scoop on your business.
- LLCs and S Corps can have benefits but also come with costs and admin obligations.
- Before forming a new entity, ask yourself if it's legal or tax-related, its purpose, new administrative tasks, costs, and if it makes sense for your business.
- Tax entity vs. legal entity: Understand the difference; tax entities affect how you're taxed, while legal entities offer liability protection.
- An LLC separates your personal and business assets, protecting your personal assets from business-related lawsuits.
- Single-member LLCs are "disregarded entities" for tax purposes, meaning there's no change to your taxes when you form one.
- Forming and maintaining an LLC: File paperwork with your state's Secretary of State, maintain separation of business and personal assets, and check for state laws that may affect you, like the New York LLC Transparency Act.
- Business liability insurance is another option for protection.
- Form an S Corp to save on self-employment tax if your profit is high enough to justify the new costs and the additional administrative challenges. Check that your state doesn't tax back all your savings—some do.

ENDNOTES

1. "Limited liability company (LLC)," *U.S. Department of Treasury, Internal Revenue Service*, last modified October 8, 2024, https://www.irs.gov/businesses/small-businesses-self-employed/limited-liability-company-llc#:~:text=For%20income%20tax%20purposes%2C%20an,still%20considered%20a%20separate%20entity.

2. "Frequently asked questions - Entities 3," *U.S. Department of Treasury, Internal Revenue Service*, last modified October 21, 2024, https://www.irs.gov/faqs/small-business-self-employed-other-business/entities/entities-3.

3. So long as you meet the IRS criteria for that entity. See this FAQ on the IRS website for more: https://www.irs.gov/businesses/small-businesses-self-employed/business-structures.

4. "Choose a business structure," *U.S. Small Business Administration*, accessed December 3, 2024, https://www.sba.gov/business-guide/launch-your-business/choose-business-structure (providing a brief overview of different types of tax entities and their formation).

5. That has not elected a separate tax entity type.

6. "Limited liability company (LLC)," *U.S. Department of Treasury, Internal Revenue Service*, last modified October 8, 2024, https://www.irs.gov/businesses/small-businesses-self-employed/limited-liability-company-llc.

7. "Sole proprietorships," *U.S. Department of Treasury, Internal Revenue Service*, last modified December 13, 2024, https://www.irs.gov/businesses/small-businesses-self-employed/sole-proprietorships#:~:text=A%20sole%20proprietor%20is%20someone,are%20not%20a%20sole%20proprietor.

8. George D. Lambert, "How to Protect Your Assets From a Lawsuit or Creditors," *Investopedia*, last modified April 11, 2024, https://www.investopedia.com/articles/retirement/07/buildawall.asp.

9. "Single member limited liability companies."

10. Marco Carbajo, "5 Ways to Separate Your Personal and Business Finances," *U.S. Small Business Administration*, February 22, 2019, https://www.sba.gov/blog/5-ways-separate-your-personal-business-finances.

11. Nikki Nelson, "Piercing the veil of limited liability results in personal exposure," *Wolters Kluwer,* last modified March 12, 2021, https://www.wolterskluwer.com/en/expert-insights/piercing-the-veil-of-limited-liability-results-in-personal-exposure.

12. "Single member limited liability companies," *U.S. Department of Treasury, Internal Revenue Service,* last modified August 22, 2024, https://www.irs.gov/businesses/small-businesses-self-employed/single-member-limited-liability-companies.

13. "When to get a new EIN," *U.S. Department of Treasury, Internal Revenue Service,* last modified November 25, 2024, https://www.irs.gov/businesses/small-businesses-self-employed/when-to-get-a-new-ein.

14. "Single member limited liability companies."

15. Ali Hussain, "Articles of Organization: Definition, What's Included, and Filing," *Investopedia,* last modified August 8, 2024, https://www.investopedia.com/terms/a/articles-of-organization.asp.

16. Matt Horwitz, "Secretary of State Business Entity Search (all 50 states)," *LLC University,* last modified April 24, 2024, https://www.llcuniversity.com/50-secretary-of-state-sos-business-entity-search/.

17. And any entity formed through a filing with your state's Secretary of State, so this may also include DBAs and more, in some states.

18. "Notice to Customers: Beneficial Ownership Information Reference Guide," *Financial Crimes Enforcement Network (FinCEN),* July 26, 2024, https://www.fincen.gov/sites/default/files/shared/BOI-Notice-to-Customers-508FINAL.pdf.

19. "Notice to Customers: Beneficial Ownership Information Reference Guide."

20. Jennifer Woodside, "I have an LLC, now what? 7 things you should do after you form an LLC," *Wolters Kluwer,* last modified July 15, 2024, https://www.wolterskluwer.com/en/expert-insights/i-have-an-llc-now-what.

21. Dave Griswold, "What is an LLC? Definition and steps on how to form an LLC," *Wolters Kluwer,* November 25, 2024, https://www.wolterskluwer.com/en/expert-insights/how-to-form-an-llc-what-is-an-llc-advantages-disadvantages-and-more.

22. "Doing business as (DBA): The "AKA" for your business," *Wolters Kluwer,* last modified June 30, 2024, https://www.wolterskluwer.com/en/expert-insights/dba-the-aka-for-your-business#definition.

23. "Register your business," *U.S. Small Business Association,* last modified February 20, 2024, https://www.sba.gov/business-guide/launch-your-business/register-your-business.

24. Each state calls this something different. Just know this when you try to Google it. In North Carolina, it's the Department of Revenue. In Massachusetts, it's MassTaxConnect. I know Heidi Klum and Tim Gunn say that "matchy-matchy" is a fashion "don't," but when it comes to the states coordinating their

tax laws, I think it would be a serious citizen "do." See Gail Cole, "What are sales tax permits and does your business need one?," *Avalara*, January 30, 2024, https://www.avalara.com/blog/en/north-america/2019/03/sales-tax-permits-a-state-by-state-guide.html.

25. "Get up to speed on the basics of sales tax," *TaxJar*, accessed December 4, 2024, https://www.taxjar.com/sales-tax.

26. "Business Insurance for LLCs: What You Need To Know," *Practice*, April 18, 2023, https://practice.do/blog/business-insurance-for-llcs-what-you-need-to-know.

27. "Forming a corporation," *U.S. Department of Treasury, Internal Revenue Service*, last modified January 16, 2025, https://www.irs.gov/businesses/small-businesses-self-employed/forming-a-corporation.

28. "What are pass-through businesses?," *Tax Policy Center*, accessed December 4, 2024, https://taxpolicycenter.org/briefing-book/what-are-pass-through-businesses#:~:text=pass%2Dthrough%20businesses%3F-What%20are%20pass%2Dthrough%20businesses%3F,companies%2C%20and%20S%2Dcorporations.

29. Tad Simons, "S corp vs. C corp vs. LLC: What's the difference, and which one is better for your business?," *Thomson Reuters*, September 8, 2023, https://tax.thomsonreuters.com/blog/s-corp-vs-c-corp-vs-llc-whats-the-difference-and-which-one-is-better-for-your-business/.

30. Prince, Samantha J., and Joshua P. Fershee. "An LLC by Any Other Name Is Still Not a Corporation." *Seton Hall Law Review*, 54 (2024): 1105, https://ideas.dickinsonlaw.psu.edu/cgi/viewcontent.cgi?article=1458&context=fac-works ("It is an egregious, nearly unforgivable, error to call an LLC a "limited liability corporation."")

31. Prince and Fershee, "An LLC by Any Other Name Is Still Not a Corporation," 1107 ("The term limited liability 'corporation' is a misnomer. Limited liability 'corporations' do not exist. LLC is the abbreviation for a limited liability company.")

32. "Business structures," *U.S. Department of Treasury, Internal Revenue Service*, last modified October 2, 2024, https://www.irs.gov/businesses/small-businesses-self-employed/business-structures.

CHAPTER THIRTEEN

LEVEL UP YOUR WEALTH

There is so much to do when you're self-employed. You have to hustle to get more work, you have to hustle to *do* the work, and then there's the admin of running your own business. It's hard to remove yourself from the day-to-day parts of the business and the nonoptional parts (like doing taxes) to do the next-level stuff. But take a moment to envision the world you would be living in by taking time to use the skills of up-leveling your money. You could:

- Build financial security for your future
- Do bigger and better projects
- Gain more visibility and serve more people with your work
- Rest and recharge
- Take time off for family or illness

So often, ethical people doing world-changing work write off the idea of their own financial security. But building wealth is not just for your clients and the people you care about in your family and your community. It's for you, too. And that's important.

BE YOUR OWN HERO

Building wealth is possible for you. Wealth is not a windfall or an accident. It's the product of habit. A lot of us dismiss the idea of learning wealth-building habits. This may be part self-protection (what if I can't?) and part self-justification (what if I don't want to put in the effort?). We might harbor a fantasy that we'll just win the lottery, and then we'll be okay. But even a windfall like that isn't the solution you might dream of. The majority of lottery winners go bankrupt within seven years.[1] Think about that. Lottery winners end up worse than if they had never won the money. Why? Because they didn't have wealth-building habits. Winning money amplified the habits they already had—habits that were often money-losing.

Wealth building is a set of skills and habits. If you have bad habits, more money will amplify those. If you have good habits, more money will become even more.

I encourage you not to slip into the daydream of the hero on the white horse coming to your rescue. You have everything you need to get started building your wealth, right here in this book. Use the tools in this section, and you can be your own hero on the white horse.

HOW TAXES HELP YOU BUILD WEALTH

Taxes can help you build wealth (really!).

Building your savings muscle is the hard part. Especially in a capitalist economy, where you're bombarded with messages training you to spend money to solve all problems, even when half the time connecting with a friend, reusing an item you already have, or getting a good night's sleep will do the trick.

Once you can work that muscle, the rest is a learnable, wealth-building skillset that I call the Power Triangle. It's a magical trio that works together to:

1. Save like a millionaire, aka using **tax-advantaged accounts**.
2. Find hidden money, aka **tax planning**.
3. Growing your wealth, aka **investing**. This is not technically a tax thing, but by investing your money *inside* tax-advantaged accounts (see #1), you accelerate the growth of your investments, by lowering the cost of them (the taxes part).

Because this is primarily a tax book, this section is short and focused on #1 and #2, the strictly tax pieces. My goal is to introduce the concepts and whet your appetite for the real possibility of building wealth. I also want you to know that in my program, Money Bootcamp, I dig even deeper into these concepts, including #3, how to invest. If you want more, you can find my program at www.sunlighttax.com/moneybootcampimpact.

Each piece of the Power Triangle is its own wealth-building skill. When used together, you maximize every dollar to full advantage. The part I love so much about the Power Triangle is that it's not about working harder. It's not about earning more money. It's about getting more out of the money you have, without additional hustle. It's not just a path to wealth; it's a path to rest.

Ready? Let's dive in.

CHAPTER SUMMARY

- Yes, you're busy. But picture the results of leveling up your money: financial security, better projects, more visibility, time off for family or illness, and rest.
- Building wealth isn't just for your clients or community; it's for you, too.
- Habits build wealth, not windfalls. More money amplifies your existing habits, whether those are good or bad.
- Taxes can help you build wealth by saving in tax-advantaged accounts, and finding hidden money through tax planning.
- The power triangle: This trio of tax-smart saving, tax planning, and investing maximizes your money without extra hustle.
- Use the tools in this section to start building your wealth habit. You have everything you need to be your own hero.

ENDNOTE

1. "The Lottery Curse: Are Lottery Winners More Likely To Declare Bankruptcy?," *American Bankruptcy Institute*, accessed December 4, 2024, https://www.abi .org/feed-item/the-lottery-curse-are-lottery-winners-more-likely-to-declare-bankruptcy.

CHAPTER FOURTEEN

SAVE LIKE A MILLIONAIRE (TAX-ADVANTAGED ACCOUNTS)

T his part of the Power Triangle is where your dollars can go further. A dollar invested in a regular brokerage account earns less than a dollar invested through a tax-advantaged account.[1] Why? While both can be invested in the same thing, one is subject to less tax. When it comes to getting the best return on your investment, even seemingly small costs like taxes and fees reduce the power of compounding within that account. A tax-smart investment account grows your money faster.

To get more power out of your money, it pays to know what tax-advantaged accounts are available to you, how they work, and how to use them. Let's go.

WHAT IS A TAX-ADVANTAGED ACCOUNT?

A **tax-advantaged account** is an account that shelters money that would normally be subject to income tax from all or part of that tax.[2] I prefer **tax-smart accounts**, because it sounds nicer, but it's the same thing.

You may also hear the term *tax shelter*. While tax-advantaged accounts *are* a type of tax shelter, that particular phrase carries some baggage, since some tax shelters are illegal. *Illegal* tax shelters are hotly pursued by the IRS, for good reason. So while that's another way to say this, I'll avoid that phrase.

Tax-smart accounts are put into the tax code as an incentive. Because incentives work. The US government creates incentives to encourage citizens to do important things with our money that are in the government/society's interest. These include saving for retirement, paying for healthcare expenses, paying for higher education (which expands the tax base because it leads to higher earnings), and helping businesses grow so they can expand, hire, pay more tax, and grow the US gross domestic product (GDP).

How Do Tax-Smart Accounts Work?

How do they work? Here's how: typically, your income is subject to income tax. In the year you earn it, you pay tax on it. If you then invest some of it, you pay tax on the earnings of those investments when you sell them.

Tax-smart accounts work by allowing money that would normally be taxed to *not* be taxed, either in whole or in part.[3] Most tax-advantaged accounts work by lowering your taxable income by the amount you contribute, in the year you contribute. If the tax advantage happens like this, you generally will still pay tax on that money in the year you take it out of the investment, as with a **traditional IRA**. But some accounts (called **Roth**-style accounts) work in reverse.[4] In a Roth IRA, for example, you get no tax savings when you put the money in, but when you take the money out, it's tax-free. Think of traditional accounts as a tax savings on entry and Roth accounts as a tax savings on exit.

WHAT ALL TAX-ADVANTAGED ACCOUNTS SHARE

Tax-advantaged accounts exist to help boost your savings for big life expenses. The most common accounts are for retirement. But there are tax-smart accounts for healthcare savings, education expenses, disability expenses, and even commuting.

All tax-advantaged accounts have the same set of attributes. I'll start with the universal things they share and then review specific accounts available to you for retirement and for healthcare.

> There are other kinds of tax-smart accounts that I'm not covering in this book. If you want to learn about them, look into 529 plans and Coverdell plans for education expenses and ABLE accounts for disability-associated expenses. Some workplaces also offer small-dollar tax-advantaged plans for things like commuting.

All tax-smart accounts share these things:

- **An account purpose** (aka the reason the government is giving you an incentive).
- **A tax-savings benefit** (either a pretax "traditional" or a post-tax "Roth-style" benefit).
- **An annual contribution limit** (which increases a little each year). You can do a quick Internet search for this limit each year.
- **A contribution deadline** (for it to count for that year).
- **Contribution rules** (minimal).
- **Rules for withdrawing the money** (which include penalties if you don't follow the rules, and exceptions where you may withdraw the money early due to various hardship reasons).
- **Catch-up contribution allowances** (additional contribution amounts allowed after certain ages to help people who didn't start early "catch up" by making larger contributions. For retirement accounts, the age of eligibility is 50+. Other accounts' contribution ages can vary.
- **Income limitations to be eligible to contribute** (often but not always). These tax advantages are here to help people *who need help*. Once you're making big money, you may become ineligible for some of these tax benefits.

Tax-Advantaged Accounts Are for One Person, Not Two

Retirement accounts are individual, not shared. Even if you're married, it's important for each spouse to fund her own account to the max. You can, and absolutely should (unless you've got reason not to), make your spouse the beneficiary of your retirement accounts, in case you die before them.[5] But these accounts are a put-the-oxygen-mask-on-yourself situation.

Tax-Advantaged Accounts Are the Container

Tax-advantaged accounts are a container. A great container that has the Kevlar coating of protecting the money inside from some of the normal taxes. Inside that container, the money is still yours, and you have control over how it is invested. You do, in fact, need to invest this money. If you don't, it's just sitting there, gathering dust and losing value as inflation eats away at it. Do not think you're done once you've opened your tax-advantaged account at a brokerage. *You then need to allocate that money into investments* so that it grows.

> I know that making investment decisions may feel intimidating. But it is an important skill for your financial health. And it's learnable. You can read a book about it and get everything you need.[6] In my program, Money Bootcamp, I teach a great module on investing. If you're interested, that's at www.sunlighttax.com/moneybootcampimpact.

Example of Tax Savings in a Traditional Tax-Advantaged Account

Say you have income of $60,000, and you put a total of $10,000 into various **traditional** tax-advantaged accounts. Instead of calculating your tax on $60,000 of income, you'll calculate your tax based on $50,000 of income ($60,000 − $10,000 = $50,000). In other words, you've reduced your taxable income and therefore lowered your tax. We'll get into a little more detail on this later.

First, let's look at an example of the tax savings in a traditional account. To follow along at home, I recommend you pull up an online tax calculator for the current year—these are easily searched online.[7]

For example, Suki, a potter, makes $69,000 profit in her ceramics studio for 2025. All of it is self-employment income. For simplicity, let's say she has no other income and files as single.

> Note that tax rates change, and the standard deduction increases slightly each year. For this reason, if you make this calculation for a different tax year, you may get a slightly different result. This is one reason I like online tax calculators—they take all that into account.

Without using tax-advantaged accounts, her tax on $69,000 profit would be **$15,532**.

Now watch Suki's taxes decrease when she puts the maximum allowable contribution into a tax-advantaged retirement plan called a SEP IRA. The limit for a SEP IRA is 20% of your business profit. Since all of Suki's $69,000 is business profit, her SEP contribution limit is $13,800 ($69,000 × 20% = $13,800).

Her tax on $69,000 of self-employment income after she puts $13,800 into a SEP IRA is **$13,876**.

That's **$15,532 vs. $13,876**—a tax savings of $1,656.

Think about that. That savings is encouraging her to set aside money for her future security. Although she has to come up with the cash and agree to some rules about leaving it in the account for a length of time (to grow), it's still *her money*. Furthermore, because she determines her maximum contribution amount at tax time, she will receive that extra $1,656 of savings near the moment she needs the cash, effectively lowering the amount she needs to gather from $13,800 to $12,144 (that's $13,800 − $1,656 = $12,144). Put another way, she is only putting $12,144 into her retirement savings account out of her own pocket, and the US government is giving her an additional $1,656 to put in it.

That additional money has a huge impact on her total retirement savings after a career's worth of time invested. If Suki invested her $13,800 of SEP IRA funds *every year* into a mix of basic investments, at the conventionally accepted rate of return on stocks (8%), at the end of her career (40 years) she would have $3.4 million without the tax savings vs. $3.9 million from the tax-advantaged account. That's $500,000 extra in retirement savings because she used a tax-advantaged account for her investments. That's 15% more money. For free. Thanks, Uncle Sam.

Retirement Savings Accounts

Retirement accounts are the big guns of tax-smart accounts. You've probably heard some of these names before: 401k, Roth, or traditional IRA, right? There are a few more beyond those (SEP IRA, solo 401k). If you focus on just one type of tax-smart account, retirement accounts are the one. With the largest contribution limits, they can generate the biggest pile of money for you. If you create a habit of maxing out all of the tax-advantaged retirement accounts that you're allowed, every year, over the course of your entire career, and make sure the money inside your accounts is invested wisely, *you will have enough money to retire.* That is by design. If you take only one habit away from reading this book, this is the one that will set you up for lifetime financial security.

CALL ME BY MY NAME: FREEDOM

The word *retirement* brings up complicated feelings. Maybe it feels distant, or just plain impossible. I get it. But let's call this what it really is. F**k-you money. You are building a giant pile of money that allows you to say no to unhealthy situations (a bad marriage, a bad boss, a dead-end job) and yes to dream opportunities. Knowing that you have a pile of money growing that is big enough to eventually sustain you is real power. It's possible. And it's freedom.

Now let's go get that coin.

You may be able to contribute to more than one type of retirement account at the same time, especially if your income is on the lower side.[8] For example, you may be able to contribute to your workplace 401k as well as to a Roth IRA (which you do outside of work, on your own). Likewise, if you're fully self-employed you can contribute to both a SEP IRA *and* to a traditional IRA, for example, as long as your income is in the required range. But pay attention to the contribution deadlines, because they are not the same for all accounts, so your order of operations matters.

401k, 403b, and Solo 401k: Traditional

Don't assume these are just for employees. While most workplace retirement plans are either a 401k (in a for-profit company) or a 403b (if you work at a nonprofit or government agency), self-employed people also have the right to form their own individual 401k plan. This is called a "solo" 401k (but it's really just a 401k).

Most 401ks and 403bs are traditional style, as in you get a tax benefit the year that you contribute. You then pay taxes at your ordinary income tax rate in the year you withdraw the money.

Here are the nine key stats on traditional-style 401ks/403bs and solo 401ks[9]:

1. **Account purpose**

   To help you save more money for retirement.

2. **Tax-savings benefit**

   Any money contributed for the year is deducted from your taxable income, therefore reducing your taxes this year. If you're low-income, you may also qualify for the **saver's credit**,[10] which gives you additional tax savings.

3. **Annual contribution limit**

   The contribution limit to these accounts is adjusted upward annually by the IRS, but it's high. As I write this, the 2025 contribution limit to 401ks and 403bs is $23,500. View the current year rates at this link: www.irs.gov/retirement-plans/plan-participant-employee/retirement-topics-401k-and-profit-sharing-plan-contribution-limits.

4. **Deadline for contributions**

   December 31. At most workplaces, you contribute by automatically transferring a percentage of each paycheck into the account. This lovely feature automates your retirement savings, so you don't have to think about it; you don't feel the pinch of the contribution, since it never arrives in your bank account; and you're much more likely to actually make the contribution.

   Importantly, the IRS allows for you to make an *additional* lump-sum contribution to a 401k or 403b. This is a nice option if you set your automatic deferral too low and you want to put in more money as a late-in-the-year decision. To do this, however, you'll need to talk to your HR department. Although the IRS allows this, your individual employer might not. So have the conversation early rather than assume it's possible and losing out.

5. **Contribution rules**

Contribute by the annual deadline. Straightforward.

6. **Rules for withdrawing the money**

Normal distributions from a traditional 401k/403b are those made after age 59½. There is no penalty for withdrawing your money at this point.

At 72, you must begin withdrawing money from your traditional 401k/403b account (or before age 70½ if you reached 70½ before 1/1/20). This is called a **required minimum distribution (RMD)**.[11] As the name implies, yes, it is required. The reasoning is that the government gives you access to a tax shelter for a specific purpose—retirement—not to give you a blanket tax shelter for an endless amassing of wealth. The RMD ensures that you actually *use* your pile of money, more or less for the stated purpose.

If you take the money out before the age of 59½, you will pay ordinary income tax plus a 10% penalty. This is a counterincentive meant to keep you from touching it too early.

That said, there are a handful of exceptions to this early withdrawal penalty that help you access the money in case of emergency. This is very important, because studies have shown that Americans' biggest reason for not contributing to retirement accounts is their fear of needing that money in an emergency. The Biden administration and Congress passed the Secure 2.0 Act to allow more emergency withdrawals.

Here are some qualified exceptions for an early withdrawal without penalty[12]:

1. Total and permanent disability
2. Loss of employment when you are at least age 55

3. A qualified domestic relations order after a divorce
4. Parents may withdraw up to $5,000 penalty-free within a year of birth or adoption for qualified expenses
5. IRS-granted disaster relief
6. Domestic abuse

The complete list of exceptions to the 10% early withdrawal penalty is available at www.irs.gov/retirement-plans/plan-participant-employee/retirement-topics-exceptions-to-tax-on-early-distributions.

7. **Catch-up contribution allowances**

   You can add an additional $7,500 to a 401k/403b if you're over 50. The Secure 2.0 Act created an additional catch-up contribution for folks aged 60, 61, 62, and 63. Starting in 2025, that higher catch-up limit is $11,250 instead of $7,500.

8. **Income limitations to be eligible to contribute**

   None. That's one reason to prioritize funding your 401k/403b over other accounts, like an IRA.

9. **Special note on prioritizing your 401k/403b**

   If you or your spouse have a workplace retirement plan, always max that out **first**, before contributing to an IRA.[13] Because:

   • There may be employer matching, aka free money.
   • Your ability to contribute to an IRA can be limited when your salary crosses a threshold and you have a workplace plan, even if you don't use it.
   • The workplace plan contribution deadline (December 31) is earlier than the IRA deadline (April 15).

Most workplace 401ks and 403bs are traditional, but more and more Roth plans are available. You might get a choice, and you might not. While there are real reasons to pick one over the other, it's awesome to have access to a 401k/403b at all. Don't get too hung up on only having access to the one

that isn't your first choice. When I see someone hand-wringing over the choice between a Roth and traditional account, my first question is always, "Are you maxing out yours?" That's a much more important question. Remember not to sweat the small stuff as a way to avoid the big stuff. If you're maxing out your account, I don't care which type it is.

Roth-Style 401k/403b

Most 401k/403bs offered by employers are traditional style, not Roth. But Roth 401ks/403bs are increasingly available. As with any Roth-style account, you don't get a current-year tax benefit, but get the tax benefit when you take the money out. The Roth 401k/403b rules are similar to the traditional 401k/403b rules, except for the withdrawal rules:

1. **Account purpose**
   To help you save more money for retirement.
2. **Tax-savings benefit**
   When you withdraw the money, it's tax-free. If you're low-income, you may also qualify for the **saver's credit**,[14] which gives you additional tax savings.
3. **Annual contribution limit**
   Same as a traditional 401k/403b/solo 401k.
4. **Deadline for that contribution to be made (to count for that year)**
   Same as a traditional 401k/403b/solo 401k.
5. **Contribution rules**
   Straightforward. By the deadline.
6. **Rules for withdrawing the money**
   When you withdraw Roth plan money, your taxes have all been paid already, so it's tax-free. This is why Roth plans have a lot fewer restrictions surrounding withdrawal: since you've already paid

your tax, the government is not all over you. There are no RMDs required from Roth accounts.[15]

When you withdraw money from a Roth account, there are two different types of withdrawal. You may withdraw the *principal* (aka your original contribution) at any time, without penalty. You've already paid tax on this money.

The requirements to withdraw the *earnings* on your money tax-free from your Roth account are that you have the money in your account for more than five years, and you are over 59½.

The same reasons for penalty-free early withdrawal in the 401k/403b section apply here. View: www.irs.gov/retirement-plans/plan-participant-employee/retirement-topics-exceptions-to-tax-on-early-distributions.

The same 10% early withdrawal penalties apply to a Roth as to a traditional account if you are taking a distribution that is not qualified.

7. **Catch-up contribution allowances**
   Same as traditional 401k/403b/solo 401k.

8. **Income limitations to be eligible to contribute**
   None. And that's one reason to prioritize funding your Roth 401k/403b over other accounts, like an IRA.

9. **Special note on prioritizing your 401k/403b**
   Same as the 401k.

Solo 401k

A solo 401k is a 401k that you set up just for yourself. The rules are the same as the 401ks described earlier, and it can be either the traditional or Roth flavor. Solo 401ks have high contribution limits and amazing perks, like employer matching. But they take some extra setup, they have an annual paperwork requirement, and you cannot flex how much you contribute each year as radically as you can with a SEP IRA. For that reason, I recommend a solo 401k only once you're making a consistent income and are ready to take on the admin of setting up payroll for yourself. A good moment for this is if you decide to elect to be taxed as an S Corporation (see Chapter 12).

The thing to note in setting one up is that while all the employee rules in the previous 401k sections apply to you, *you are also the employer*. So the employer rules *also* apply to you. This can make the solo 401k a little trickier to administer than, say, the SEP IRA (which I cover next).

Consider this if you're ready for a little extra admin. Once your plan has a certain dollar amount in it, you must file annual paperwork for your 401k. This sounds annoying, but the brokerage where you open the account can help you with it, and there are great plan administrators out there, like Guideline (which I use), that administer your plan and make it simple.

With a solo 401k, there are two types of contribution you can make. Think about this as the employee vs. employer contributions. Remember, you are both the employee and the employer here.

On the "employee" side, you can make all the contributions that I listed in the 401k/403b sections (traditional or Roth). This is your **elective contribution**.

In addition to this amount, you are also allowed to make an **employer nonelective contribution**. Typically, you set this up as an employer match, where you match up to a certain percentage of your employee's 401k contribution. When you combine your elective contribution with your nonelective contribution, they must not exceed an annually adjusted maximum (which is high). For the current year, see www.irs.gov/retirement-plans/plan-participant-employee/retirement-topics-401k-and-profit-sharing-plan-contribution-limits. In 2025, this combined maximum was $70,000. Think about that for a minute: up to $70,000 that you can put away in a tax shelter. Wow.

What's a SEP IRA?

If you report your business income on a Schedule C, a **SEP IRA** is an excellent option for you to put away a big chunk of money for future you and get a tax benefit. It's got a lot of contribution flexibility and little admin, which makes it a great option for self-employed people. SEP IRA stands for **Simplified Employee Pension (SEP) Individual Retirement Arrangement (IRA)**.[16]

1. **Account purpose**

   To help you save more money for retirement.

2. **Tax-savings benefit**

   SEP IRAs were all traditional style until the passage of the Secure 2.0 Act in 2022, meaning that most SEP IRAs give you tax savings in the year you put the money in. When you withdraw the money, you pay ordinary income tax on it. If yours is Roth style, you'll get no immediate tax benefit the year you contribute but can withdraw the earnings tax-free when you withdraw funds.[17]

   In either case, If you're low-income, you may qualify for the **saver's credit**,[18] which gives you additional tax savings.

3. **Annual contribution limit**

   You can put up to 20% of your self-employed profit into it, up to a maximum income that increases each year (in 2025, that's $350,000 of profit) to a maximum contribution amount (in 2025 that max is $23,000). See updated rates at www.irs.gov/retirement-plans/ plan-participant-employee/sep-contribution-limits-including-grandfathered-sarseps.

   Note that this 20% limit can make the SEP IRA contribution limit really high or really low, depending on your income. If you make $115,000 in profit, then you can make the 2025 maximum contribution of $23,000 (20% of $115,000 = $23,000). If you make $300,000 of profit, you can still only put in $23,000. If you make only

279

$10,000, then your maximum contribution allowance would be only $2,000 (20% of $10,000).

4. **Deadline for that contribution to be made** (to count for that year) Your 20% contribution limit is determined when you file your tax return. For this reason, the SEP IRA is the only retirement account that you can contribute to up to the tax deadline *including extensions* to count for the prior year.[19]

Other IRAs have an April 15 deadline but won't allow you to contribute past that, even if you file a tax extension. The SEP IRA requires your finalized Schedule C, so until you do your tax return, you can't know your exact contribution allowance. For this reason, they have to allow extensions.

You must do your Schedule C calculation to see what your down-to-the-dollar SEP contribution limit is. That said, you can still budget for it all year, and even contribute the money to the account, based on what you estimate to be 20% of your profit, as long as you withdraw any excess contributions before the tax deadline.

5. **Contribution rules**

By the deadline, up to the limit, if you're eligible based on having self-employed profit. Important note: As the name implies, a SEP IRA is actually a pension plan for you and any employees.[20] If you have employees, they cannot contribute to their accounts—only you, the boss, can. You also need to know that whatever percentage of your income you contribute to your own SEP you must contribute to any employees' SEPs as well. For example, if you have $100,000 of profit, and you have one part-time employee whose salary is $10,000, if you contributed your maximum contribution of 20%, then not only would you need to put $20,000 into your SEP IRA, but you would need to contribute $2,000 to *their* SEP IRA. Note that you must contribute the same *percentage*, not the same dollar amount. If you don't have any employees (and remember that contractors are not employees), then this is moot. But keep it in mind once you make your first hire.

6. **Rules for withdrawing the money**

SEP IRAs follow the same withdrawal rules as other IRAs, either traditional or Roth. See the following sections, depending on if your SEP IRA is traditional style (most common) or Roth style. You can roll over your SEP contributions and earnings tax-free into other IRAs.

Like goes to like, so a traditional-style SEP IRA can be tax-free rolled over into a traditional IRA, and a Roth-style SEP IRA can be rolled into a Roth IRA.

7. **Catch-up contribution allowances**

Not allowed.

8. **Income limitations to be eligible to contribute**

None.

The reason I love SEP IRAs for self-employed people is their flexibility. Setup is easy through any brokerage, without much paperwork. And you can contribute a different amount every year, or nothing at all, a great feature when your business has unpredictable income. In one year, you may be flush with cash and looking for a way to lower your tax bill. A large SEP IRA contribution will do that. Then you might have a really lean year and need every dollar you've got. That's okay—make a tax time decision about whether you want to contribute to your SEP or not.

Traditional and Roth IRAs: What They Share

Individual Retirement Arrangements (IRAs), whether **traditional** or **Roth**, are retirement accounts available to almost everyone.[21] They are like fraternal twins. They share a lot of DNA (like contribution amounts, structure, and timing), but in a couple key zones, they're unique. Think pretax vs. post-tax contributions, taxed vs. untaxed withdrawals, and two different contribution eligibility tables, with the Roth having an allowance for higher incomes than the traditional. Before we review key stats, let's look at what traditional and Roth IRAs *share*.

You can use an IRA whether you're self-employed or employed. If your income falls within the limits, you can contribute to an IRA *on top of* an employer-based plan or your self-employed plan (such as a SEP IRA or a solo 401k). The "I" in IRA stands for Individual, and that means this is an individually directed fund that is totally independent from your employment.

Both IRAs have the same contribution limit amounts, which is a total limit, meaning that you may contribute to both a Roth and a traditional IRA in the same year, but the sum of both contributions may not exceed the overall annual contribution limit. This limit is about one-third the size of the 401k/403b limit, but it increases yearly. It's also okay to have a Roth IRA and a traditional IRA and switch back and forth between contributing to one vs. the other as it suits you, every year. It's more like "What's the best for me this year?" than "Which do I commit to for life?"

Another important IRA consideration is that it has a later contribution deadline than a 401k or 403b, with limits on contributing if your income is high or if you have access to a 401k, a 403b, or a SEP IRA. If you want to max out multiple accounts, it is important to max out the 401k/403b or SEP IRA *first*. If not, you run the risk of relying on your IRA and realizing too late that you're ineligible to make a bigger contribution elsewhere.

There are two different sets of income limit tables for both traditional and Roth IRAs, called **covered** and **noncovered** limits.[22] If you are covered by a workplace retirement plan *and* meet covered income limits, you may still be able to make a tax-advantaged contribution to an IRA. If you don't have access to a workplace plan, then you have a higher income limit for making a deductible IRA contribution (you are noncovered). This rule applies to each spouse independently.

The idea is that you get a certain amount of tax-free help in saving for retirement, but not infinite help. If you have access to a workplace plan, definitely use it. If you have access to one but don't use it, your ability to contribute to an IRA may be limited because of your (potentially unused) workplace plan. If you don't have a workplace plan, the government gives you a higher income threshold, since an IRA may be your only retirement plan option.

Now, the stats on each type of IRA.

Traditional IRAs

1. **Account purpose**

   To help you save more money for retirement. These boost your workplace retirement plan (including a solo 401k or SEP IRA when you're self-employed), if your income is below certain thresholds; if they're your only option for retirement savings, the income threshold to contribute is higher.

2. **Tax-savings benefit**

   You receive a current-year tax benefit. If you're low-income, you may also qualify for the **saver's credit**,[23] which gives you additional tax savings.

3. **Annual contribution limit**

   It increases yearly and is about one-third the amount you can put in a 401k. In 2025, the maximum contribution amount was $7,000.

For the current year contribution limit, see www.irs.gov/retirement-plans/plan-participant-employee/retirement-topics-ira-contribution-limits.

4. **Deadline for that contribution to be made**

Up to the April 15 tax deadline, with no extensions, to count toward the prior tax year.

5. **Contribution rules**

Contribute by the annual tax deadline.

6. **Rules for withdrawing the money**

Same as a traditional 401k. The money is taxed as ordinary income upon withdrawal.

7. **Catch-up contribution allowances**

An additional $1,000 if you are over age 50.

8. **Income limitations to be eligible to contribute**

If you are covered by a workplace plan (like a 401k, 403b, solo 401k, or SEP IRA), then you must have income below the **covered limit**. If you are *not* covered by a workplace plan (like a 401k, 403b, solo 401k, or SEP IRA), then your income must be below the **noncovered limit**. For an up-to-date income contribution table, see www.irs.gov/retirement-plans/plan-participant-employee/amount-of-roth-ira-contributions-that-you-can-make-for-2024.

Roth IRAs

1. **Account purpose**

Same as a traditional IRA, with the tax benefit flipped (see #2).

2. **Tax-savings benefit**

The money you put in gives you no current-year tax benefit, but when it's withdrawn, it's tax-free. If you're low-income, you may also qualify for the **saver's credit**,[24] which gives you additional tax savings.

3. **Annual contribution limit**

   Same as the traditional IRA.

4. **Deadline for that contribution to be made**

   Same as the traditional IRA.

5. **Contribution rules**

   Same as the traditional IRA.

6. **Rules for withdrawing the money**

   Same as a Roth 401k, except you can also take a qualified distribution for a first-time home purchase. No RMDs are required from a Roth IRA.

7. **Catch-up contribution allowances**

   Same as the traditional IRA.

8. **Income limitations to be eligible to contribute**

   If you are covered by a workplace plan (like a 401k, 403b, solo 401k, or SEP IRA), then you must have income below the **covered limit**. If you are *not* covered by a workplace plan (like a 401k, 403b, solo 401k, or SEP IRA), then your income must be below the **noncovered limit**. For an up-to-date income contribution table, see https://www.irs.gov/retirement-plans/plan-participant-employee/amount-of-roth-ira-contributions-that-you-can-make-for-2024.[25]

OTHER TAX-SMART ACCOUNTS (NONRETIREMENT)

While retirement accounts are the biggest tax-advantaged accounts you can access, there are a handful of additional ones that exist to pay for other important things, like healthcare. The following is a quick rundown of some other types of the best nonretirement tax-advantaged accounts.

Medical/Health Savings

There are two similarly named healthcare savings accounts that are very different from each other.

Flexible Spending Accounts (FSAs)

The first, **flexible spending arrangements (FSAs)** is generally offered as a workplace benefit. If you're self-employed while reading this, I understand you might want to skip ahead. But it's good to get a sense of FSAs in case your spouse has access to one through their workplace or if your own employment situation changes.

1. **Account purpose**

   FSAs are a workplace-based perk that offer you a tax-advantaged way to set aside a part of your salary for medical expenses.[26]

2. **Tax-savings benefit**

   Employer contributions can be excluded from your gross income. This is a nice benefit, as usually, anything your employer contributes to you financially must be reported as income. No employment or federal income taxes are deducted from the contributions.

3. **Annual contribution limit**

   For 2025, the maximum contribution amount is **$3,300 per spouse**.[27]

4. **Deadline for that contribution to be made**

   Must be withdrawn from payroll within the relevant calendar year.

5. **Contribution rules**

   These are made through payroll deductions. Self-employed folks aren't eligible.

6. **Rules for withdrawing the money**

Withdrawn money is tax-free only if used for qualified medical expenses (these are generous and include stuff like sanitary supplies, sunscreen, dental cleanings, contacts and Band-Aids, as well as copays and more "official" stuff).[28] The FSA contribution level maximum increases slightly each year, and you can look up the current year at www.irs.gov/newsroom/irs-2024-flexible-spending-arrangement-contribution-limit-rises-by-150-dollars.

The downside of FSAs is that they **don't** roll over to the next year (*some* plans allow a small amount to roll over—$660 in 2025—don't assume this is true of yours).[29] You need to use up what's in your account each year. If you've ever wondered why your local optometrist runs so many ads at the end of the year, it's because glasses and contacts are allowable medical expenses, and they know that there are people with FSA money to spend before December 31.

7. **Catch-up contribution allowances**

None.

8. **Income limitations to be eligible to contribute**

None.

Health Savings Accounts (HSAs)

Health savings accounts (HSAs) are actually very different from FSAs (much better), and HSAs are independent of your workplace. As a self-employed person, you can set one up.

1. **Account purpose**

To save for the costs of healthcare, *when you have a high-deductible health plan (HDHP)*.

Unlike an FSA, an HSA is "portable." It stays with you if you change employers or leave the workforce.[30] You can also set up your own. Lively and Fidelity Investments offer fee-free individual HSAs for self-employed folks, independent contractors, and gig workers.

The benefits are lovely. HSA contributions remain in your account until you use them. Unlike FSAs, *HSAs do roll over* year to year.[31] The interest or other earnings on the assets in the account are tax-free.

When you invest the money in your HSA, which you're allowed to do, you get a multifold benefit. The money grows with compound interest, it's yours forever, and, when you turn 65, you can withdraw money for uses other than medical ones. You will pay the same tax as you would on withdrawals from a traditional 401(k). It's like a secret back-up retirement account. Although the annual contribution is relatively modest, HSAs are the secretly most powerful tax-advantaged account that the US tax code has to offer.[32]

2. **Tax-savings benefit**

You can claim a tax deduction for contributions you, or someone other than your employer, make to your HSA even if you don't itemize your deductions on Schedule A (Form 1040).[33] This is nice, because most US taxpayers don't itemize deductions and therefore can't deduct medical expenses.

Like an FSA, contributions to your HSA made by your employer (including contributions made through a cafeteria plan) may be excluded from your gross income.

3. **Annual contribution limit**

The HSA contribution limit increases yearly. Find this year's limit at www.irs.gov/publications/p969. The 2025 limit for HSA contributions is $4,300, and for a family is $8,550.[34]

4. **Deadline for that contribution to be made**

By the tax deadline, April 15, without extension.

5. **Contribution rules**

To qualify, you need to have an HSA-eligible HDHP.[35] I think of this as a "shit sandwich." An HSA is a really nice account with massive tax and investment benefits, but it's there primarily to help you pay the high costs of your crappy healthcare plan. So you need a crappy healthcare plan to get one (technically, a HDHP). Check the website for your health plan to see if it is a qualifying HDHP.

6. **Rules for withdrawing the money**
    When you take a distribution from your HSA for qualified medical expenses, the money comes out tax-free.

7. **Catch-up contribution allowances**
    You and your spouse, if you have separate HSAs, are each allowed to contribute your own catch-up contribution, if you're over 55. The catch-up contribution limit for those over age 55 remains at $1,000 for 2025.[36]

8. **Income limitations to be eligible to contribute**
    None.

CHAPTER SUMMARY

- Tax-smart accounts shelter money from income tax, saving you money. They are a government-provided incentive that helps you save for retirement, healthcare, education, and business growth.
- How they work: your contributions lower your current year taxable income or provide tax-free withdrawals, depending on the account type (traditional vs. Roth).
- All tax-advantaged accounts share some things: a tax benefit, contribution limits, deadlines, rules for withdrawal, and some have catch-up allowances for people close to retirement age.
- Retirement accounts are individual; each spouse should fund their own account to the max.

- Money in tax-advantaged accounts needs to be invested to grow; simply opening the account isn't enough.
- A SEP IRA is one (of several) great option for freelancers. It's flexible and can significantly reduce your taxable income and grow your retirement savings over time.
- Besides retirement accounts, consider FSAs and HSAs for health-care savings.

ENDNOTES

1. Hayden Adams, "Tax-Efficient Investing: Why Is It Important?", *Charles Schwab*, May 8, 2023, https://www.schwab.com/learn/story/tax-efficient-investing-why-is-it-important.
2. "What is a tax shelter?", *Tax Policy Center*, last modified January 2024, https://taxpolicycenter.org/briefing-book/what-tax-shelter#:~:text=Tax%20shelters%20are%20ways%20individuals,way%20to%20reduce%20tax%20liabilities.
3. Rachel Murphy, "Tax shelters: What are they and how do they work?", *Prudential*, April 16, 2024, https://www.prudential.com/financial-education/tax-shelter#:~:text=A%20tax%20shelter%20provides%20a,tax%20and%20capital%20gains%20taxes.
4. "Traditional and Roth IRAs," *U.S. Department of Treasury, Internal Revenue Service*, last modified August 20, 2024, https://www.irs.gov/retirement-plans/traditional-and-roth-iras.
5. "Retirement topics - Beneficiary," *U.S. Department of Treasury, Internal Revenue Service*, last modified August 26, 2024, https://www.irs.gov/retirement-plans/plan-participant-employee/retirement-topics-beneficiary.
6. I like these two: Suze Orman's Action Plan, and Ramit Sethi's I Will Teach You to Be Rich. See Suze Orman, *Suze Orman's Action Plan: New Rules for New Times* (Random House, 2010); Ramit Sethi, *I Will Teach You To Be Rich* (Workman Publishing, 2010).
7. I like this one. Don't forget to put your self-employed income into the self-employed income category. Otherwise, you'll skip calculating your self-employment tax, and your tax will appear much lower than it's going to be in real life. John Waggoner, "1040 Tax Calculator," *AARP*, last modified February 6, 2025, https://www.aarp.org/money/taxes/1040-tax-calculator/.

8. "401(k) limit increases to $23,500 for 2025, IRA limit remains $7,000," *Department of Treasury, Internal Revenue Service*, last modified November 12, 2024, https://www.irs.gov/newsroom/401k-limit-increases-to-23500-for-2025-ira-limit-remains-7000.

9. "401(k) plans," *Department of Treasury, Internal Revenue Service*, last modified January 30, 2025, https://www.irs.gov/retirement-plans/401k-plans.

10. The saver's credit is a credit that reduces the taxes on low-income taxpayers who contribute to retirement savings. See "Retirement Savings Contributions Credit (Saver's Credit)."

11. "Retirement plan and IRA required minimum distributions FAQs," *Department of Treasury, Internal Revenue Service*, last modified January 29, 2025, https://www.irs.gov/retirement-plans/retirement-plan-and-ira-required-minimum-distributions-faqs#:~:text=Roth%20IRAs%20do%20not%20require, required%20from%20designated%20Roth%20accounts.

12. "Retirement topics - Exceptions to tax on early distributions," *U.S. Department of Treasury, Internal Revenue Service*, last modified December 11, 2024, https://www.irs.gov/retirement-plans/plan-participant-employee/retirement-topics-exceptions-to-tax-on-early-distributions.

13. "Retirement topics - IRA contribution limits," *U.S. Department of Treasury, Internal Revenue Service*, last modified August 20, 2024, https://www.irs.gov/retirement-plans/plan-participant-employee/retirement-topics-ira-contribution-limits.

14. The saver's credit is a credit that reduces the taxes on low-income taxpayers who contribute to retirement savings. See "Retirement Savings Contributions Credit (Saver's Credit)."

15. "Traditional or Roth account? 2 tips to help you choose," *Fidelity*, accessed December 4, 2024, https://www.fidelity.com/viewpoints/retirement/spender-or-saver.

16. "Simplified Employee Pension plan (SEP)," *U.S. Department of Treasury, Internal Revenue Service*, last modified August 19, 2024, https://www.irs.gov/retirement-plans/plan-sponsor/simplified-employee-pension-plan-sep.

17. Nell Adkins and B. Charlene Henderson, "SECURE 2.0 developments and guidance for 2024," *The Tax Adviser*, January 1, 2024, https://www.thetaxadviser.com/issues/2024/jan/secure-2-0-developments-and-guidance-for-2024.html.

18. The saver's credit is a credit that reduces the taxes on low-income taxpayers who contribute to retirement savings. See "Retirement Savings Contributions Credit (Saver's Credit)."

19. "Retirement plans: FAQs regarding SEPs," *U.S. Department of Treasury, Internal Revenue Service*, last modified July 31, 2024, https://www.irs.gov/retirement-plans/retirement-plans-faqs-regarding-seps.

20. "Simplified Employee Pension plan (SEP)."

21. "Individual retirement arrangements (IRAs)," *U.S. Department of Treasury, Internal Revenue Service*, last modified August 19, 2024, https://www.irs.gov/retirement-plans/individual-retirement-arrangements-iras.

22. U.S. Department of the Treasury, Internal Revenue Service. Publication 590-A (2023), Contributions to Individual Retirement Arrangements (IRAs). 2024, Pub. 590-A, Washington, DC.

23. The saver's credit is a credit that reduces the taxes on low-income taxpayers who contribute to retirement savings. See "Retirement Savings Contributions Credit (Saver's Credit)."

24. The saver's credit is a credit that reduces the taxes on low-income taxpayers who contribute to retirement savings. See "Retirement Savings Contributions Credit (Saver's Credit)."

25. "Amount of Roth IRA contributions that you can make for 2024."

26. "People with coverage through a job," *HealthCare.gov*, accessed February 9, 2025, https://www.healthcare.gov/have-job-based-coverage/flexible-spending-accounts/#:~:text=A%20Flexible%20Spending%20Account%20(FSA%2C%20also%20called%20a%20%E2%80%9Cflexible,the%20money%20you%20set%20aside.

27. "IRS: Healthcare FSA reminder: Employees can contribute up to $3,300 in 2025; must elect every year," *U.S. Department of the Treasury, Internal Revenue Service*, last modified November 25, 2024, https://www.irs.gov/retirement-plans/plan-participant-employee/retirement-savings-contributions-credit-savers-credit.

28. "FSA qualified medical expenses (QME)," *HealthEquity*, last accessed December 13, 2024, https://www.healthequity.com/fsa-qme.

29. "IRS: Healthcare FSA reminder: Employees can contribute up to $3,300 in 2025; must elect every year."

30. *Health Savings Accounts and Other Tax-Favored Health Plans*. Pub. 969, 5.

31. *Health Savings Accounts and Other Tax-Favored Health Plans*. Pub. 969, 15.

32. William D. Johnson, "The triple tax benefits of health savings accounts," *Ameriprise Financial*, accessed February 2025, https://www.ameripriseadvisors.com/william.d.johnson/insights/benefits-health-savings-accounts/.

33. *Health Savings Accounts and Other Tax-Favored Health Plans*. Pub. 969, 20.

34. *Health Savings Accounts and Other Tax-Favored Health Plans*. Pub. 969, 5.

35. *Health Savings Accounts and Other Tax-Favored Health Plans*. Pub. 969, 6.

36. *Health Savings Accounts and Other Tax-Favored Health Plans*. Pub. 969, 6.

CHAPTER FIFTEEN
FINDING HIDDEN MONEY (AKA TAX PLANNING)

W ant free money? Want to generate compounding wealth—
without any extra hustle?

Year-end tax planning is the sexiest concept in taxes (with the unsexiest name). Hear me out. Tax planning is not about hustling; it's about taking time to find money that you *already have* that is lazing around and making it work for you. This is one level-up financial strategy you shouldn't ignore. It's the ultimate "work smarter, not harder."

Tax planning rule #1: be gentle with yourself. Tax planning is a habit that improves with practice. If this is new, you might feel left behind or too late, and that's hard. This is your signal to make note of the option and ensure *you don't miss it next year*. If this list gives you new strategies to consider, you're making improvements. Even if you can manage only one thing that you've never done before, that is improvement to be proud of. Increasing your awareness of what you've been missing out on is a step toward claiming it in the future. Remember that tax planning is a habit that you repeat *yearly*. Do what you can now, and in a year, plan to tackle more of this list.

PUMPKIN SPICE TAX PLANNING: DO IT IN THE FALL

The concept of tax planning is that you take time to evaluate your financial situation as the year is winding down, while there's still time to change things. You know that scene in action movies, where the hero is in a dangerous place, and the door to safety is closing, and at the last moment, the hero dives through it? That's you and tax planning. You're diving through, clutching as much extra money as you can, right before the door closes on this tax year.

It goes like this: in late fall, you do some math and estimating, and then you play with these three planning tools to lower your expected tax (you may not be able to use all of them):

- Accelerating business expenses and deferring business income
- Maximizing money you put into tax-advantaged accounts
- Evaluating you/your spouse's workplace benefits for additional tax-advantaged savings

The first task you must do for effective tax planning as a self-employed person is to *get your year-to-date bookkeeping done.* This tells you where things stand now and what leeway you have to make adjustments before the tax year ends.

> Remember that your profit is your taxable income from your self-employment, but it may not be all of your taxable income. How close your business profit is to your total taxable income depends on what income you have outside your business, like a spouse's income, investment income, a day job, etc. To get a sense of the fuller picture, get last year's tax return and review the income sources summary on the bottom of page 1 to remind yourself of your income types from last year.

With your bookkeeping up-to-date, evaluate your profit so far this year. Your taxable business income is roughly the same as your net profit in your business. If you have bookkeeping software, find the report called **profit and loss statement** (also known as an **income statement**) and run that report from January first until the current date. If you use a spreadsheet for bookkeeping, do the math to find your year-to-date profit.

Estimate the income and expenses you expect to have in the remaining weeks of the year and add any additional profit to your year-to-date profit. You need the gist, not the exact number.

Use a Tax Calculator to Estimate Your Tax

The cool thing is that you're doing year-end planning *before* your tax number becomes real, rather than after. Estimating your tax due while there's still time allows you to make decisions that can reduce it.

The easiest way to roughly calculate your tax due is to plug your approximated full-year profit number into an online tax calculator.

Remember to identify it as self-employment income in the tax calculator, or you'll underestimate your tax.

Do an Internet search for "online income tax calculator." I like the one from the AARP.

Knowing roughly what tax you would owe if you did nothing, you can now play with the following tips to see how much you can save. This is the fun part of tax planning. Are you feeling the sexy nerd vibes like I am here?

Accelerate Business Expenses and Defer Income

Since taxes are based on a calendar year, a year-end evaluation allows you to shift income and expenses so they fall within a more advantageous timeframe. The idea is to defer income to after January 1 that you don't imminently need so that it falls into the next tax year.[1] Conversely, with a holistic view of your expected expenses, you can prepay expenses or buy big-ticket items that you already planned for so they fall within the current calendar year, thus lowering your taxable profit for this tax year. This trick doesn't move mountains, but it does shift the edges.

Don't overuse it. Don't spend money you wouldn't have spent anyway or deplete the cash you need to operate. But if there are expenses you know you plan to incur in the near future, say, the next six months, it's worth considering.

Review last year's business expenses to see if any will repeat in the upcoming year. Are any prepayable or you could buy now instead of after 12/31? Some ideas:

- Prepay for coaches, online courses, memberships
- Office supplies

- Book headshots now (ask about a prepayment discount)
- Services: web design, accounting, legal, product photography, software, etc.
- Large equipment purchases (pre- or post-holiday sales? Sweet!)

Remember the broader context of your business. If you're trying to spend less, then *spend less*. This isn't an excuse to spend business money that you shouldn't be spending. But as long as it's in your budget and you planned to get it for your business anyway, then go for it.

To defer income, there's not always much you can do. If you invoice clients, consider holding end-of-year invoices and sending them after January 1. If you are receiving a grant and have any degree of input on when the grant is paid out, try requesting the payment be made after January 1.

CASH VS. ACCRUAL ACCOUNTING

Does deferring income and accelerating expenses bring up questions about how you report your income and expenses for your taxes? Most small businesses operate as **cash basis** taxpayers. Cash basis means that you report your income when you receive it, and you report expenses when you spend the money.[2] In other words, it's about when money enters and leaves your business bank account. This is simple and intuitive, and that's why it's what most businesses do, especially small ones.

Even if your bookkeeper delivers your financial statements using the accrual method, you're likely still a **cash basis** taxpayer.

Here's another place where the differences between your book-keeping and your taxes can create confusion. I hope that under-standing that your taxes and your books can follow different rules eases your mind.

Note that line F of your Schedule C asks if you use accrual or cash basis, and this refers to how you pay taxes, *not* how you do your books.[3] For 99.9% of the people reading this book, you are a **cash basis** taxpayer.

Work Your Tax-Advantaged Accounts

Next, try to reduce your taxable income with tax-smart accounts. This means looking at the tax-advantaged accounts you could be using (see Chapter 14) and ensuring you have put the maximum amount of money allowed in each one that you're able to. The more money you stash in a 401k, SEP IRA, HSA, etc., the further you reduce your taxable income and therefore your tax bill. Huge bonus: when you put money into these accounts, *it's still your money*. You are choosing to hold it for the right time and right reason (as in retirement, healthcare expenses, etc.). It's still yours. The tax savings is total gravy. Have I swooned enough for you yet? Tax-advantaged accounts are awesome.

Review the rules and limits for each account type in Chapter 14. And sock away every dollar you can.

Maximize You/Your Spouse's Workplace Benefits

Finally, if you or your spouse is a W2 employee, quickly review your workplace benefits and ensure that you are maximizing every available one. Again, Chapter 14 will remind you of benefits you might have access to and the annual limits. Some workplaces have tax-advantaged benefits that include childcare savings plans, student loan repayment matching plans, commuter benefits, and flexible spending accounts (FSAs). Each dollar you put in these accounts becomes tax-free and reduces your taxable income. In the case of an FSA, you should evaluate any funds left in your account for the year and use up the money. FSAs don't roll over year to year.[4] If you don't have upcoming medical expenses that you can prepay, stock up on eligible supplies.

Charitable Giving Is Probably Not Deductible

At year end, many nonprofits send solicitations for donations, courting people in the holiday spirit, and/or in the more self-interested year-end tax planning spirit (no shade here—if you can align your giving with a tax deduction, great). But before you send a huge donation thinking you'll get a tax deduction, remember that most middle-class people don't get any deduction for charitable contributions. That's because most people take the standard deduction.[5] Only people who itemize deductions get a deduction for their charitable, medical, mortgage, and state/local tax expenses (please recall that itemizing has no relationship with taking all your business expenses—you get to take that regardless).

If you can't remember if you itemize or take the standard deduction, last year's tax return (page one, line 12) will tell you. I'm not saying don't donate to charity. Not at all. Just don't donate thinking that you get a tax break. You might, but you probably don't.

Review Your Health Insurance: Year-End Open Enrollment

My final note is actually not about tax planning. But while you're in this mode, now is the time to review your health insurance plan. November is the open enrollment period for health insurance—the one time of year you're allowed to change your plan without a qualifying health event.[6] This is true whether you are covered by private insurance or through the Healthcare.gov marketplace.[7] Either way, add this to your year-end tax planning list, since it happens at the same time of year.[8]

Now Celebrate

With your year-end tax planning done, celebrate! This work can feel uncomfortable and even make you feel like you've missed the boat. For example, the first time I tried it, I realized that I had missed a few deadlines, that my then-workplace didn't allow lump-sum 403b contributions, and that I didn't have enough cash to max out the HSA I wanted to open. Live and learn. Even this is valuable. Really. You've now identified a few things for next year's year-end tax planning, and you have a year to budget for it and plan out your options. Year-end comes around, literally, every year. So I absolutely mean it when I say take a moment to celebrate what you've done. Go have a glass of eggnog and hug a friend.

CHAPTER SUMMARY

- Year-end tax planning gets you free money without extra hustle. It's about finding hidden money you already have.
- Rule number one: Be gentle with yourself. Tax planning is a habit that improves with practice. Celebrate even small wins, and keep improving.
- Tax planning happens at pumpkin spice time: do it in the fall. The trick is to evaluate your situation while there's still time to make changes.

- The three key strategies:
  - Accelerate your business expenses and defer income.
  - Maximize contributions to tax-advantaged accounts.
  - Evaluate any workplace benefits, including your spouse's.
- Get your bookkeeping up-to-date.
- Estimate your tax due while there's still time to reduce it. Use a tax calculator.
- Open enrollment is the time to make changes to your health plan, and it happens in November. So add this to your tax planning checklist, even if it's not strictly tax planning.
- Even if you miss some stuff, you've learned what to look for next year.
- Tax planning is about working smarter, not harder. Celebrate *any* progress and keep improving each year.

ENDNOTES

1. "4 Last-Minute Ways to Reduce Your Taxes," *TurboTax*, January 7, 2025, https://turbotax.intuit.com/tax-tips/tax-planning-and-checklists/4-last-minute-ways-to-reduce-your-taxes/L3eJ81kRC.
2. *Accounting Periods and Methods*, Pub. 538, 8.
3. "2024 Instructions for Schedule C (2024)."
4. "IRS: Healthcare FSA reminder: Employees can contribute up to $3,300 in 2025; must elect every year."
5. "Expanded tax benefits help individuals and businesses give to charity during 2021; deductions up to $600 available for cash donations by non-itemizers," *U.S. Department of the Treasury, Internal Revenue Service*, last modified May 7, 2024, https://www.irs.gov/newsroom/expanded-tax-benefits-help-individuals-and-businesses-give-to-charity-during-2021-deductions-up-to-600-available-for-cash-donations-by-non-itemizers.
6. "A quick guide to the Health Insurance Marketplace®," *HealthCare.gov*, accessed February 9, 2025, https://www.healthcare.gov/quick-guide/dates-and-deadlines/.
7. "A quick guide to the Health Insurance Marketplace®."
8. "A quick guide to the Health Insurance Marketplace®."

PART VI

THE FIX: OH SHIT! (HOW TO FIX THINGS)

S ometimes, things break. This is taxes for *humans*, after all. Not to worry. This section is about fixing—or making the best of—a bad situation. If you're reading this book to get your taxes done and you don't have any "oh shit!" tax situations happening right now, hear me out. Remember this chapter is here for you. Because sooner or later, most of us get a letter from the IRS.

If you want that moment to be a lot less painful, your best option is to follow the rules in the first place. Before you skip this chapter, I will tell you that knowing how an audit works and what the IRS is actually looking for can help de-stress your tax process. Often, it helps you realize that you're doing a good job already and that even if the scary thing happens, you'll be okay.

If you're managing a tax situation gone awry, first, my condolences. This part will help you navigate that. Let's normalize tax breakdowns. You're human 365 days a year, and things sometimes go wrong—like owing back taxes, for example (if you don't know, back taxes are unfiled taxes from years' past, often in a multiyear string). Why do people's taxes go sideways? It's usually because of something awful in their life; in my experience, it's divorce, cancer, addiction, or other breakdown. This is when you need the *most* empathy and care—not a guilt trip. These are legit problems requiring steady guidance to fix.

The tax problems I outline here are fixable, and there's no judgment about your past mistakes or traumas. In fact, anyone facing their tax mess is someone who's putting on her big girl pants. Read this section, and you get an adulting merit badge. Plus, you'll stay clear of jail.

CHAPTER SIXTEEN

OOPS! FILING AN AMENDED RETURN

Name someone who's never made a mistake, and I'll show you someone I don't want as a friend. Sometimes, you make a mistake on your tax return. Here's the good news: it's fixable.

The way to fix a mistake on your tax return—this includes discovering that you missed a tax credit or a bunch of deductions you were entitled to—is to file an **amended return**, called a **1040X**.[1]

HOW AN AMENDED RETURN WORKS

An amended return isn't as hard as you might fear. It requires only that you report the change. You don't redo the entire tax return. If the change you are making on your 1040X changes the amount of tax, your software will recalculate your tax due or refund owed to you. Should you *owe* additional taxes because of the change, then yes, of course you need to pay those (there's no statute of limitations on paying your taxes, sorry).[2] Often, you won't need to file an amended return with your state, unless your amended return changes your *state* tax liability.[3] Then you do.

The 1040X is considered a "continuous" tax form, meaning the IRS updates it as needed, rather than issuing a new updated form each tax year.[4] All you need is the latest version of the 1040X. A separate 1040X must be filed for each tax year you are amending.

How Far Back Should You Go?

The statute of limitations on *getting* money that you are owed from the IRS is either three years from the date you filed the return or two years from the date you paid the tax, whichever is later.[5] Sadly, if you realize you missed out on the Obama-era first-time homebuyer tax credit (which expired in 2010), that money is gone.[6] But if you put your kids in summer camp two years ago so you could work and you didn't realize that made you eligible for the child and dependent care tax credit, then get your amended return in ASAP and get your money![7] Likewise, if reading this book has made you aware of Schedule C deductions you were eligible for but never took, I recommend locating those receipts and filing amended returns up to the money-back statute date.

If you do, consider dropping me a quick email: hello@sunlighttax .com. This kind of win fuels my happiness.

You can file amended returns for years beyond that statute of limitations, but understand that you won't receive any money you are owed past that date.[8] You should still file if you find a misstatement of income or you failed to make an important tax election.[9] Always file an amended return to correct a filing status error[10] such as if your accountant filed a return for you as "single" when you are "married filing separately."

Correct a Filing Status or Dependent

A common and important reason to amend a filing is to add a dependent to your return who was incorrectly claimed on another tax return.[11] This tends to happen when people get divorced and don't have a clear agreement on who claims the kids (or, different story, someone doesn't act in good faith). I had a fresh-out-of-college client who filed his first tax return as an adult, only to find the return rejected because his mom, probably through force of habit, had already claimed him on *her* tax return. This made my client ineligible for all sorts of tax credits he was owed. In the end, his mother had to file an amended return to unclaim her son, and only then could we file his return.

The one filing status you cannot change is "married filing jointly." If you realize that you filed a joint return and meant to file separate returns, your only opportunity to change it is to file a **superseded return** *before the due date of the tax return*, including extensions. While similar to an amended return, a superseded return is filed before the due date and replaces the original before the original is processed, so it *becomes* the original return.[12] Once the tax deadline has passed, you are irrevocably stuck "married filing jointly" for that year.

As of 2022, there is a checkbox on electronically filed tax returns for a superseded return. You need to submit this new tax return before the deadline, *with that box checked*, to have it supersede the original filing.[13]

Pro tip: I recommend using the same software to file your amended return that you used to prepare the original. That allows the software to pull the info directly from your original return to make the new calculations.

If you use a different software, you effectively have to prepare your entire tax return again. Ugh. If you don't want to or can't use the same software as the original filing, you may consider preparing your 1040X on paper and mailing it in.[14]

You can always ask your accountant to file an amended return for you. Depending on their fee, it may or may not be worth it, since the 1040X is so simple. That said, if you're filing an amended tax return because your accountant made an error, then they should prepare and file your amended return at no charge. That's what's right, and you should insist on it. But to extend the same kindness here that I offer to you, please remember that accountants are human, too.

Lastly, the IRS has a handy "Where's My Amended Return?" tool, where you can check the status of your amendment.[15]

CHAPTER SUMMARY

- You're human. Mistakes happen, even on tax returns. Good news! They're fixable, with an amended return (1040X).
- How an amended return works: You only report the change. You don't have to redo the entire return. Your software will recalculate your tax due or refund. If you owe more, you need to pay it.
- You have three years from the date you filed the return or two years from the date you paid the tax to get money owed to you.
- Amend your return to correct errors like filing status or adding a dependent. This is common in cases of divorce or between parents and their recently adult children.

- A "superseded return" is a checkbox that turns your amendment *into* your actual tax return, but it only works before the tax deadline.
- It's easier to file an amended return using the same software as your original return. If you can't do that, consider preparing your 1040X on paper.
- You can use the IRS "Where's My Amended Return?" tool to track your amendment.

ENDNOTES

1. "Amended returns & Form 1040X," *U.S. Department of the Treasury, Internal Revenue Service*, last modified September 17, 2024, https://www.irs.gov/faqs/irs-procedures/amended-returns-form-1040x/amended-returns-form-1040x.
2. "Time IRS can assess tax," *U.S. Department of the Treasury, Internal Revenue Service*, last modified January 27, 2025, https://www.irs.gov/filing/time-irs-can-assess-tax.
3. "If I Filed an Amended Federal Tax Return, Should I Amend My State Return?," H&R Block, accessed August 1, 2024, https://www.hrblock.com/tax-center/support/online/online-tax-filing/after-filing-online-return/amend-state-return-if-federal-amended/#:~:text=Usually%2C%20you'll%20file%20an, filing%20the%20federal%20amended%20return.
4. "Instructions for Form 1040-X," *U.S. Department of the Treasury, Internal Revenue Service*, last modified September 25, 2024, https://www.irs.gov/instructions/i1040x.
5. "Time You Can Claim a Credit or Refund," *U.S. Department of the Treasury, Internal Revenue Service*, last modified January 27, 2025, https://www.irs.gov/filing/time-you-can-claim-a-credit-or-refund#:~:text=The%20latest%20date%2C%20by%20law,date%20you%20paid%20the%20tax.
6. "First-Time Homebuyers Tax Credit," *Mark Warner for Senate*, accessed July 2024, https://www.warner.senate.gov/public/index.cfm/firsttimehomebu yerstaxcredit#:~:text=An%20%248%2C000%20tax%20credit%20is,their%20 2009%20or%202010%20return.
7. *See* U.S. Department of the Treasury, Internal Revenue Service. *Child and Dependent Care Expenses*. 2023, Pub. 503, Washington, DC, 10.

8. "File an amended return," *U.S. Department of the Treasury, Internal Revenue Service*, last modified June 17, 2024, https://www.irs.gov/filing/file-an-amended-return.

9. "File an amended return."

10. "File an amended return."

11. "File an amended return."

12. "IRS: Taxpayers now have more options to correct, amend returns electronically," *U.S. Department of the Treasury, Internal Revenue Service*, last modified April 16, 2024, https://www.irs.gov/newsroom/irs-taxpayers-now-have-more-options-to-correct-amend-returns-electronically.

13. "Amended and superseding corporate returns," *U.S. Department of the Treasury, Internal Revenue Service*, last modified June 14, 2024, https://www.irs.gov/businesses/corporations/amended-and-superseding-corporate-returns.

14. "Instructions for Form 1040-X."

15. "Where's My Amended Return," *U.S. Department of the Treasury, Internal Revenue Service*, accessed August 1, 2024, https://sa.www4.irs.gov/wmar/login.

CHAPTER SEVENTEEN
WHAT IF I CAN'T PAY MY TAX BILL?

I t happens. Sometimes you do not have the money to pay your tax bill. In my work with self-employed people, I've seen people not pay estimated quarterly taxes, get busy with their new business that is suddenly making money, and then get pulled up short when the tax bill presents itself. A good year turns bad—fast. It's so common, and so painful, that it's one of the main reasons I wrote this book.

If it happens, first, understand that this means you made money. That's little consolation at this terrible moment, but it's true. It also means you need to get religious about factoring tax-paying into your rhythm throughout the year, or the cycle will continue. Taxes are due every year. And the more money you make, the higher your tax rate, so this problem gets worse.[1] The last thing you want to do while dealing with a past-due tax bill from the last year (or few years) is to keep on top of *this year's* estimated taxes. But until you gain the muscle memory of paying what you owe each quarter, the huge tax bill problem will keep recurring. Balance your recovery with modifying your habits so the awfulness does not repeat. If it sounds like I've seen many harrowing client journeys with this vicious cycle, you guessed right.

You must make sure you've got bookkeeping set up, do your books at least once per quarter, and calculate and pay your estimated taxes each quarter *from now on*.

With that warning in place, let's proceed to how to face that past-due bill.

FILING VS. PAYING: YOU SHOULD STILL FILE

Remember that filing your taxes and paying your bill are separate things. If you suspect a large bill is coming but you can't pay it, you should still file your tax return.

First, you'll avoid a **failure to file penalty**, even though you'll receive a **failure to pay penalty**.[2] One less penalty is good when you're scraping pennies. There's a temptation to not bother with your taxes when you know you're in tax trouble—I am here with a load of client experience to tell you that that's how to dig yourself an even deeper hole of back taxes. As hard as it feels, you definitely need to get your tax return done. This way, you know what you owe, and you can make plans to pay it and anticipate the potential problem for next year before it happens. Putting on your big girl pants now will stop this year's bill from turning into a multiyear tax snowball.

Another reason to file even when you can't pay is that the IRS will be nicer to you. Funny, right? But the logic is simple. The IRS tends to have a different level of humor depending on which direction the bad news is traveling. If you approach the IRS—by filing your return, showing what you owe, and being honest that you can't pay—the IRS tends to give you a lot of options and will work with you. If the IRS has to track you down, they are a lot less understanding.

PAYMENT PLAN OPTIONS

There are different ways to handle your bill. They get more formal the larger the dollar amount owed and more difficult if you ask to pay less than what you owe.

Paying Your State

Don't forget that your state taxes are due as well. Usually, when you're struggling to pay your tax bill, you're struggling to pay *all* of your tax bills, both federal and state. I can't review each state's tax attitude or its payment plan options here. But I will share with you one wisdom nugget: it's better to deal with one tax entity than two. If I had to choose a tax authority to negotiate with, I'd choose the IRS over most states. Why? The IRS is nicer. Truly. Consider this: the federal government can print money and can run on a deficit. Many states have balanced budget amendments, which deny them all breathing room when it comes to collecting monies owed. Your state can't print money. These state-level restrictions tend to foster a much less flexible attitude. And don't get me started on New York, with its historic bad budget issues plus a culture of assertiveness. The New York Department of Taxation and Finance can be downright cheeky.[3] Do I recommend negotiating with New York over unpaid bills vs. the IRS? Fuhgeddaboudit.

I cut my teeth in Brooklyn, so New York City was my training ground and tax motherland.

If possible, I suggest you pay off your state tax bill fully. This gets one tax authority out of your hair. Then do the best you can with payment plans with the IRS.

The DIY Payment Plan

The DIY version of a payment plan is the easiest. If you can pay the full balance due within a few months, then I recommend this informal option. Pay as much of your bill as possible on the due date. This demonstrates good faith and reduces your interest and penalty. You will be charged interest only on the *unpaid portion* of the balance, at the federal interest rate, plus a 0.5% per month late payment penalty, up to a 25% maximum.[4]

An IRS letter will arrive in a month or two with your remaining balance listed. Pay that balance when that letter comes.

Alternatively, you could put your remaining outstanding balance on a credit card. You will pay the credit card's interest rate until you pay off the balance, plus pay the IRS's credit card convenience fee.[5] I get *very* squeamish about racking up credit card debt and hate presenting this option. But if you need it, it will work. Proceed with caution.

Installment Agreements

Installment agreements are formal agreements with the IRS that allow you to pay your taxes due in installments.[6] It's important to understand that you must follow the rules strictly here. It's your last chance before the ugly side of tax collection. Paying your taxes is the law. By not paying your taxes when they are due, even if it was a mistake, a lack of planning, or not realizing that you were meant to be paying quarterly taxes, you have not obeyed the law. The IRS doesn't want to get mean. They deeply prefer that you realize the error and commit to good behavior from now on. But this is your second chance. If you start leaning on them for third and fourth chances, you're joining the company of tax evaders and cheats, and the IRS will bring out the heavier enforcement tools, which are no longer voluntary. Not to freak you out, but here's the unvarnished truth: the IRS has the power to withhold your refunds, garnish your wages, lien your property, and even put you in jail.[7] Appreciate their forgiveness after your first strike, and prove your good intentions by meeting every deadline and making good on your promises. Your life will get very hard if you don't.

Think of installment agreements as the "Girl Scout" agreements, as in, you better behave like a Girl Scout. This is your last chance to do things voluntarily, so deliver on what you agree to. It's a little like you had a night of passion with an old flame and you've confessed it to your spouse. She'll forgive you once. And now she'll be watching if you do everything you promised to do to make it up to her. But if you dally again, she's changing the locks. You are going to meet every deadline, make every payment, file every tax return, etc.

There are a few options for paying an installment agreement. If you owe less than $10,000, you may be eligible for a **guaranteed installment agreement**.[8] This is lovely (relatively speaking), because the IRS is required to accept the agreement, if you meet the requirements. That certainty is the main benefit of this agreement. To get a guaranteed installment agreement, you must meet these requirements:

- You owe $10,000 or less in income tax (excluding penalties and interest)
- You agree to pay the full amount within three years
- You don't have any other installment agreements from the last five years
- You've filed every tax return and paid your every tax due for the past five years
- You agree to file and pay all upcoming tax returns during the period of the agreement[9]

Other payment agreement types are not guaranteed to be accepted by the IRS. The options vary based on what you owe and how quickly you can pay it. Those factors also determine if you're allowed to pay by check or credit card vs. mandatory checking account withdrawals. The agreement options are:

- A long-term agreement (pay in more than 180 days)
- A short-term agreement (pay in 180 days or less)

You apply for them online or using **Form 9465, Installment Agreement Request**.[10] Both applications can be found at IRS.gov.

Offer in Compromise

If your tax situation is far past your ability to pay and you need to negotiate with the IRS to get in the clear again, the last option is an **offer in compromise (OIC)**. An offer in compromise is a negotiated agreement (emphasis on *negotiated*), where the IRS agrees you can pay less than what you actually owe.[11] Consider this route only if you have multiple years of outstanding tax bills and no savings, current income, or saleable property to pay it with.

If you thought applying for an installment agreement was tricky, you ain't seen nothin' yet. The offer in compromise is a last-ditch option. It takes time and technical knowledge to apply for one, and it's a specialty area for some tax experts. Don't try this at home. If you need this option, you need to find a reputable OIC specialist. Expect to pay a substantial amount for their skill (thousands), but do not hire them if they can't point to a track record of client success stories. Many tax professionals who are good at what they do have no experience in this area, and you need the experience to get a good OIC deal.

CHAPTER SUMMARY

- What if you can't pay your tax bill? It happens. Especially if you haven't been paying estimated quarterly taxes.
- You must factor estimated tax-paying into your yearly rhythm to avoid getting stuck in a tax-debt loop.
- Filing vs. paying: Always file your tax return, even if you can't pay. Filing avoids a failure to file penalty and shows the IRS good faith, which opens more options.
- If possible, pay off your state tax bill fully. The IRS is generally more flexible than state tax authorities.
- DIY payment plan: Pay as much as you can on the due date, then pay the remaining balance when the IRS sends a letter. You'll still owe some interest.
- Installment agreements with the IRS are an option. Follow the rules like a Girl Scout to avoid harsher enforcement.
- If you can't pay at all, you can negotiate an offer in compromise (OIC) with the IRS to pay less than what you owe. This is a complex process requiring an OIC specialist.
- It's hard, but by facing up to your tax bill, you end anxiety, plus get an adulting merit badge.

ENDNOTES

1. Amanda Lott, "What Happens When You Change Tax Brackets," *J.P. Morgan Wealth Management*, last modified February 27, 2024, https://www.jpmorgan .com/insights/wealth-planning/taxes/what-happens-when-you-change-tax-brackets#:~:text=Like%20any%20progressive%20tax%20system,and %20reduce%20your%20tax%20burden.

2. E. Napoletano, "What Happens If You File Your Taxes Late—And How to Avoid Big Penalties," *Buy Side from the Wall Street Journal*, last modified January 3, 2025, https://www.wsj.com/buyside/personal-finance/taxes/what-happens-if-you-file-taxes-late.

3. E.J. McMahon, "New York State Has Dug Itself Into Its Deepest Hole On Record," *Empire Center for Public Policy*, last modified September 16, 2020, https://www.empirecenter.org/publications/new-york-state-has-dug-itself-into-its-deepest-hole-on-record/.

4. "Failure to pay penalty," *U.S. Department of the Treasury, Internal Revenue Service*, last modified December 12, 2024, https://www.irs.gov/payments/failure-to-pay-penalty.

5. "Pay your taxes by debit or credit card or digital wallet," *U.S. Department of the Treasury, Internal Revenue Service*, last modified January 13, 2025, https://www.irs.gov/payments/pay-your-taxes-by-debit-or-credit-card.

6. "Additional Information on Payment Plans," *U.S. Department of the Treasury, Internal Revenue Service*, last modified May 30, 2024, https://www.irs.gov/payments/payment-plans-installment-agreements.

7. "Levy," *U.S. Department of the Treasury, Internal Revenue Service*, last modified August 22, 2024, https://www.irs.gov/businesses/small-businesses-self-employed/levy#:~:text=An%20IRS%20levy%20permits%20the,estate%20and%20other%20personal%20property.

8. 26 U.S. Code § 6159.

9. "Topic no. 202, Tax payment options," *U.S. Department of the Treasury, Internal Revenue Service*, last modified January 2, 2025, https://www.irs.gov/taxtopics/tc202.

10. "Instructions for Form 9465 (07/2024)," *U.S. Department of the Treasury, Internal Revenue Service*, accessed June 25, 2024, https://www.irs.gov/instructions/i9465.

11. "Topic no. 204, Offers in compromise," *U.S. Department of the Treasury, Internal Revenue Service*, last modified July 22, 2024, https://www.irs.gov/taxtopics/tc204#:~:text=An%20offer%20in%20compromise%20(OIC,an%20OIC%20in%20most%20cases.

CHAPTER EIGHTEEN
BACK TAXES: BETTER THAN DEATH OR HEARTBREAK (THEY'RE FIXABLE)

Back taxes are the name for multiple years of unfiled tax returns.[1] They usually begin when someone gets overwhelmed and can't face their tax return. Sometimes this is because they know they can't pay. If that's you, I understand the impulse but hope the preceding chapter helped you realize it is much better to fess up and make a plan with the IRS than to let the problem grow worse. That said, I've seen the problem grow worse many times. Sometimes the reason is a disruptive life event, like an illness, an addiction struggle, or divorce.

When you're going through something traumatic, you need kindness. The thought of being dressed down by a judgmental accountant is enough to send you back into the cycle again, rather than face the unpleasantness of fixing it.

Please understand that this is something that happens to good people. You're not horrible, broken, or alone. You're probably sleeping terribly.

There's good news. Back taxes are better than death and heartbreak. Why? They're fixable. It takes courage to face them, but once you do, they can be resolved with surprising speed. In fact, the feelings you're already sitting with are the worst part. The taxes part of back taxes, in the hands of a competent tax professional, are no big deal. Tax preparers handle these all the time, and once you have your paperwork gathered, the tax filings—even across multiple years—can be knocked out in a couple days.

Take a moment to visualize the feeling of being done: being caught up with your taxes, and freedom from that constant low-level anxiety haunting you. Sink into that feeling of relief. You can do it. The hardest part is the feelings you're already having. The second hardest part is reaching out to a tax pro or taking the step of gathering documents. Once you move in that direction, the rest will fall into place quickly. You've got this.

Here's the game plan.

YOUR GAME PLAN FOR BACK TAXES

First, stop the bleeding.

File This Year's Tax Return

If it's tax season, your first move is to file the current year's taxes before the deadline. Don't fall into the trap of missing another deadline and compounding your problem. If there's a current deadline, that is your first priority and starting point.

Meeting that deadline and filing your current tax return is also an important signal to the IRS that you're starting to deal with things. As I mentioned in the previous chapter, when *you* approach the IRS, they tend to have a kinder attitude toward you than if they have to chase you down. It is much better for your IRS dealings to begin resolving your back taxes before they mail a letter about them. That letter might come quickly, and it might come slowly, but it is coming.

File Your Tax Returns Backward, Starting with the Current Year

There's an important logic to doing your tax returns backward in time starting from today: the statute of limitations. If you are owed any tax refund money, you can claim it only for three years from the date you filed the tax return or two years from the date you paid the tax.[2] Filing returns in reverse order from the current year will ensure that you receive money owed to you before it's too late to claim it.

Sadly, paying the tax you owe doesn't expire. You must do that for each year you owe taxes. Chapter 17 highlights that your payment plan options are limited if you haven't kept current on your taxes.

CALL A PRO IF YOU CAN, BUT THE TAXPAYER ADVOCATE SERVICE CAN HELP

Negotiating a payment plan with the IRS is possible on your own. That's a good place to start if your funds are limited and paying a tax

---

pro isn't in the cards. If you hit a roadblock when working with the IRS, there's a service called the Taxpayer Advocate Service (TAS). The TAS is an independent body within the IRS that exists to help taxpayers navigate situations they can't handle on their own. Find them at www.taxpayeradvocate.irs.gov/.

Chronic underfunding of the IRS has impacted their customer service. Wait times can be long. Sometimes you get someone who is wonderful and helpful, and sometimes you get a dud. If they're a dud, pretend your toilet just exploded and call back.

Gathering your tax documents for this year's taxes will likely get you into the swing so that gathering the next most recent year's documents becomes a little easier. Also, the further back you go, the more the details get lost to time and memory. Frankly, you'll probably have fewer little things to track, because you won't remember them anymore.

I'm not saying to half-ass your tax returns or to exclude reporting income. You have to follow the law, and that means reporting all your income. It also means gathering and reporting any tax documents you received. I'm saying that some of the finer details of business deductions and options that were available to you when the year was current, like IRA contributions, are moot now. It's a bummer to miss stuff, but it also means your tax return is a little easier. In my experience, preparing tax returns for prior years tends to be quicker than a tax return for the current year. A lot of back and forth is eliminated because many discussion points become irrelevant once you're past the original tax deadline.

A NOTE ABOUT PAYING A TAX PRO

Perhaps surprisingly, back taxes clients are some of my favorites. The reason is simple. They have a problem that is 9/10ths emotional, and the technical part is something I can 100% solve for them. I am happy to hold space for the client's pain and grateful that the problem is usually easier to resolve than they expect. I really care about the human side of taxes[3]; a lot of accountants don't think the *human* part is their job. That's why many of us, but especially people who work in the humanities, often feel alienated and ill served when it comes to this stuff.

I once got a thank-you note from a back taxes client for letting him have extra time to gather his documents. This was an accomplished artist, with accolades like the Whitney Biennial and a huge museum retrospective.[4] He was freshly out of drug rehab and knew that he'd be triggered to use again by walking back into his apartment and had needed time to gather the support of friends, or he risked relapse. We were able to get all his back taxes filed without ever triggering the addiction that had caused the spiral in the first place. It was a beautiful reminder that we can all use a little grace.

But also, real talk: when you're a back taxes client, expect to pay your accounting fee in advance. I learned the hard way that a client in financial dire straits, despite their best intentions, will look at the IRS bill, look at the accountant's bill, and decide to prioritize the one that risks sending them to jail. For my first back taxes case, a man who had gone through an emotionally devastating divorce, I put in several diligent weeks of work over multiple years of past tax returns. He was kind, promised to pay me promptly, and was very grateful for my work. And once I filed the returns, he ghosted me. It was several thousand dollars of work, and I never got paid. That's the origin of my own non-negotiable payment-in-advance policy on back taxes. Any experienced professional will have one. Don't take it personally.

CHAPTER SUMMARY

- Back taxes happen. You're not alone. You're not horrible or broken. You're probably going through a really hard time.
- Back taxes are fixable. The hardest part is facing them. But once you do, they can be resolved quickly.
- Game plan for back taxes:
  - Stop the bleeding: File this year's tax return before the deadline to avoid compounding the problem.
  - Start with the current year and work backward to ensure you claim any refunds within the statute of limitations.
  - Call a pro if you can. If funds are limited, consider the Taxpayer Advocate Service for help.
  - Start by gathering this year's documents and work backwards. The further back you go, the fewer details you'll have.
- Back taxes are emotionally hard, but from a tax standpoint, they're easy.
- Expect to pay your accounting fee in advance.
- Facing your back taxes takes courage, but it's a huge relief once done. You've got this.

ENDNOTES

1. "Filing past-due tax returns," *U.S. Department of the Treasury, Internal Revenue Service*, last modified February 7, 2025, https://www.irs.gov/businesses/small-businesses-self-employed/filing-past-due-tax-returns.
2. "Taxpayer Claims Refund," *Taxpayer Advocate Service*, accessed August 1, 2024, https://www.taxpayeradvocate.irs.gov/tax-terms/refund-statute-expiration-date-rsed/#:~:text=Submitting%20a%20Claim%20for%20Refund&text=Generally%2C%20you%20must%20file%20a,the%20tax%2C%20whichever%20is%20later.
3. Perhaps you noticed the title of my book?
4. I fan-girled pretty hard.

CHAPTER NINETEEN

AUDITS: A GREAT WAY TO LOSE WEIGHT[1] (WHY, HOW, AND WHAT TO DO ABOUT THEM)

There's a halo of horrible surrounding audits that creates more fear than necessary. Occasionally, a particular audit gets messy or is an especially rotten experience. Those are the ones people talk about—and fear. The reality is that most audits are routine, straightforward, and easily resolved. In this chapter, I'll dispel the myths and give you the knowledge and tools to deal with one, should it happen.

WHAT IS AN AUDIT?

Audit is an accounting term meaning an official inspection of an individual or organization's accounts by an independent body.[2] Accountants use the term *audit* frequently to describe things that have nothing to do with the IRS. You might hear about "audited financial statements," which means financial statements that have been reviewed and verified by an independent party, usually a CPA.[3] The IRS version is really called an **examination**.[4] I use the term *audit*, because it is colloquially known that way—but you should know the official term.

Understand that a tax examination, aka audit, is neutral. It's a checkup, not an accusation. The United States has a **voluntary tax system**. This means that taxpayers have the responsibility to complete a tax return, report income, and pay taxes.[5] Audits are the only check and balance in this system. If they didn't exist, people would be less likely to file tax returns and pay taxes each year. Audit enforcement is actually pretty gentle when you think about it. Any taxpayer is subject to examination for anything they put on a tax return. The knowledge that the government has the right to take a look keeps most people in compliance.

An audit examines the correctness of a tax return. Also understand that if your tax return is correct, there is no punishment, and you can proceed on your merry way. Yes, it is possible to be audited when you have done nothing wrong. If that's the case, and as long as you've got all the records the law requires you to have, you have nothing to worry about. Sure, there's annoying paperwork to get through, but you'll be fine.

Neutrality is the baseline, but in practice, with limited dollars to spend, the IRS doesn't waste resources examining returns that appear correct on their face. To remain efficient, the IRS usually selects returns with a higher likelihood of income underreporting, misapplication of the law, or downright fraud.[6] If you are audited, even if your filing is correct and legally compliant, you are likely in a category of taxpayer that has some history of underreporting or legal fudging.

Five Important Things to Know About Audits

If you're skimming, here are your baseline rights when it comes to an audit:

1. You have a right to counsel. While often not necessary in a **correspondence audit** (an audit by mail—more on this in a moment), having a representative look at your letter/guide you to provide the correct information to prove the item under scrutiny is a good idea.[7] Counsel is highly recommended in an in-person audit.

2. The **taxpayer burden of proof** is to provide: receipts, canceled checks, invoices, year-end statements, logs/journals, reconstruction, your testimony, affidavit to prove "intangible items."[8] Be ready.

3. The Cohan rule: the court can grant reasonable deductions, even without proof. They must be substantiated with detail.[9] Testimony of the taxpayer is admissible. This does *not* apply to travel, gifts, or listed property (property that is mixed use between business and personal). For those, deductions are granted only with proper proof. Proving an expense without the receipt is harder, and you'll need to have appealed your audit and be in court to apply the Cohan rule.[10] A receipt will *always* make your life/case easier.

4. Your right to appeal the initial finding is *absolute*.[11]
5. The Taxpayer Advocate Service (TAS) is an independent body within the IRS that helps when the normal channels are not working.[12]

Statute of Limitations

How far back can an audit go? When is there no more chance of an examination? The IRS has three years from the filing date to assess tax.[13] The IRS has six years if more than 25% of gross income was omitted from the return (note: this is a felony) or greater than $5,000 of income from offshore activity is omitted from the return.[14] There is no statute of limitations when there is fraud or when no tax return was ever filed.

Reasons for an Audit

How do tax returns get picked for examination? There are several methods, many of them automated. This means that in a number of situations, if you meet all criteria for a certain trigger, the IRS computers will automatically select your return for audit, and you'll get a form letter about it.

Common reasons for audit include the following:

Math errors. An automated letter will kick out to correct the math error. This is why you need not file an amended return if you notice a math error on your return. Turns out the IRS has gotten pretty accustomed to working with *humans*.

Automated substitute for return program (ASFR) for nonfilers. The ASFR program finds taxpayers who have not filed a tax return at all but owe substantial tax. It creates an IRS-version of that taxpayer's tax return for them, using information available to the IRS, such as mortgage interest statements, W2s, and 1099s.

The program also computes penalties and interest owed on the nonfiled income. If you have back taxes (see Chapter 18), it's in your interest to come forward and start filing your returns ASAP, because once your case gets into the ASFR system, you're not talking to "good cop" anymore; you're talking to "bad cop."

Automated underreporter program (AUP).[15] The automated underreporter program is just that: IRS computers match taxpayers' tax returns with their information returns (like W2s, 1099s, etc.) to select returns that show underreporting of income. Any return selected gets a full review by a tax examiner (a human) to determine areas of underreported income or overreported deductions.[16] The taxpayer is sent a notice and has a chance to explain or prove that what's in the tax return is correct.

The Discriminant Inventory Function System (DIF), called a "dif score" by pros, rates returns for:

- Probability of inaccurate information
- Probability of omitted income[17]

Certain categories may get flagged if they fall too far outside statistical averages for your region and **North American Industry Classification System (NAICS) code** (the code for what profession you are in).[18]

Not all flagged returns get audited. But all audits are selected from the flagged returns. Now, I want to help keep your heart rate down. Keep in mind that your expenses for categories in your business will naturally vary, but they will tend to be *in proportion* to your overall income level for the business. Beyoncé and I are both in NAICS code 711500, Independent Artists, Writers, and Performers.[19] We both spend money on photo shoots for publicity purposes. But I *suspect* that Bey's hair, makeup, and set design, not to mention her famously meticulous prop sourcing, all run her publicity photo budget up several zeros past the $750 every other year I spend on headshots.

Beyoncé's income is also several zeros past mine. Even if she spends several hundred thousand dollars on publicity photography each year, that high dollar amount is looked at within the context of *her* business.

The Three Types of Audit

Not all audits are created equal. Here are the three types of audit in order from most intensive and least likely to simplest and most likely:

1. The **field audit.** Highly skilled IRS agents come to your place of business and use forensic accounting techniques to assess what is happening in the business.[20] This is the kind of audit that happens only if you're, say, an all-cash pizza joint reporting suspiciously low amounts of income despite your Times Square location. The IRS algorithm is good at smelling unreported cash, and this kind of trigger will get an agent quietly monitoring your business and counting how many transactions you have over a certain time period to prove that you're not reporting all your income. Because these are expensive, they're rare, and the IRS is usually pretty dialed in on your shenanigans, and you're about to come-to-Jesus.

2. The **desk audit.** You are asked to come to an IRS office and sit down with an agent in person to discuss (typically) several items in a tax return or multiple returns.[21] While none of my clients have had a desk audit, friends of mine have. In other words, they're not unheard of. I highly recommend engaging a tax professional (an EA, CPA, or tax lawyer) to represent you if you're called to a desk audit. You do not need to be present, though you have a right to be. A representative has key advantages in this situation, including knowing how to limit the scope of the audit, ensuring it's valid before it proceeds, playing to the strengths of your case, and knowing when to keep their mouth shut. Since they don't know every detail that you do, they are unlikely to accidentally open up other areas for

examination, or nervous-talk. This is key, because the IRS has discretion to open up other areas in a desk audit, depending on what they find.

3. **Correspondence ("paper") audit.** This is the most common type by an order of magnitude. A letter states the disagreement/proposed change within the tax return and the adjusted balance due.[22] If you disagree with the change, you provide the documents to prove the legitimacy of the original numbers on the tax return and write a response letter.

Many people mistakenly think the IRS letter is final and indisputable. They never realize that it's their right to disagree with the finding and that they have recourse. Ironically, these rights are spelled out in the documents you're sent.[23] This is further evidence that people have been so effectively trained to fear the IRS or feel that the situation must be hopeless that they don't read through the documents.

Not every letter you get from the IRS is an audit notification. Usually it'll be something more mundane, like ID verification. But every audit notification comes in the mail.

Format and Timing

All audits begin with a letter mailed from the IRS to the address listed on your most recent tax return.

You will *never* get a phone call announcing an audit; 100% of these calls are scams.[24] The IRS will never surprise you with a phone call. They will call you only if you're in the middle of an open case with them and you've established with the person(s) on your case that they might call you.

What Are the Most Common Reasons for an Examination?

These are the top six reasons that tax returns get flagged for examination:

1. Offshore accounts
2. Employment tax issues (i.e., employers not paying the proper payroll tax/Social Security/Medicare)
3. Nonfilers
4. Flow-through entities (this means businesses that are taxed at their owner's tax rate; yes, *Schedule Cs are included in this category*, in addition to S Corporations and Partnerships)[25]
5. *Profit motive of a business (Schedule C)*
6. *Individual Schedule C deductions*

Notice anything there? Schedule Cs are listed three times. Why are Schedule Cs so often selected for examination? Unlike a person with a W2, there is no third-party verification of a Schedule C income or expenses. The IRS has to take your word for it. For that reason, it is reasonable that the IRS checks up regularly on Schedule C taxpayers to make sure they

a. Are reporting income accurately
b. Are not fabricating deductions
c. Are not using losses to shelter other taxable income (verify profit motive)

Remember this from Chapter 3? This is the tricky side of having a loss. You may be fully entitled to it, but there are taxpayers abusing the tax-sheltering quality of losses. So yes, a loss puts you in a category that is frequently audited.

Common Areas of Examination for Schedule Cs

If you can curb that worried feeling and look objectively at the universe of taxpayers filing Schedule Cs, it's easy to understand why some categories on the Schedule C get an IRS looksie. They tend to be "fun stuff." In other words, you can imagine that a lot of Schedule C travel and meals expenses are not really for business. The IRS is savvy about this, and they look at these categories *a lot*.

Schedule C categories that the IRS audits the most:

1. **Vehicles and mileage**[26]: A mileage log is required to substantiate the business portion, and you may not deduct more miles than the business portion. The IRS checks up on this. Make sure you've got that log.

2. **Travel and meals expenses:** Makes sense, right? You've seen a friend wave their business card after a hangout and jokes about having "talked business"? Tread lightly. There is a higher burden of proof for business meals than regular deductions. The IRS is looking to see that you meet it: you'll need your receipt *plus* who was met with and for what business purpose. For travel, the IRS will dig into your business trips to ensure they were really all business and, if not, that only the business portion was deducted. A log is helpful, plus documentation of all your scheduled meetings, etc.

HOW TO TALK TO THE IRS

Take notes. Any time you are talking to the IRS, it's good practice to take notes: include the date and nature of the call, and always note the name and badge number of the IRS worker you're speaking to. This is standard practice, so don't be shy. If you can't get a badge number, if

> the person uses pressure tactics, or if they will not let you call back, you are speaking with a scammer, not the IRS. In fact, if a scammer contacts you posing as the IRS, the IRS would love to know about it. They have a reporting system for these scams, and you can report it at this address: phishing@irs.gov (Subject: IRS Phone Scam).[27]
>
> Your notes from your IRS phone calls become part of your documentation if things go sideways. They can help you in tax court. They can update the next agent on where your case last left off. They can be your resource to refer to and cite in future letters to the IRS and as proof in your case.

All letters from the IRS are dated, and audit responses must be postmarked within 30 days of that date. In fact, the IRS calls them **30-day letters.**[28]

Never ignore mail from the IRS. You will lose the audit automatically if you fail to respond within the given timeframe, *regardless of the merits of your case.*

You can always request more time (call the number listed on the letter to do that). This is generally seen favorably by the IRS, because it means you're responding and not ignoring.

HOW TO ASK THE IRS FOR MORE TIME

There should be a number listed on the letter you received. If not, look up the taxpayer help line at IRS.gov. Pop in some earbuds, learn to love the hold music, and start folding laundry. It's going to be a minute.

Be prepared for the call with the letter in front of you, and open a fresh Google doc/Word doc/actual paper document with today's date and what you're calling the IRS about. While you're at it, note the time you first got put on hold and how long that goes on for. This document will become your **contemporaneous notes**. That's a legal term, and it means notes taken during or immediately after an event, representing your freshest memory of what happened.[29] If your case drags on, if you spend a godforsaken amount of time on hold and need to move your case to the Taxpayer Advocate Service, or if you end up in court, you will use and rely on these notes.

You should be able to reference each phone call you've made to the IRS and what happened on it, including the agent's name and badge ID number.

When you get someone on the phone, they will immediately say their name and badge ID number. Write it down in your notes, and if you miss it, ask them to repeat it.

Once you've done that, explain that you got a letter from the IRS. They may ask you what kind of letter it is: read them the title on the top. This letter type reveals to the IRS and any accountant assisting you, what is being asked of you, the deadline you're under, and what the stakes are.

You'll want to say to the person on the phone, "I received this letter, and I am doing my best to gather everything I need to in order to respond, but I need more time. May I have more time to gather my documents?"

With that magic ask, they will generally grant you a new deadline. WRITE. IT. DOWN. If you're missing the date of the phone call, the name and badge ID of the person who granted you a new deadline in your contemporaneous notes, you have no proof that you've got more time. Do not forget.

That's it. Now you've got more breathing room to gather documents, write a response letter, and if needed, reach out to an accountant for help.

THE KEY TO AN EASY AUDIT

The key to audits being smooth and relatively easy is *following the law in the first place*. The real way to be ready for any audit is to read and follow the *first part* of this book—knowing and following the rules all along. Don't put anything on your tax return that you don't have proper documentation for. Obviously, don't hide a bunch of personal expenses on your Schedule C. If you file a Schedule C, be 100% sure that you are operating in a businesslike manner, and maintain all records that demonstrate that you have a profit motive. If you stick to those basics, any audit letter you get will be pretty straightforward to respond to. I'm not here to say it'll be fun (it won't! It's an annoying day of paperwork!), but it'll be relatively painless, and it won't turn ugly. Always treat your Schedule C business like a *business*.

Remember That You're Running a Business

Reading about audits can feel scary. The important thing to remember is that as long as you follow the rules, you will be fine. Go back and read Chapter 4 on how to document business deductions, and review Chapter 3 on the importance of proving your profit motive, and you will have everything you need to respond to an audit, should one come your way.

With these things in hand, you are likely to emerge from the audit with no changes to your tax due. In other words, you will be able to prove that you were doing things above board and be allowed to continue operating that way, without penalty. What you're looking for, in IRS terms, is called a *no-change audit*.[30] Basically, *no change* means you've won. You successfully proved that all your business deductions were legitimate, and the IRS accepts this.

WHAT DOES AN AUDIT ACTUALLY LOOK LIKE?

Let me take some of the fear away, by showing you what a typical audit looks like.[31] A letter arrives from the IRS, and it typically says that the IRS has made an adjustment to your income. It shows you the calculation and the resulting difference (up or down) in tax. If you agree with the finding, you pay the difference (it can go the other way, too, in which case you'll get a refund).

Missing 1099

Missing 1099s are a super common way to get an IRS letter. This can happen if someone is late getting their 1099 you and you've already filed your taxes. The IRS receives its copy of the 1099, and an automatically generated letter is sent with the adjusted tax due reflecting the tax on the unreported 1099. If the IRS is correct and that 1099 income was never listed on your tax return, pay the bill. That's the end of it. There's no recourse here, because you actually didn't report that income, the IRS knows it, and you owe the tax.

If you did report that income, but you had not received a 1099 yet when you filed, then you have already paid the tax on it and should respond to the IRS proving this. Simply follow the instructions on your letter in the area that says "what if I disagree."[32] In broad strokes, write a letter to the IRS, within 30 days of the letter's date, stating that the 1099 income was reported in your gross income/sales on your Schedule C, but at the time you did not have a 1099 for it. This is where splitting your Schedule C income into two categories, "reported on a 1099" vs. "not reported on a 1099" comes in handy. Show your own records of your column of "not reported on a 1099," and include any business bank statements or bookkeeping that proves the total amount of income you reported is correct and, therefore, that you've already paid the tax on it.

Hobby Loss Audit

If the IRS letter says that it finds your business to be a hobby, denies your business expenses and losses, and recalculates your income, then write a response letter detailing your profit motive. Include receipts, business calendars, and any other proof demonstrating your intent to make a profit. I taught you how to prove and document your profit motive in Chapter 3, with specific tips for each point in the "IRS nine point test to prove profit motive." Refer to that as you gather the documents for your response.

Verification of Certain Expense Categories

Lastly, a letter asking for proof of various Schedule C deduction categories is the next most common audit and it's pretty straightforward. If the letter asks for your documentation of specific categories, that's exactly what you send. For example, if the letter asks for travel and meals documentation, send all of that. It's not fun to gather this stuff, but this is where you get rewarded for following the rules in the first place. If you've kept your receipts by year, as recommended in Chapter 5, you can pull out just that year's folder (physical and the one in your inbox), and your only sorting will be to find receipts pertaining to travel and meals (or whatever the requested category was). If the IRS asks about your car expense, you'll just log in to your mileage app, print the PDF mileage log for the relevant year, and send it in.

THERE'S ALWAYS HELP

If you get such a big stomachache from looking at the IRS letter that you can't make sense of it or you presume the worst possible result, then I recommend reaching out to a tax pro.

While a pro isn't free, they may save you a lot of time and heartache by having a better sense of the scope of the audit (I often see clients that are so scared that they don't read the letter carefully and don't realize that the IRS request is small and the response will take a tax pro 20 minutes). Pros also have experience in responding and know what works. In my own tax practice, I read and interpreted any clients' IRS letter for no charge. I charged only if the client wanted me to do the work of responding; I would often tell them how they could do it on their own. If someone else prepared your tax return, then I recommend you share the letter with them and ask what you should do. Just be quick about it. Accountants won't interrupt their vacation because you waited to the end of your 30-day window.

CHAPTER SUMMARY

- Audits seem scary, but most are routine and straightforward.
- An audit, or "examination," is an official inspection. It's a neutral check-up, not an accusation.
- Five important things to know:
  - You have the right to counsel.
  - Burden of proof: You must provide receipts, canceled checks, invoices, etc.
  - Cohan rule: Courts can grant reasonable deductions without proof, except for travel, gifts, or listed property.
  - Your right to appeal the initial finding is absolute.
  - Taxpayer Advocate Service: Helps when normal channels aren't working.
- The IRS can audit up to three years from the filing date, six years for significant omissions, and indefinitely for fraud or non-filing.
- Reasons for an audit: Math errors, non-filers, underreporting, and certain flagged categories.

- Types of audits:
  - Field audit: Intensive, rare, and expensive.
  - Desk audit: In-person at IRS office, I recommend you bring a tax professional.
  - Correspondence audit: Most common, happens through the mail.
- Common audit triggers: Offshore accounts, employment tax issues, non-filers, "flow-through" entities (including Schedule Cs), profit motive, and Schedule C deductions.
- How to respond: Gather documents, write your response letter, and request more time if needed.
- The keys to an easy audit: Follow the law in the first place, keep proper documentation, and treat your business like a business.
- Reach out to a tax pro if needed. They can save you time and heartache.

ENDNOTES

1. Kidding! Please, you're gorgeous just as you are.
2. Alicia Tuovila, "Audit: Meaning in Finance and Accounting and 3 Main Types," *Investopedia*, last modified June 2, 2024, https://www.investopedia .com/terms/a/audit.asp#:~:text=Investopedia%20%2F%20Daniel%20Fishel-, Understanding%20Audits,audit%20of%20their%20financial%20statements.
3. Tuovila, "Audit: Meaning in Finance and Accounting and 3 Main Types."
4. "IRS Audits," *U.S. Department of the Treasury, Internal Revenue Service,* last modified September 9, 2024, https://www.irs.gov/businesses/small-businesses-self-employed/irs-audits.
5. John T. Manhire, "What Does Voluntary Tax Compliance Mean?: A Government Perspective", *University of Pennsylvania Law Review Online,* 164 (2015): 11.
6. *See* U.S. Department of the Treasury, Internal Revenue Service. *The Examination (Audit),* 2022, Pub. 535, Washington, DC.
7. "Topic no. 311, Power of attorney information," *U.S. Department of the Treasury, Internal Revenue Service,* last modified September 26, 2024, https://www.irs.gov/taxtopics/tc311#:~:text=You%20have%20the%20 right%20to,a%20Low%20Income%20Taxpayer%20Clinic; "Lifecycle of a Tax

Return: Correspondence Audits: Increased Communication Alternatives Are in Progress," *Taxpayer Advocate Service*, last modified February 8, 2024, https://www.taxpayeradvocate.irs.gov/news/nta-blog/nta-blog-lifecycle-of-a-tax-return-correspondence-audits-increased-communication-alternatives-are-in-progress/2021/09/.

8. "Burden of Proof," *U.S. Department of the Treasury, Internal Revenue Service*, last modified September 30, 2024, https://www.irs.gov/businesses/small-businesses-self-employed/burden-of-proof#:~:text=The%20responsibility%20to%20prove%20entries,of%20expenses%20to%20deduct%20them.

9. See Patricia S. Chappell v. Commissioner of Internal Revenue, *T.C. SUMM. OP. 2024-2*, (U.S.T.C. 2024) ("If a taxpayer clearly shows that she incurred a deductible expense but is unable to substantiate the exact amount, the "*Cohan rule*" permits the Court to estimate the amount of the expense, provided there is a reasonable basis for doing so. *See Cohan v. Commissioner*, 39 F.2d 540, 543—44 (2d Cir. 1930)").

10. John K. Cook and Sarah Webber, "Cohan Rule" Estimates, *The CPA Journal*, last modified December 15, 2021, https://www.cpajournal.com/2021/12/15/cohan-rule-estimates/.

11. "Taxpayer Bill of Rights 5: The Right to Appeal an IRS Decision in an Independent Forum," *U.S. Department of the Treasury, Internal Revenue Service*, last modified January 23, 2025, https://www.irs.gov/newsroom/taxpayer-bill-of-rights-5.

12. "About Us," *Taxpayer Advocate Service*, accessed August 8, 2024, https://www.taxpayeradvocate.irs.gov/.

13. "Assessment Statute Expiration Date (ASED)," *Taxpayer Advocate Service*, accessed August 8, 2024, https://www.taxpayeradvocate.irs.gov/tax-terms/assessment-statute-expiration-date-ased/.

14. "4.63.3 Offshore Voluntary Disclosure Program, Streamlined Filing Compliance Procedures and Voluntary Disclosure Practice," *U.S. Department of the Treasury, Internal Revenue Service*, last modified April 27, 2021, https://www.irs.gov/irm/part4/irm_04-063-003r.

15. Gerard H. Schreiber, Jr., "Business meal deductions after the TCJA," *The Tax Adviser*, last modified December 31, 2008, https://www.thetaxadviser.com/issues/2009/jan/irsautomatedunderreporter.html.

16. Beware Schedule C folks: that's you.

17. J. Eric Butler, "IRS Examination and Collection Functions—A Basic Overview," *Lewis Thomason*, accessed December 9, 2024, https://www.lewisthomason.com/wp-content/uploads/2016/05/IRS-Collections.pdf.

18. "What is a NAICS Code and Why do I Need One?," *NAICS Association,* November 15, 2024, https://www.naics.com/what-is-a-naics-code/.
19. "711510—Independent Artists, Writers, and Performers," *NAICS Association,* accessed December 9, 2024, https://www.naics.com/naics-code-description/? code=711510.
20. "IRS Audits."
21. "IRS Audits."
22. "Lifecycle of a Tax Return: Correspondence Audits: Increased Communication Alternatives Are in Progress."
23. "IRS Audits."
24. "IRS Audits."
25. Tina Orem, "7 Reasons the IRS Will Audit You," *NerdWallet,* last modified April 28, 2023, https://www.nerdwallet.com/article/taxes/reasons-irs-audit.
26. Joy Taylor, "12 IRS Audit RedFlags for the Self-Employed," *Kiplinger,* last modified January 25, 2023, https://www.kiplinger.com/taxes/604179/self-employed-irs-audit-red-flags.
27. "Report phishing and online scams," *U.S. Department of the Treasury, Internal Revenue Service,* last modified July 12, 2024, https://www.irs.gov/privacy-disclosure/report-phishing.
28. "Letter 525: Examination Report Transmittal Audit Report/Letter Giving Taxpayer 30 Days to Respond," *Taxpayer Advocate Service,* last modified August 9, 2024, https://www.taxpayeradvocate.irs.gov/notices/audit-report-letter-giving-taxpayer-30-days-to-respond/.
29. Robert Merriott, "Contemporaneous Notes," *Forensic Notes,* accessed 2024, https://www.forensicnotes.com/contemporaneous-notes/#:~:text= Contemporaneous%20Notes%20are%20notes%20made,as%20defined %20by%20Lawin.org.
30. Janet Hotlzblatt, "Too Many IRS Audits of Big Businesses Result In No Change In Tax Liability," *Tax Policy Center,* April 19, 2021, https://taxpolicycenter.org/ taxvox/too-many-irs-audits-big-businesses-result-no-change-tax-liability.
31. "The Examination (Audit) Process," *U.S. Department of Treasury, Internal Revenue Service,* January 2006, https://www.irs.gov/pub/irs-news/fs-06-10 .pdf.
32. "What to do when a W-2 or Form 1099 is missing or incorrect," *U.S. Department of Treasury, Internal Revenue Service,* December 5, 2024, https:// www.irs.gov/newsroom/what-to-do-when-a-w-2-or-form-1099-is-missing-or-incorrect.

CHAPTER TWENTY

HOLY MATRIMONY OR HOLY SHIT: WHAT TO DO IF YOU ACCIDENTALLY MARRY A CON ARTIST

t can happen. You're swept away in love, and you never talk money with your betrothed until you're hitched. And then it hits you: your spouse brought some bad money history to the marriage.

Ideally, you never get into this situation. If you're considering marriage, I strongly advise you to have financial heart-to-hearts with your beloved and get deep into the bank accounts, the debts owed, and the actual numbers. If what you discover isn't pretty, I recommend holding off the wedding until your partner cleans up their act—settling up their debts, child support, and back taxes.

But sometimes you're already up shit creek, and the prevention window is closed. Sometimes it's a rude surprise. And sometimes, you fall for someone who is straight-up scamming you. You just need a paddle. This chapter is that—how to untangle yourself from the bad deeds of a spouse.

FIRST: DON'T FILE JOINTLY, AND DON'T SIGN A TAX RETURN YOU DON'T UNDERSTAND

I covered Married Filing Joint tax returns in Chapter 9. It's important to understand that when you file a joint tax return, you can be held responsible for 100% of it—even if your spouse disappears off the face of the planet.[1] Your signature on that return says that you know and attest to what's in it. Recall that the one filing status that you're stuck with and can't undo (at least for the year of that tax return) is Married Filing Joint. If you suspect sketchy business, I am here to validate the inner alarm bell. Review your return or get it reviewed by someone you trust before you sign it, or stop the presses and file your own return as Married Filing Separately.

FINANCIAL ABUSE IS REAL

I want to acknowledge a hard truth. Financial abuse is real. In 99% of all cases where there is physical abuse, there is financial abuse.[2] This makes sense. If someone is trying to control you, controlling your access to money works as well as, if not better than, violence. You're not moving out if you'll be instantly cut off from your money. And if you can't access the cash for a security deposit or your own car, you're stuck. I am well aware that saying "just don't sign the tax return" is not an option for you if you're living under threat of violence or losing access to your money. Take heart, the IRS has a path for you (read on).

Assuming you're past that point and you've discovered bad news you didn't realize was filed with your joint tax return? You have two options. Joint returns have existed only since 1948, and while they have advantages, deceit between the members of the joint unit is a possibility.[3] For that reason, there are ways to disentangle a joint mess that you didn't have knowledge or control of.

Injured Spouse Relief

The first and simplest path is **injured spouse relief**, which is available when you file a joint tax return and one spouse has a past debt owed.[4] You (the non-owing spouse) must meet two requirements:

- The debt must belong *entirely* to the other spouse.
- You, the injured spouse, must have refund money at risk of being lost to your spouse's tax debt. That is, you must have either W2 withholding, expect a refundable tax credit, or have paid estimated tax payments, with the expectation that your overpayment will be refunded to you. Sadly, if you're self-employed and *haven't* paid any estimates, you're unlikely to qualify.

To apply for injured spouse relief, file **form 8379**.[5] This form is pretty simple; pull one off the IRS website and complete the questions that indicate whether you qualify. You can either file it with your 1040, your 1040X or file it on its own. Put all the forms in the order the IRS directions tell you to, and write "Injured Spouse" in the upper-right corner of the first page of the tax return. The IRS does the calculation for you of what your spouse owes due to their income and past debts vs. what you are owed by the IRS.

Before the pandemic, this filing took the IRS about 11–14 weeks to process; since then, wait times have grown. Hang tight. You should see your refund again, if a little slowly.

It's worth noting that you might prefer to handle this situation directly with your spouse. If your refund is eaten up by their past debt and you keep your finances separate, you may want to simply ask your spouse to pay you what your refund would have been. This takes less time and paperwork, though it requires you (or your accountant) to work out the math.

Consider adjusting your withholding or estimated tax payments to not overpay in the future. This means you will no longer be owed a refund, since you'll keep the money throughout the year. But you won't lose your refund to their tax debt.

If past debts like child support or an IRS installment agreement will exist for years into your marital future, consider filing "Married Filing Separately."

Innocent Spouse Relief

While "injured spouse relief" often pops up at the beginning of a marriage, **innocent spouse relief** is often triggered by divorce.[6] This is usually a surprise to one spouse, triggered by an IRS action, like an audit, a notice, or the withholding of a refund. If that is you, my condolences.

It's smart to get help with this from a tax pro, if you can. The four types of innocent spouse relief are complex, and it's an indicator that you have tax info to navigate that is brand new to you. Find someone without a conflict of interest and who will listen with empathy. If you're in this situation, you're likely dealing with some hard stuff.

Conflict of Interest: Your Ex's Tax Pro Has One

If you had a tax pro helping you both when you were married and now you're getting divorced or are divorced, that tax pro now has a conflict of interest. A licensed tax professional must alert both people whose interests could be averse. Divorcing spouses are in this category.

This is an ethical concern that they are *required by law*[7] to take seriously. It's important that you are aware of this and that they are, too. Conflicts of interest should be discussed up front. They should have you sign an agreement that says you are working with them with full knowledge and consent. If they don't, they're violating their license's ethics requirement, which is a big red flag.

In other words, if you're not absolutely certain your tax pro can represent *your* interests without bias or favor, now is the time to find a new one. Anyone not representing your spouse will keep your interests primary.

There are four brands of innocent spouse relief, for four types of situations. You are an innocent spouse if you want to avoid (1) losing your share of your tax refund or (2) paying more than your share of a tax bill because your spouse didn't report income, improperly reported income, or claimed credits/overreported expenses—*and* you had no knowledge of it or reason to know about it. This IRS flowchart will help you determine if you qualify for **innocent spouse relief**[8]: www.irs.gov/publications/p971#en_US_202112_publink100098691.

The first of the four types of innocent spouse is **innocent spouse relief**.[9] To qualify, you must meet five criteria:

1. You filed a joint return.
2. There was an understatement of tax because of an erroneous item(s).

3. You didn't know/had no reason to know about the erroneous item(s).[10]
4. It would be inequitable to hold you responsible for the erroneous item(s).
5. You must file form 8857 within two years of the IRS collection action (aka when the IRS attempts to get the money).

To translate, this means you must have filed a joint return; if you filed separately, then your taxes state items that are only yours, so there's no way to not have knowledge of those items. Your spouse has to have been taking shady deductions/credits or not reporting all the income they're required to. You have to have not known or had reason to know about it, or been under threat, such that it would be unfair to hold you responsible for the spouse parts of the tax. You need to file the paperwork (form 8857) as soon as you can, within two years of the IRS attempting to collect the money.

If you've been the subject of spousal abuse, this tool is for you. There is a section of the form that you complete where you describe any abuse or threat. Doing so puts a flag on your file alerting the IRS not to share any information, especially your address, with your spouse or ex-spouse.

See this IRS flowchart to determine if you qualify for **innocent spouse relief**[11]: www.irs.gov/publications/p971#en_US_202112_publink100098691.

Separation of Liability Relief: Innocent Spouse Relief Type #2

The next brand of innocent spouse is called **separation of liability relief**.[12] For this, you must have been divorced, or either separated from your spouse for more than a year or not a member of the same household for over a year. This relief retroactively splits a married filing joint return into two "married filing separately" returns. You will not receive any refund that may have been due to you this way, but you benefit from separating your tax liability from your spouse/ex-spouse's and owing only yours.

For this separation relief, you must have had no knowledge of the understatement of income, and you must file the paperwork within two years of IRS enforcement action.

This flowchart will help you determine if you qualify for separation of liability relief: www.irs.gov/publications/p971#en_US_202112_publink 100098691.

Equitable Relief: Innocent Spouse Relief Type #3

If you don't qualify for either of the other types of innocent spouse, the last resort is **equitable relief**.[13] There are seven factors the IRS uses to determine whether it would be fair to make you pay the joint tax:

1. Your marital status
2. Economic hardship you might suffer without relief
3. Whether you knew or had reason to know about your spouse's understated or unpaid tax
4. Whether you're legally obligated to pay the tax
5. Whether you significantly benefited from not paying tax or under-reporting your tax
6. Whether you complied in good faith with tax laws after requested
7. Your mental and physical health

This flowchart will walk you through whether or not you qualify: www.irs.gov/publications/p971#en_US_202112_publink100098691.

Equitable Relief for Community Property States: Innocent Spouse Relief Type #4

There is one final type of **equitable relief for people who live in community property states**. This matters, because if you live in a community property state, your income when married is considered joint income. These states are:

- Arizona
- California
- Idaho
- Louisiana
- Nevada
- New Mexico
- Texas
- Washington
- Wisconsin

To meet the requirements of the community property equitable relief, you must:

- Be in a community property state but didn't file a joint return.
- Didn't include the income item belonging to your spouse under community property laws.
- Not know or have reason to know about the income item.
- It must be unfair to include the item of community income in your gross income.
- File form 8857 within *six months* of the statute of limitations on assessment of the tax.

You will need to read up on the specifics of your situation if you are in a domestic partnership or in a state that allows the election of community property treatment. This IRS document has more info: www.irs.gov/irm/part25/irm_25-015-005#idm139948152383040.

If you find yourself in a situation where your spouse or your ex was not reporting income as they should have and you didn't know about it, were incapacitated, or were under threat, you may qualify for relief from the taxes on what your spouse didn't report. The forms can be complex, the timing is important, and you are in a position of discovering tax items you didn't know about, so this is when employing the help of a tax professional is a good idea.

CHAPTER SUMMARY

- It can happen. You fall in love, get married, and discover too late that your spouse has been playing games with your taxes.
- You're on the hook for a Married Filing Joint tax return, so don't file jointly or sign a tax return that you don't understand.
- Financial abuse is real: If you're under threat, the last point can be impossible. Take heart, the IRS has a path to help you.
- Injured Spouse Relief is available if your spouse has past debts. File form 8379 to protect your refund.
- Innocent Spouse Relief is often triggered by divorce. There are four types:
  - **Innocent Spouse Relief:** For joint returns with erroneous items you didn't know about.
  - **Separation of Liability Relief:** For those divorced or separated for over a year.
  - **Equitable Relief:** For those who don't qualify for the other types but meet certain fairness criteria.
  - **Equitable Relief for Community Property States:** Specific to community property states with joint income.
- Get help. If you're in this situation, a tax pro can guide you through the complex forms and timing.

ENDNOTES

1. "Innocent spouse relief," *U.S. Department of Treasury, Internal Revenue Service*, last modified November 8, 2024, https://www.irs.gov/individuals/innocent-spouse-relief.

2. Adrienne E. Adams, Cris M. Sullivan, Deborah Bybee, and Megan R. Greeson, "Development of the Scale of Economic Abuse," *Violence Against Women* 14, no. 5 (2008): 563–588, https://doi.org/10.1177/1077801208315529.

3. Nick Kasprak, "Joint Filing in the Tax Code," *Tax Foundation*, June 26, 2013, https://taxfoundation.org/blog/joint-filing-tax-code/.

4. "Injured spouse relief," *U.S. Department of Treasury, Internal Revenue Service*, last modified November 8, 2024, https://www.irs.gov/individuals/injured-spouse-relief.

5. "Injured spouse relief."

6. "Innocent spouse relief," *U.S. Department of Treasury, Internal Revenue Service*, last modified November 8, 2024, https://www.irs.gov/individuals/innocent-spouse-relief.

7. Specifically they are required by IRS Circular 230, the code of conduct that governs licensed tax professionals including CPAs and EAs. "Office of Professional Responsibility and Circular 230," *U.S. Department of Treasury, Internal Revenue Service*, last modified August 20, 2024, https://www.irs.gov/tax-professionals/office-of-professional-responsibility-and-circular-230.

8. 26 U.S. Code § 6015(b). See *Publication 971 (12/2021), Innocent Spouse Relief*. 2021, Pub. 791, Washington, DC. Note that has been modified to be accurate as of 2024.

9. 26 U.S. Code § 6015(b). See U.S. Department of the Treasury, Internal Revenue Service. *Publication 971 (12/2021), Innocent Spouse Relief*. 2021, Pub. 791, Washington, DC.

10. Weirdly, this is almost impossible to know, which means you should assume the shortest timeline, and get your paperwork in as soon as possible.

11. *Publication 971 (12/2021), Innocent Spouse Relief*. Note that this has been modified to be accurate as of 2024.

12. "Separation of liability relief," *U.S. Department of Treasury, Internal Revenue Service*, last modified October 9, 2024, https://www.irs.gov/individuals/equitable-relief.; 26 U.S. Code § 6015(c).

13. "Equitable relief," *U.S. Department of Treasury, Internal Revenue Service*, last modified October 9, 2024, https://www.irs.gov/individuals/equitable-relief.

PART VII

THE BIGGER PICTURE: HOW TO SHIFT THE CULTURE FOR GOOD

Your business creates good in this world, by providing value to a community that you care about. It's creating good by providing money to you and your family. When it grows, that beneficial circle of impact widens to a larger community. When you build a business that embodies your values, serves people you care about, and provides for people you love, you change the world for the better.

Your taxes change the world on a societal level (local, state, and national) as well. Taxes are our agreement about our society and how we fund the machinery of our culture. The taxpaying public elects people to office to distribute taxes in a way that reflects the society we want. So what do we value? What do we want our taxes to build?

It's important to connect our taxes with the representatives we elect and the policies they propose and enact. When we don't connect these dots or don't have the tax knowledge we need to distinguish an equitable policy from a regressive one, we can't advocate well.

And yet, there is no tax education in this country. Even smart, engaged citizens have trouble discerning what a fair tax even looks like. When we the people lack the ability to identify a fair vs. an unfair tax law, politicians can easily say one thing and do another.

If you're reading this, you're a person who cares. It's become unpopular in recent years to believe in our government's power to do good, but let me highlight the power in play when the government adjusts tax policy. It's huge. More than a third of all public support for families is delivered through tax benefits.[1]

Take, for example, the Biden administration's 2021 expansion of the existing child tax credit. With that one move, child poverty was cut in half.[2] Thousands of nonprofits, advocates, and small businesses couldn't match what the US government did for poor kids overnight by expanding one tax credit.

Is that power something we want to cede to megacorporations, billionaires, and lobbyists who put in the work to understand it? Or is this democracy *ours*, and could we claim it to help our communities and advance the cause of equity? Maybe the idea of tax policy makes you want to recoil, but tax policy is power. When we tune in, we can claim that power for our communities.

These last few pages include a quick primer on what tax fairness looks like and how to understand the broader power of taxes for doing good in our society.

ENDNOTES

1. *Center on Poverty and Social Policy*, Poverty Measurement research, accessed December 9, 2024, https://povertycenter.columbia.edu/poverty-measurement.
2. Hope Karnopp and Matthew Crowley, "In Milwaukee radio interview, Biden says Black child poverty was cut in half. Is he right?," *Milwaukee Journal Sentinel*, May 15, 2024, https://www.jsonline.com/story/news/politics/politifact wisconsin/2024/05/15/is-biden-right-that-black-child-poverty-was-cut-in-half-in-2021/73701556007/.

CHAPTER TWENTY-ONE

TAX EQUITY 101

There are two sides to fair taxation. There's the paying side, which is the most visible to us. This means **who pays more in tax**? And there's the spending side, which is about **who receives the benefit of those taxes**, in the form of government spending.

First, let's understand the paying side.

WHAT IS A PROGRESSIVE TAX VS. A REGRESSIVE TAX?

When it comes to *paying* taxes, a tax is more equitable if it's **progressive**. A **progressive tax policy** is one that is borne more heavily by those with the most ability to pay (the wealthiest) and borne the least heavily by those least able to pay (the poorest). **Tax credits** are an example of progressive tax policy. Most tax credits offer the same *dollar* amount of money to everyone, where the benefit is larger in proportion to the income of a poorer person and smaller in proportion to the income of a wealthy person.[1] In other words, the poorest people get the biggest benefit, relative to their income. Another progressive tax is our graduated earned income tax rates. All US taxpayers pay nothing on their first chunk of income, a little bit on their next chunk, and on up until only those taxpayers with very high incomes pay the highest tax rates.[2] Even then, they only pay the high rates on those last dollars of earnings. Graduated income tax rates make calculating your tax rate more complex, but they're more equitable.

A **regressive tax** gives the largest benefit to the wealthy and the least benefit to the poor. Tax is regressive if it is flat, meaning that the tax is the same for everyone, either in percentage or in dollar amount. Put another way, the burden of the tax decreases the more money you have. An example of this is **tax deductions**: the higher your income tax rate, the bigger your deduction benefit. If you have a low income tax rate, you get less benefit from a tax deduction. Other regressive tax examples are sales tax, property taxes, excise taxes, and payroll tax.

Overall, the US federal system of tax is progressive.[3] This may surprise you, but it's true. Look at the data for yourself, but to give you one summarizing point, in 2021, the latest year available at the time of writing, taxpayers in the top 50% of income paid 97.7% of all federal individual income taxes, and the bottom 50% paid the remaining 2.3%.[4]

A 2024 briefing article from the Tax Policy Center of the Urban Institute and the Brookings Institution summarizes it like this:

"Most low-income households do not pay federal income taxes, typically because they owe no tax (as their income is lower than the standard deduction) or because tax credits offset the tax they would owe. Some receive substantial rebates via refundable tax credits. However, nearly all low-income workers are subject to the payroll tax."[5]

Households in the lowest quintile of income have a tax rate that is negative; that is, they receive back more in tax credits than they pay in tax, largely due to two refundable tax credits, the Earned Income Credit (EIC) and the Child Tax Credit (CTC).[6]

So when it comes to *paying* taxes, our federal system on the whole is progressive.

TAX DISTRIBUTION: THE OTHER SIDE OF TAX EQUITY

But that's not the whole story. Our tax *spending* is not nearly as progressive as our tax collection.

Tax distribution is how we spread the benefit from taxes among groups in our society. While some tax distribution takes place on the taxation side, through refundable tax credits like the EIC and the CTC, most tax distribution (60% in the United States vs. 75% in OECD countries) happens through spending policies.

In their 2019 article "Are Taxes (and Also Spending) Progressive?" William Gale and Zachary Obstfeld of Brookings and Econofact write:

"Relative to other countries, the [United States] has a fairly progressive tax system but less than average redistribution. This is because the [United States] generates far less revenue, 26% of GDP,[7] than the other OECD countries who collect an average of 33% of GDP. Taken together, US taxes and transfers do less to redistribute income than 26 out of 30 OECD countries."[8]

OECD countries raise more tax revenue than the United States (33% of GDP vs. 26% in the US[9]), and 26 out of 30 of them redistribute more of that revenue to benefit low-and middle-income citizens[10] than the United States does.

CHAPTER SUMMARY

- Fair taxation is two-sided: There's paying taxes and there's receiving the benefits of government spending.
- Progressive vs. regressive taxes:
  - Progressive taxes are borne more heavily by the wealthy, and less by the poor. Examples include tax credits and graduated income tax rates.
  - Regressive taxes: Flat taxes that burden the poor relatively more than the wealthy. Examples include sales tax, property taxes, excise taxes, and payroll tax.
- Overall, the US federal tax system is progressive. In 2021, the top 50% of income earners paid 97.7% of all federal individual income taxes.
- Tax distribution: US tax spending is less progressive than its tax collection. Most redistribution happens through spending policies.
- In comparison with OECD countries, the US raises less tax revenue (26% of GDP vs. 33% in OECD countries) and redistributes less to benefit low-and middle-income citizens.

ENDNOTES

1. "Progressive Tax," *Tax Foundation*, accessed December 9, 2024, https://tax foundation.org/taxedu/glossary/progressive-tax/.
2. "Graduated Rate Income Tax," *Tax Foundation*, accessed December 9, 2024, https://taxfoundation.org/taxedu/glossary/graduated-rate-income-tax/.
3. William G. Gale and Zachary Obstfeld, "Are Taxes (And Also Spending) Progressive?," *Econofact*, November 11, 2019, https://econofact.org/are-taxes-and-also-spending-progressive.
4. Erica York, "Summary of the Latest Federal Income Tax Data, 2024 Update," *Tax Foundation*, March 13, 2024, https://taxfoundation.org/data/all/federal/latest-federal-income-tax-data-2024/#:~:text=High%2DIncome%20Taxpayers

%20Paid%20the%20Majority%20of%20Federal%20Income%20Taxes,of%20 all%20federal%20income%20taxes.

5. "How does the federal tax system affect low-income households?," *Tax Policy Center*, last modified January 2024, https://taxpolicycenter.org/briefing-book/ how-does-federal-tax-system-affect-low-income-households#:~:text= The%20Urban%2DBrookings%20Tax%20Policy,child%20tax%20credit %20(CTC).

6. "How does the federal tax system affect low-income households?"

7. "How do US taxes compare internationally?," *Tax Policy Center,* last modified January 2024, https://taxpolicycenter.org/briefing-book/how-do-us-taxes-compare-internationally.

8. "Are Taxes (And Also Spending) Progressive?"

9. "How do US taxes compare internationally?," *Tax Policy Center,* last modified January 2024, https://taxpolicycenter.org/briefing-book/how-do-us-taxes-compare-internationally.

10. "Are Taxes (And Also Spending) Progressive?"

CHAPTER TWENTY-TWO

TALKING ABOUT TAXES: AVOID MANIPULATION

D o you like being manipulated? Me neither. But much of the language used to talk about taxes was designed to manipulate our assumptions about taxes for the benefit of wealthy people. Let's deprogram from our corporate overlords with a quick primer on manipulative tax language—so you can avoid it.

In his book *Don't Think of an Elephant*, professor of Cognitive Science and Linguistics at UC Berkeley George Lakoff unpacks the concept of political framing. When you frame an issue, you create the lens through which someone will view it. Even if you negate the issue, you reinforce the frame. A good example of this is Richard Nixon saying "I am not a crook." The frame is whether Nixon is or isn't a crook. Most Americans ended up using his frame, even when they took the opposite position that he did. People thought, "Nixon *is* a crook."

The biggest beneficiaries of tax dollars are the lower and middle class. The rich pay a large portion of our tax dollars and receive fewer of the benefits, because (duh) they don't need help buying food for their kids. A dollar more in income, food assistance, or medical care for someone on the lower end of the income spectrum is proportionally worth more than a dollar to a billionaire. I believe that spending tax dollars on public benefits like healthcare, education, safety, and food are important for the health, safety, and wellness of our society overall.

You might not like this if you're a billionaire—particularly one without much sense of gratitude to the United States for being the most nurturing climate for business growth the world has ever known. Instead of looking at your relative ability to pay and the relative painlessness of those tax payments compared to a middle class family struggling to afford housing, you might see just the total dollars you pay and feel salty.

But being a billionaire who complains about paying money into the education and food security of poor kids while your personal chef whips you up caviar blinis on your private jet is a bad look. You might instead push the public to frame taxes as something dreadful. Never mind that taxes are what fund 30% of the social benefits distributed in the United States.[1] Never mind that a public-school-educated population forms the bulk of your workforce, that you drive your delivery trucks on public roads, and that you feel safe in your life because of an imposing military. Never mind the hypocrisy alarm blaring as you take billions in US government subsidies ($2.5 billion: Tesla, $3.5 billion: Amazon).[2] You want people with less money than you to think of the tax dollars that benefit them as bad.

So you deploy a new frame: "tax relief."[3] Lakoff tells you the rest:

"When the word *tax* is added to *relief*, the result is a metaphor: taxation is an affliction. And the person who takes it away is a hero, and anyone who tries to stop him is a bad guy. This is a frame. It is made up of ideas, like *affliction* and *hero*. The language that evokes the frame comes out of the White House, and it goes into press releases, goes to every radio station, every TV station, every newspaper. And soon the *New York Times* is using *tax relief*. And it is not only on Fox; it is on CNN, it is on NBC, it is on every station because it is 'the President's tax-relief plan.' And soon the Democrats are using *tax relief*—shooting themselves in the foot."[4]

Another successful billionaire frame on the progressive and good **estate tax** is the phrase "death tax." Ultra-wealthy family dynasties designed that phrase, on purpose, to make you believe the estate tax will be *your* problem (because death happens to all of us, right?). Guess what? The estate tax is progressive and is one of the few tools we have to make the ultra-wealthy pay their share. Only about 1,500 estates in the United States are wealthy enough to pay even one dollar of estate tax.[5] If you are reading this book, it means that the estate tax will never touch you. How do I know? If you don't have a team of family tax lawyers and accountants on staff, then you don't have enough money to be touched by the estate tax. You and your spouse can pass on $27.22 million[6] to your children without paying one dollar of federal estate tax. And I think that threshold should be much lower.

BETTER WAYS TO FRAME TAXES

Taxes are an *investment*. . .in our people, in communities, in infrastructure, in our physical well-being and safety, and in our future. Investing is critical to growth. If we want to grow our economy, our population, our safety, our security, and our health, then we need to invest tax dollars in those things.

For the people at the very top, who were either born lucky or derived the peak benefit from a US system that is set up for maximum capital growth, if they don't want to pay their fair share of investment back into the system they've benefited most from, that is unpatriotic and ungrateful. Not every country is the business-growth accelerator that the United States is, and we do it uniquely well. Elon Musk did not build Tesla in South Africa. He came here.

As billionaire investor Warren Buffett put it, "If you're in the luckiest 1% of humanity, you owe it to the rest of humanity to think about the other 99%."[7]

Rather than use the anti-tax, anti-society frame of *tax relief*, we should speak of **investment in our people** and our infrastructure. Taxes are the fertilizer in the soil of America. We can only pull out nutrients without replenishing them for so long until we've got a dust bowl. But when we invest in a rich soil, everyone has the conditions to grow strong and thrive.

CHAPTER SUMMARY

- Boost your political effectiveness by not using tax language that's designed to manipulate you, and benefit the ultra-wealthy.
- George Lakoff explained how framing shapes our views.
- Lower and middle class people benefit most from tax dollars. The ultrarich pay more but need fewer benefits, and use framing to manipulate our views on cutting taxes on the wealthy, and reducing benefits to the middle class.

- Billionaire framing: Terms like "tax relief" and "death tax" are designed to make taxes seem dreadful and to protect wealthy interests.
- Only about 1,500 US estates are wealthy enough to pay estate tax. Most people will never be affected by it.
- Better ways to frame taxes: Taxes are an investment in our people, communities, infrastructure, and future. It's patriotic for the wealthy to pay their fair share.

ENDNOTES

1. "Payroll Taxes: What Are They and What Do They Fund?," *Peter G. Peterson Foundation*, last modified May 1, 2023, https://www.pgpf.org/article/budget-explainer-payroll-taxes/.
2. Scott Galloway, "Elon Musk, Welfare Queen," *No Mercy/No Malice*, February 14, 2025, https://www.profgalloway.com/elon-musk-welfare-queen/; "Subsidy Tracker Megadeals," *Good Jobs First*, accessed February 18, 2025, https://subsidy tracker.goodjobsfirst.org/megadeals.
3. Emily Horton, "The Legacy of the 2001 and 2003 'Bush' Tax Cuts," *Center on Budget and Policy Priorities*, last modified October 23, 2017, https://www.cbpp .org/research/the-legacy-of-the-2001-and-2003-bush-tax-cuts.
4. George Lakoff, *Don't Think of an Elephant!: Know Your Values and Frame the Debate--The Essential Guide for Progressives*, (Chelsea Green Publishing, 2004), 3–4.
5. Steve Wamhoff, "The Estate Tax is Irrelevant to More Than 99 Percent of Americans," *Institute on Economic and Tax Policy*, December 7, 2023, https:// itep.org/federal-estate-tax-historic-lows-2023/.
6. This is the 2024 estate tax threshold. This amount increases each year. You can find the current year limit at https://www.irs.gov/businesses/small-businesses-self-employed/estate-tax.
7. "Warren Buffett Gave This Brilliant Advice to Billionaires But It Can Instantly Improve Your Life Too," *INC.*, April 23, 2018, https://www.inc.com/marcel-schwantes/warren-buffett-gave-this-brilliant-advice-to-billionaires-but-it-can-also-improve-your-life-fast.html.

CHAPTER TWENTY-THREE

THE SHORTEST PATH TO $600 BILLION/YEAR? FUND THE IRS

I f you're reading this book, you care about others, your community, and, I hope, our democracy. Taxes are our most powerful way to change it for the better. This chapter, while outside the "how-to" part of the book, is for people who believe in democracy and care about fixing it. I'm hoping that's you.

You probably didn't open this book for tax policy, so I'll be brief. The following are changes we could make (and advocate for, to our elected representatives) that would make our system fairer.

FUND THE IRS

The **tax gap** is the amount of money that is owed in tax in the United States every year but goes unpaid. It's about $600 billion dollars annually.[1] The large majority of that unpaid bill is owed by. . .wait for it. . .the wealthiest individuals in the United States.[2]

Dear reader, the second most tax-evading group is self-employed folks like you and me. I say that to give you the full and honest facts but also because it's just not cool.

The IRS knows this, as do the 1%. For every dollar of funding the IRS receives, it collects between $5 and $12 in revenue. And when the IRS budget is cut, the tax gap grows even more.[3]

When the IRS budget is cut, audits of wealthy taxpayers go down, and audits of lower-and middle-income people go up.[4] Why? Because you and I have relatively simple tax returns. The IRS doesn't need much more than a form letter and a postage stamp to audit folks like us. But to audit the wealthy (especially wealthy tax cheats), it takes more money. You get this money back and then some, but it takes money up front, because the wealthy are armed with savvy accountants and tax lawyers.

So why are we cheering when the IRS budget gets cut? We have been trained to have a knee-jerk hate for the IRS. This is coming from the same lobbyists who are paid by those wealthy tax cheats, and the politicians those tax cheats give money to. Makes sense, right? This is another way that the private jet set succeeds in manipulating us into wanting what's best for *them* rather than what's best for *us*.

Fully funding the IRS is good for *us*. It means audits on folks like us go down, and audits go up on wealthy tax cheaters. It means collecting more of the $600 billion outstanding yearly bill. And every dollar we spend on the IRS brings back $5—$12, so it pays off.

The Biden administration's Inflation Reduction Act of 2022 added $80 billion to the IRS budget, stepped up IRS enforcement activity specifically targeted at wealthy taxpayers, and was projected to generate $240 billion in additional revenue.[5]

In June 2024, Republicans clawed back $20.2 billion of this funding in exchange for raising the debt limit and keeping the government open.[6]

Cutting the IRS budget represents bald hypocrisy for a party that claims to care about fiscal responsibility. I hope it's clear that sowing hate for the IRS and cutting its funding serves the interests of the wealthy— and the most law-breaking contingent of the wealthy, at that. Funding the IRS multiplies revenue collected, improves your experience with them (think: reduced hold times and more help when you need it), enforces existing law, prevents taxpayer cheating (especially by the wealthy), and makes the system more fair.

Many equity-focused folks have proposed a wealth tax. I'm not opposed to one, but because of the structure of our tax system, a wealth tax will be difficult to construct, enact, and enforce. Before we fight the uphill slog of a new wealth tax, I suggest the simple fix of funding the IRS first. A new law is worthless when the current laws aren't enforced to begin with. Let's fix the leaky bucket first.

If you care about a fair system and fairer taxes, care about funding the IRS. It doesn't require a single new law. Every dollar spent generates $5—$12 back, and it is a simple fix to get the wealthy to follow the laws they are currently breaking, and pay the money they rightfully owe.

In Conclusion

If you've read this far, thank you. I hope you feel how much I care about you, your work, your community, your economic security, and your success. I hope I've given you concrete tools to improve all of those things.

It is my honor to help a person like you; an ethical, caring, community-building, creative person. In this day and society where division rules and it feels like we've forgotten how to love each other, be civil with each other, care for each other, disagree respectfully with each other, and build connections with each other, it's *your work* that repairs this brokenness. Creative people and vision-driven people are the ones helping people have transformative experiences together and rebuild our lost connections. Whether you do this through performances that help the audience connect with an emotion, through writing that illuminates an important issue or a new perspective, through a design that helps someone move through a space with more ease, or through visual art that inspires someone or makes them want to call their mom, through a statement piece of jewelry that makes them feel fabulous or a mug that gives comfort and keeps their tea warm, *your work* is changing our world for the better. From the bottom of my heart, thank you for doing it. You are exactly what the world needs right now. And *you* are the reason that I do this work.

I want you to pay taxes like your contribution matters. Advocate like you and your community matter. Set up your books and your business systems like your work matters. Use planning and tax-smart accounts to squeeze out more like your dollars matter. Invest like your financial safety and ability to rest matter. Build a business that serves people you care about with the unique thing that only you can do, like your vision matters.

And that is why I wrote this book like you matter.

Because you do.

CHAPTER SUMMARY

- Fully funding the IRS means collecting the $600 billion annually that is mostly owed by wealthy tax cheats.
- For every dollar spent on the IRS, $5–$12 is collected. Cutting the IRS budget increases audits on lower-and middle-income people and decreases audits on the wealthy.
- Rich tax cheaters and their lobbyists push for IRS budget cuts to avoid paying their fair share.
- Biden's Inflation Reduction Act added $80 billion to the IRS budget, mostly for enforcement targeted at the wealthy. It was projected to generate $240 billion in revenue. Recent cuts undermine this progress.
- Funding the IRS ensures that tax cheaters pay what they owe, making the system fairer and improving IRS services for all of us.
- Your work is important, and I hope I've helped you. Because the world needs you right now. And you matter.

ENDNOTES

1. "IRS updates tax gap projections for 2020, 2021; projected annual gap rises to $688 billion," *U.S. Department of Treasury, Internal Revenue Service*, October 12, 2023, https://www.irs.gov/newsroom/irs-updates-tax-gap-projections-for-2020-2021-projected-annual-gap-rises-to-688-billion.
2. "Give IRS the tools it needs to enforce tax rules and catch cheaters," *The Brookings Institute*, September 1, 2021, https://www.brookings.edu/articles/give-irs-the-tools-it-needs-to-enforce-tax-rules-and-catch-cheaters/.

3. "The IRS is Significantly Underfunded to Serve Taxpayers and Collect Tax," *Taxpayer Advocacy Service*, last modified 2012, https://www.taxpayeradvocate .irs.gov/wp-content/uploads/2020/08/Most-Serious-Problems-IRS-Significantly-Underfunded.pdf.

4. "IRS Audits Few Millionaires But Targeted Many Low-Income Families in FY 2022," *Transactional Records Access Clearinghouse*, January 4, 2023, https://trac .syr.edu/reports/706/.

5. "Empowering the IRS: Understanding the Full Potential of the Inflation Reduction Act's Historic Investment in the Internal Revenue Service," *The White House*, accessed December 9, 2024, https://www.whitehouse.gov/cea/ written-materials/2024/02/08/empowering-the-irs-understanding-the-full-potential-of-the-inflation-reduction-acts-historic-investment-in-the-internal-revenue-service/#:~:text=Even%20after%20accounting%20for%20IRS%27s, by%20the%20wealthiest%20tax%20evaders.

6. Dustin Stamper and Colin Wilhelm, "IRS loses $20.2 billion in funding," *Grant Thornton*, March 26, 2024, https://www.grantthornton.com/insights/newsletters/ tax/2024/hot-topics/mar-26/irs-loses-billion-in-funding.

INDEX

Page numbers followed by *f* refer to figures.

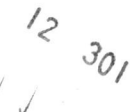

Printed and bound by CPI Group (UK) Ltd, Croydon, CR0 4YY

07/12/2025

14785990-0002